MERCER
street

2013-2014

a collection of essays from the expository writing program

Editors:
Pat C. Hoy II
Stephen Donatelli
Darlene A. Forrest
Georgia Halliday
Evan Bobella

Senior Production Editors:
Ingrid S. Nuñez
Richard Larson
Christopher Cappelluti

Development Editors:
Alyssa Böehle
Hanna Novak
Megan Steiner
Victoria Olsen
Tara Parmiter

EXPOSITORY WRITING PROGRAM
NEW YORK UNIVERSITY
COLLEGE OF ARTS & SCIENCE

Advisory Editors:
Denice Martone
William M. Morgan

MERCER
street

To the Class of 2017:

Welcome to the challenging world of New York University. This collection of fine essays can make your own intellectual journey less daunting. Savor the essays; they have been left for you by your predecessors.

We know, from years of classroom experience, that learning rarely happens instantaneously. Pen-in-the-hand experience continually trumps talk and easy reading. Doing is of utmost importance. So too is failure.

If your writing courses do not unsettle you in serious ways, we will have failed you. We must necessarily ask of you things that you do not yet know and understand how to do.

In the film *Iris*, Dame Iris Murdoch plays seriously with her audience: "Education doesn't make you happy. Nor does freedom. We don't become happy just because we're free, if we are, or because we've been educated, if we have, but because education may be the means by which we realize we are happy. It opens our eyes, our ears—tells us where delights are lurking, convinces us that there is only one freedom of any importance whatsoever, that of the mind—and gives us the assurance, the confidence, to walk the path our mind, our educated mind, offers."

Several years ago, during the first semester, I noticed that my students were only partially reading the assigned essays. I had asked them to select a single written text and to put that text in conversation with two or three other like-minded but different texts. The resulting conversation—staged in the students' minds and on the page—would, I had hoped, eventually yield ideas worthy of serious essays.

I discovered that my students were paying primary attention to personal connections with the texts, showing little interest in the larger body of ideas, or the way those ideas were presented. Their resistance, coupled with impatience, often led to hasty conclusions about meaning—to an erasure of parts of the various texts. They were looking for a single point instead of a network of complementary ideas. The thesis chase diverted them from the pleasures of the texts and kept them from making discoveries that could eventually lead to an understanding of complex issues.

Later, when I asked my advanced course students what they considered the most difficult thing they had to learn in the college writing classroom, their answer repeatedly came down to this: a different kind of thinking. One student put her difficulty this way: "I have struggled with inductive reasoning, with a form that starts with evidence and progresses to idea, rather than the other way around. High school did not prepare me for this kind of writing."

Many of you have learned to take shortcuts, to intuit a thesis, to intuit propositions to support it, and to find examples to support the thesis, moving habitually from thesis to evidence—leaving out contradictions, challenges, complications. The learned emphasis has been not on the rigorous analysis of evidence but on a fact-based, highly structured response: thesis, proposition, examples.

In your work with us in the Expository Writing Program, you will learn to reverse the emphasis, setting in motion a progression from evidence to idea to essay. The examination of evidence begins with inductive reasoning—reasoning that does not lead to certainty or to a thesis that can, out of necessity, be proved; it leads instead to discovery, to the rigorous combination and application of analysis and imagination, to ideas that must, like the evidence itself, be continually reassessed and re-conceptualized to represent more accurately whatever truth the evidence suggests to you, the researching writer. The focus will always be on developing a dialectical frame of mind— a questioning, a weighing of contradictions and dichotomies, that leads not to certainty but to ideas that will forever be subject to reassessment by others.

At the heart of this inductive and dialectical process of discovery lies the complex business of reading complex written texts, texts that do not reveal themselves to cursory examination. Reading these more complex texts is similar to reading any body of evidence (essays, books, research findings, newspapers, movies, visual art, music). Central to such reading is the presumption that conceiving an idea is exciting, complicated work and that all one needs to know to express that idea cannot be contained in a simplified thesis statement and a series of topic sentences. This new kind of work leads to the delights that are lurking in the texts and in your minds, waiting for you to discover them.

To grapple is to begin to understand the meaning of thought. For the writer, such grappling leads eventually to clarification and the use of nuanced language, to a form of expression more complex than a formulaic set of declarations and a series of examples. The act of writing—writing itself—is central to this learning process and the development of ideas.

The inductive process is, of course, the same process that leads to discovery in science or in any other academic discipline. It provides the foundation for making sense. It lies at the heart of all reasoning and reading. Without it, we have no way of discovering what the evidence means.

Essays, you will learn, do not prove, repeat, or reiterate. They do not confine themselves to making a single point. Instead, essays, like ideas, develop, change, expand, turn on themselves—and captivate the reader, when the writer gets the words right. As you read the essays in this collection for your own pleasure and instruction, know that the student writers are asking you to *see*—just for a moment—as they see. They are trying to persuade you that their ideas have merit.

When one of these essays surprises you—or perhaps confuses you—pause to figure out what the writer is doing. During that long moment, you may unearth a hidden secret—a writing technique that enlivens the essay and gives you an idea for your own writing. Assume always that both surprise and confusion warrant further study and that the secret is worth discovering.

All of us in the Expository Writing Program, along with a group of amazing student editors, wish you the very best during your first year at New York University.

Pat C. Hoy II
Director, Expository Writing Program
Professor of English

We thank Dean G. Gabrielle Starr, College of Arts and Science, for her generous support of this publication.

Cover Photography: Spandrel: "*Pax melior est quam iustissimum bellum.*" Translation from Latin: "Peace is better than the most just war" by Denice Martone.
Cover Illustration: "Mercer Street 2013-2014" by Lisa Klausing.

VI - MERCER STREET

MERCER street

CONTENTS

EDUCATION AND THE PROFESSIONS

POLY

SPECTRUM OF ESSAYS

Beyond Death: The Aesthetics of the Human Corpse

KATHLEEN ZHANG

Against a sanguine backdrop a skinless man stands tall. This is quite a feat considering he has been bisected down the center of his body, a foot for each side to stand on. Through the gap between his separated sides, his organs have been neatly shuffled to the left or right, providing a jigsaw view of the human abdominal cavity. Despite his exposure, the man is confident: he's got one fist against each hip, as if inviting the viewer to peruse his innards. And why shouldn't he be confident? He's been gifted with a new lease on life. His fat has been melted away, his fluids replaced by silicon. As a display in *Bodies: The Exhibition*, he will never rot, ignominiously, in the ground; instead, medical students, children, and the curious can pay Premier Exhibitions for the privilege of staring into unseeing eyes, but whose? The process this nameless, skinless man has gone through is called "plastination," an invention of German doctor Gunther von Hagens, who founded the *Body Worlds* exhibition, featuring preserved human and animal corpses ("Plastination"). In 2011, the then 66-year-old anatomist announced that he was dying. He requested that his body be plastinated after death and put on display.

Von Hagens' life work is, to say the least, shrouded in controversy. Numerous allegations over ethical concerns, body sourcing, and violated social mores have dogged *Body Worlds* and its later rival, Premier Exhibition's *Bodies: The Exhibition*. As concerns over exhibits featuring human remains still garner controversy after two decades, it's important to note that this is not the first time these issues have been raised. In 1988, David J. Williams, a professor of medical illustration at Purdue University, wrote "The History of Eduard Pernkopf's *Topographische Anatomie des Menschen*," a work detailing the anatomical obsession of one Eduard Pernkopf, the head of Vienna University during WWII and a notorious Nazi. Williams was deeply interested in Pernkopf's atlas of the human body, which is sometimes referred to in English simply as *The Pernkopf Anatomy*. While he did not side-step Pernkopf's Nazism in his paper, he did say that the *Anatomy* would "unfortunately, never be acknowledged by some as the masterpiece it truly is" (Williams).

These words would make Williams infamous. They would cost him relationships and damage his reputation. In 2002, journalist Michael Paterniti interviewed Williams for his essay, "The Most Dangerous Beauty." Paterniti's inquiry follows Professor Williams's fear of his own impending mortality as he seeks redemption for his defense of a Nazi work as well as the work of Franz Batke, the last living contributor to the *Anatomy* and a former brownshirt whom Williams met in 1980. Paterniti also turns back to the original source, scrutinizing Pernkopf's approach to his subjects, finding it worthy both of condemnation and sympathy.

It's difficult to ascertain precisely where Paterniti stands on the issue, entrenched as he is in these narratives. As a journalist, he restrains his own opinions, yet he constantly calls for "understand[ing]," all the while knowing that what he's asking for is huge: that we turn a blind eye to the development of plastination by perpetrators of a great atrocity (737). He approaches the beauty of the artwork in *The Pernkopf Anatomy* with vivid language. He grants equal favor to the Nazi atrocities committed in Vienna, and to the life stories of each of his main subjects. The connection seems damning because the artwork is inherently dehumanized. But Paterniti's ecstatic descriptions of the drawings from the *Anatomy* are described with the same lush ardor. The use of words like "otherworldly" suggests that Paterniti sees in Pernkopf's individual body parts a transcendance, a presence beyond mere flesh and blood, as if by becoming objects of art they had become something more than what they used to be in life (741). At ground level, the *Anatomy* is an atlas of the human body for functional use, but on the plane of the visual artists who created and endorsed it, it is an ambitious endeavor that marries scientific needs to the dizzying heights of fine art. The body becomes a beautiful object, and Paterniti seems aware of this. But, after death, is the body necessarily granted transcendence? A body preserved in art has lost its personhood; a pair of kidneys does not make a man. The elusive beauty that draws people to the *Anatomy* is the same one that draws them to the plastinated body that seemingly exists only on the other side of death. Virginia Woolf's "The Death of the Moth" looks into the life and death of a trifling moth. She describes it as "pathetic" in life, but finds that in death it attains a quiet dignity and is "decently and uncomplainingly composed" (385, 386). Could a body part—a kidney, the delicate sacs inside the lung—achieve a similar dignity after death?

Paterniti seems to suggest so given his vivid descriptions of the body parts in question, but his true judgments are not so simple. He also has a preoccupation with "sin" throughout the work, but refrains from openly judging all but the least defendable subjects in his narrative (746). In the case of David Williams, easily the most sympathetic voice in an essay where all other subjects are Nazis, one can apply what Paterniti chooses to include or exclude as clues to the author's judgment. In this case, the most damning, personal, and raw moment is Paterniti's portrayal of Williams's hypocrisy. Though this professor of anatomical art can find anonymous, fragmented bodies beautiful beyond death, he has a far different reaction to the exhibited corpse of a close family member. Paterniti dedicates an entire passage to the apparent suicide of David Williams's brother Greg, in a work where, under different circumstances, Greg would be but a minor character. The reaction that Williams has to his brother's corpse (he finds it without beauty, a "lifeless slab") is important to our understanding of his view of the other bodies after death (743). Greg dies alone in New York of an overdose. His brother comes to identify him. In a New York morgue, Williams finds Greg "in severe rigor mortis, with the back of his head resting on a wooden block, exactly like a cadaver in a gross-anatomy lab" (743). Despite Paterniti's comparison of Greg's body and a cadaver (the professor would have dealt with many cadavers over his career), Williams is so affected by his brother's death that he actually "fell" into the arms of a nearby police officer (743). Yet he still finds the anonymous and dismembered bodies in *The Pernkopf Anatomy* beautiful. They do not touch him. It becomes evident over the course of his essay that he does not revere them the way he does his brother's body—does not see them as human. Greg dies without the objectification of his body: instead, Williams retains Greg's personhood in his memory. Paterniti describes Greg's body just as explicitly as the "otherworldly vaginas" of *The Pernkopf Anatomy*, but instead of transcendental, ecstatic language, he focuses on the gross and vivid detail—the track marks on Greg's arms (741). This work rests so heavily on the shoulders of Paterniti's subjects that it's amazing that Greg, a man we first meet in his teens, before his struggle with his sexual identity, before his suicide, is allowed, in death, to be human. Thanks to Paterniti's description we see through the body to the man himself: messy, complex, intensely human, and deserving of dignity despite his darker moments.

Greg's parents worry about his body after death, concerned that he won't be buried with his family in a Catholic cemetery. This preoccupation defines the struggle Greg's family has with death and Greg's individuality. Though Williams is a conflicted supporter of the *Anatomy*, the death of his brother

Greg shadows his own research. Paterniti writes, "If his brother's death left no mark on the greater world, the rest of those dark days in 1978 are part of David Williams's personal history" (743). And yet in only two years Williams would meet Franz Batke in Germany during his first pilgrimage to learn the origins of *The Pernkopf Anatomy*. After this meeting, he would write the infamous, laudatory review of the book for an obscure journal. Then, as he faces losses to his reputation and in his personal life, he meets several times with a local rabbi who "tells him that his sin may be one of perspective" (746). The rabbi instructs him to imagine the grief of the Holocaust victims, or those who lost family members. For them, the book would not hold the aesthetic, transcendental value it has for Williams; instead, it would be a "dirty crime scene" (746). The fact that he could never make the connection between the fervor of his detractors and his own feelings after his brother's death is baffling. Williams sees Greg 's dead body in a human light.

But understand that we are meeting Williams as he nears the end of his own life; in the face of his own mortality, he is changing. As of Paterniti's writing in 2002, the professor has suffered three heart attacks. In the spring of that year, Williams would pack his bags to make another pilgrimage to consider again the origins of *The Pernkopf Anatomy*. His inner revelations were not expected to be the same as those he experienced on the journey that led him to write that original article in 1988. Years before, Williams's mind had been preoccupied by beauty and transcendence; in 2002, he embarked on a search for sin. On this journey, he is met by former-Nazis-turned-professors, and the faint stain of decades-old atrocities.

When a large group is dehumanized, atrocity is not long in following. But Lawrence Weschler's collection of essays *Vermeer in Bosnia* shows how the individual may subvert the traditional dehumanization through art or action. Acting can break the cycle of rhetoric and violence associated with the loss of humanity. Weschler's work opens, like Paterniti's, in the confusion that follows great atrocity. Weschler is sitting on the Yugoslav War Crimes Tribunal in the Netherlands, with the trial of Serbian war criminal Dusko Tadic underway. Despite the intensity of the trial, he finds his answer to centuries of conflict and blood feud not in the courtroom, but in an art museum. Weschler undergoes Paterniti's transfiguration in reverse: *his* work deals with the transcendence of a mere art object into a human being! He examines the situation in the Balkans through the lens of Dutch painter Johannes Vermeer. Vermeer could take trite and hackneyed tropes and create a transcendent work of humanity. Weschler cites Edward Snow, author of *Study of Vermeer*, who argues that Vermeer's work celebrates autonomy, and thus individual humans. Specifically, Snow sees sexuality in Vermeer's female subjects, but rather than depicting the subject with an objectifying gaze, Vermeer portrays his women as autonomous and individual, and above all, as human.

Weschler argues that by going beyond genre, Vermeer imbued his subjects with personal worth. The humanization of the subject became the focus of Vermeer's artistic transcendence. With this in mind, Weschler asks a jurist at the tribunal if ethnic violence can ever stop in the Balkans. The jurist replies yes, if "specific individuals bear the major share of the responsibility" for the violence, "and it is they, not the group as a whole, that need to be held to account" (784). Weschler's interpretation of Vermeer and his artistic focus on the individual, when applied to the human body, sheds a new light on Paterniti's discussion of transcendence. Weschler lets us ask: what if these anatomical works were no longer subject to our gaze? Just as Vermeer's subjects were freed from the male gaze, can the subjects of *The Pernkopf Anatomy* be recognized as individuals? It isn't easy to see an anonymous spinal cord, a pair of lungs, as the human they once belonged to.

But Williams cannot revive his brother Greg. He cannot raise the dead, but he certainly continues to see his dead brother's corpse as human. So too did the Jewish critics regard the other cadavers as "brethren" and considered their exhibition a desecration. Some thought they came from concentration camps, though an investigation found that untrue. Even though Jews as "subjects" did arouse sympathy, it would still be shortsighted to think of *The Pernkopf Anatomy* as concerning only one group. Some may have been thrown from the roof of the university, while others may have been petty criminals. Before their deaths, it's hard to fathom any of them consenting to what would be done to their bodies. This problem persists, no matter who they were. To ethically confront the controversy surrounding the *Anatomy*, one must avoid thinking of the human form only in an artistic sense. One must never forget the human.

Weschler sat as Tadic stood accused and then convicted of torture, and of overseeing torture and rape. As of 2008, Tadic has been released. The controversy surrounding Pernkopf's *Anatomy*, too, continues on in other forms: using the technique of body plastination, *Bodies: The Exhibition* is still open in three cities, New York included, despite concerns from the government and mainstream media about body sourcing. Most of the corpses on display in that exhibition come from China, where there is no cultural tradition or legal procedure for the donation of bodies. Instead, executed prisoners are the primary source of organ transplants and anatomy specimens. Out of China's prisoners, hundreds of thousands are believed to be political prisoners or prisoners of conscience. So who were the murderers, who the oppressed? Without a skin as evidence, it almost becomes impossible to know. For Paterniti, the transformation from human into commodity is the transfiguration of fragmented body parts into art. However, the literal commodification of the body flouts any aesthetic aim: plastinated bodies can be purchased on Chinese websites, and thirty-five dollars can buy entrance to the whole exhibition of plastinated people. It is important, now, when lines between the body and commodity remain blurred, that we follow Vermeer's example, and turn this process back on itself. The next time you see the advertisement with that sanguine man, take a moment to consider who he was, rather than what he has become, and wonder what could have happened to his name, and his skin.

WORKS CITED

Bodies: The Exhibition. Premier Exhibitions, 2012. Web. 10 June 2013.

Paterniti, Michael. "The Most Dangerous Beauty." *Occasions for Writing: Evidence, Idea, Essay*. Ed. Robert DiYanni and Pat C. Hoy II. Boston: Wadsworth, 2008. 735-49. Print.

von Hagens, Gunther. "The Idea behind Plastination." *Body Worlds: The Original Exhibition of Real Human Bodies*. Premier Exhibitions, 2012. Web. 10 June 2013.

Weschler, Lawrence. "Vermeer in Bosnia." *Occasions for Writing: Evidence, Idea, Essay*. Ed. Robert DiYanni and Pat C. Hoy II. Boston: Wadsworth, 2008. 778-85. Print.

Williams, David J. "The History of Eduard Pernkopf's *Topographische Anatomie des Menschen*." *The Journal of Biocommunication*, 15.2, 1988. N.pag. *Purdue U School of Veterinary Medicine*. Web. 10 June 2013.

Woolf, Virginia. "The Death of the Moth." *Occasions for Writing: Evidence, Idea, Essay*. Ed. Robert DiYanni and Pat C. Hoy II. Boston: Wadsworth, 2008. 385-86. Print.

Play On

DEANNA KIM

In *Listen to This*, Alex Ross explores the value of music in a transient life. In a world that is seemingly indifferent to our existence, where we struggle to somehow inject significance into our lives, Ross believes that music gives us meaning. It has a way of allowing us to glimpse the inner workings of our nature, to express the inexpressible, to be heard by others. This relationship between our mortality and the significance of music in our lives reveals Ross's ultimate belief that music is a way to escape death. He appears to fear living without meaning, and dying without being remembered, but this fear is ultimately assuaged by the existence of music, that undying testament to the human experience.

Ross reveals in his interpretations of music a fixation on melancholy, even in the works of Johannes Brahms, where it is subtle. He describes one symphony as "whirl[ing] away in a fast diminuendo, like a group of revelers vanishing down an empty street" ("Blessed" 295). That the music evokes in him images of emptiness and the passing of time suggests his preoccupation with the transience of life and the imminence of death. Ross suggests that a note in one of the composer's Intermezzos represents a "bell tolling from whatever unknown church Brahms chose for his doubting faith," and adds that this is "the music that you will hear when you die" (307, 308). His interpretation of such music exposes more about himself than about the composer: his dread of death, and perhaps his own agnosticism. And in his characterization of Brahms's music as "one troubled mind commiserating with another," Ross reveals himself to be, at least in that moment, full of grief (296). But why such sadness? Perhaps it stems from a "primal fear of being weighed in the balance and found wanting"—the subconscious anxiety that, when all is said and done, his life will have amounted to nothing (73). He dreads such senselessness, dreads dying without meaning.

Yet as much as music fills him with melancholy, as much as it reminds him of his mortality, it also gives him intense joy. Ross says of one Brahmsian movement, "What does the movement evoke, if not the triumph of darkness?" and describes another piece as "unadulterated C-major joy" (311, 301). When Ross listens to music, the distinction between emotions is blurred. Hope and misery intermingle to reflect the reality that lies between; what he experiences cannot be neatly separated and classified. Yes, Ross asserts, music can make him melancholy for no discernible reason, but it is "a pleasing melancholy" ("Walking Blues" 32). Such conflicts of emotion transport him from the "hurly-burly" of everyday life into a "twilight realm where time stops for a while"—a place where he can immerse himself in emotion, experience it more richly and acutely (32). To be able to feel anything with such intensity is a luxury to Ross, not a burden. His complex, shifting reactions to the music parallel his attitude towards life as a whole: that it is not only full of loneliness and sorrow, but also joy and love. The full spectrum of the human condition, the "entire gamut of emotion," lies waiting to be experienced in chords and symphonies ("Great Soul" 126). One need only listen. For Ross, there may be nothing more than this in life, but he wants nothing more.

It might seem overly romantic, however, to view music as anything other than a hobby or a plaything for the privileged. After all, Ross asks, "Isn't it simply a self-indulgent fantasy to think that German chamber music could change the world of a girl whose mother is living on food stamps?" ("Learning" 237). Yet Ross contends that there is more substance to music than one might think. He would agree with the Pythagorean Greeks who spoke of a duality between astronomy and music: while astronomy concerned itself with the relationship between tangible, external objects, music studied the invisible and the internal. Ross wants us to realize that music is not simply a pastime but an inextricable part of our being, a science of human nature. He asserts that music has the ability to "have it all, uniting Romanticism and Enlightenment, civilization and revolution, brain and body, order and chaos"—a reflection, an embodiment, of life itself ("Listen" 7). Perhaps we have music because it allows us to make sense of our lives, to express ourselves when science and language fall short. Could it be, then, that music is somehow necessary to understanding ourselves?

Ross asserts that music is indeed an essential facet of our nature, precisely because it affects what we cannot put a finger on. He writes, "It has long been understood that music has the ability to stir feelings for which we do not have a name" ("Walking Blues" 32). Where do these emotions come from? What significance do they hold in our lives, if any? These are questions that John Berger addresses in his essay "The White Bird." He writes that we are born into a world that "lends itself to as much evil as good," whose "energy is fearsomely indifferent" (7). In other words, the universe is a blank, impartial force; it does not lean in our favor or promise us happiness. Therefore, we react to art so strongly because it seems to exist "always [as] an exception, always *in despite of*" our condition, a condition that is very often ugly and unsympathetic (7). We find art beautiful because it is a symbol of defiance; it reminds us that if foulness can exist in this world, so too can beauty.

Perhaps these seemingly polar opposites are interwoven. Perhaps that is how art makes life bearable, by giving sound or shape to inner chaos and thereby "tam[ing] the edges of emotion" ("Walking Blues" 26). One is reminded of the emotional dance that Ross experiences when listening to music: "Sobs and kisses, pleasure and anguish, coincide" (35). Berger gives us this premise: we are organisms living in a non-sentient universe, one that has the potential for both great beauty and great ugliness, and Ross believes that music makes our tension-filled lives bearable.

But art still does not explain the problem of death. How does one escape the fate that Ross regards with such fear and sadness? The seemingly cruel coexistence of the brevity of human life and the inevitability of death is something that we have grappled with since biblical times, and Ross echoes Job's sentiments: "Why go on? What do we have that is better than death?" ("Blessed" 311). In the end, Job had God, but the agnostic composer Brahms had music. His compositions reflect both pain and joy, and they serve as a kind of storyline of his experiences. Strip away this music, Ross asserts, and you will find nothing but a "gray void" in its wake (311).

Perhaps, then, Ross sees music as an attempt to preserve one's voice, to keep one's story alive. Indeed, he confesses that when he listens to music, he "map[s] out a little more of the imaginary world . . . invent[s] stories for each thing as it happens" ("Listen" 20). This need to tell stories stems from Ross's desire to preserve life. To tell a story is to remember; to remember is to bring what was lost into the present. Berger writes that "[all] the languages of art have been developed as an attempt to transform the instantaneous into the permanent," and that "the transcendental face of art is always a form of prayer" (9). The prayer is for salvation from oblivion, for the preservation of what hope and beauty exists in a world where suffering is rampant. This prayer is passed down for as long as people are willing to hear it. As Ross says of one of Beethoven's works, "The symphony becomes a fragmentary, unfinished thing. . . . It becomes whole again only in the mind and soul of someone listening for the first time, and listening again. The hero is you" ("Listen" 21). The composer, the player, and the listener reciprocate and engage in conversation. The story goes on; there is no end. After all, as Ross writes, "Since the oldest art forms, such as music, have transcended time, they can become part of any time" ("Learning" 237). And thus, whatever Brahms or any ordinary listener endeavored to express can be heard and understood even centuries after they have died. We are immortalized by the stories we write and play and hear in music.

Of course, our physical deaths are inevitable. Even then, however, Ross believes that we use music as a way to assert our existence and cope with mortality. Like the sonata Brahms composed after his friend's suicide, we are "broken but still colossal" in the face of death ("Blessed" 299). To be alive at all is miraculous, but to create art even despite our circumstances is even more miraculous. In his final years, the composer Schubert wrote an Adagio that to Ross reflects "an awareness, a defiance, and then an acceptance of death" ("Great Soul" 136). Again, there is the fixation on death and mortality, but it seems now that Ross is not preoccupied with the sadness of dying. Rather, he is fascinated by the beauty with which humans contend with death, the art we create in response to it. One is reminded of the wooden birds Berger speaks of: simple yet profound symbols of the human desire to replicate and thus preserve beauty, even after its source—the actual bird—has long gone. By the same token, we play and listen to music without realizing that we are carving wooden birds ourselves. A composer like Brahms cannot die because every time someone listens to a symphony of his, the essence of his being is brought back to life. The death of his body is rendered irrelevant when everything else—those elements that made him human, like joy, melancholy, love, and loss—remains so fully expressed in his music.

The apparent transience and insignificance of life answers to music, which continues to exist even after the passing of its makers. Music, in itself, is rooted in a language of cycles and repetition. It displays a reluctance, a desire to draw things out: the first movement of a symphony ends, but then there is the second, and the third, and the fourth. The vibrato of a violin lengthens and varies the sound of a string; the pedal on a piano sustains what would otherwise be a short and choppy note. And there is the often-used *da capo al fine*, an Italian musical term that means "from the beginning to the end." The notes end, but the performer is expected to play on, repeating the piece from the very beginning. When the music is over, we are transported back to the dauntingly apathetic world Berger speaks of. Here we are given the choice of what to do in such a situation, and Ross chooses music, every single time. He may not be able to escape physical death, but he can outlive himself so long as he engages in the call and response, the remembrance that music embodies. He ultimately seems to agree with Berger, that our search for beauty in the world means "that we are more deeply inserted into existence than the course of a single life would lead us to believe" (8-9).

WORKS CITED

Berger, John. "The White Bird." *The Sense of Sight*. New York: Random, 1993. 5-10. Print.
Ross, Alex. *Listen to This*. New York: Farrar, 2010. Print.
    "Blessed are the Sad." 293-311.
    "Chacona, Lamento, Walking Blues." 22-54.
    "Great Soul." 124-37.
    "Learning the Score." 226-38.
    "Listen to This." 3-21.

Life, Liberty, and Lincoln

RAJ MATHUR

Rain pours down on the young woman, mingling with her stream of tears. Hundreds of feet away, the most powerful office in the world is being transferred, as it has been forty-two times before, to a new man: George W. Bush—a hopeful revival for some, utter ruination in the minds of others. For Sarah Vowell, it is ruination, and she sobs "tears of rage" as the oath of office is given ("Patriot" 169). There are thousands of protesters on the Washington Mall, but through blurry eyes and hazy weather, Vowell's gaze falls upon a pro-Bush family, praying hand-in-hand with their heads down as the chaplains give the invocation. The dichotomy between the family and the hate sign of a nearby protestor strikes her as the national anthem begins to play ("Nerd" 93). Many protestors refuse to sing—an affirmation of their steadfast belief that the Death of Democracy is occurring before their very eyes. And yet, however much she may agree with their politics or abhor President Bush, Sarah Vowell puts her hands over her heart and sings ("Patriot" 169).

Singing loudly is much of what Sarah Vowell does in her terse yet compelling essays—she presents her political convictions as incontrovertible. "The modern mocha is a bittersweet concoction of imperialism, genocide, invention, and consumerism served with whipped cream on top," she quips in "God Will Give You Blood to Drink in a Souvenir Shot Glass" (42). When a veterans' group leaves American flags on Vowell's lawn to celebrate Independence Day, she screams, "The whole point of that goddamn flag is that people don't stick flags in my yard without asking me!" ("Patriot" 159). Addressing people who make grandiose analogies between themselves and historical figures of great import, she suggests that "perhaps people who compare themselves to Rosa Parks are simply arrogant, pampered nincompoops with delusions of grandeur who couldn't tell the difference between a paper cut and a decapitation" ("Rosa Parks" 123). Vowell, attentive to hypocrisy in others, appears so resolute in her own ideology that she tends to dismiss those who believe otherwise.

Yet she is quick to remind us that her strong convictions do not always engender resolution. After singing the anthem, Vowell's gaze falls upon President George W. Bush embracing his father, former President George H.W. Bush, and begins to "cry harder" ("Nerd" 96). She seethes in frustration, dismayed "that Bush doesn't . . . come clean" about the fact that he lost the popular vote ("Nerd" 98). This is how her narrative of the 2001 Inauguration ends—not with her proudly singing the national anthem, or waxing poetic about the endless possibilities of American democracy, or even discussing how the Democrats are favored in the 2002 midterm elections—but in trepidation, leaving us uneasy and disconcerted about the future.

Just days after the 2001 Inauguration, Philip Hamburger, a young East Coast liberal like Vowell, wrote an essay for *The New Yorker* entitled "Visiting the Declaration." He too admits to feeling disturbed and forlorn about the prospect of a Bush presidency. Seeking solace, Hamburger goes to the site of George Washington's first inauguration, Federal Hall in downtown Manhattan. He is struck by the "poetic . . . freedom of [the] design" of the balcony on which Washington took the oath of office (33). He then visits a curator, Mimi Bowling, guardian of an original copy of the Declaration of Independence. She recounts some of the document's history, including its secret transfer out of D.C. for safety during the Second World War. Its most recent trip to Paris for display at the Bibliothèque Nationale almost ended in disaster: Bowling and the Declaration got stuck in traffic and "[she] was sure [they] would miss the plane," but luckily they "boarded . . . just as the door slammed shut and the plane took off" (33). This is the resonant and heroic image Hamburger leaves us with. The Declaration, and the ideal of American democracy it symbolizes, has always endured—through far more trying times than this—and the Bush presidency cannot possibly halt America's inexorable march towards a more perfect union. This assuring impression of continuity stands in stark contrast to Vowell's lament, which makes no overt attempt to leave us inspired or hopeful. Whereas Hamburger's tone begins pessimistically and then slowly but surely winds towards hopefulness, Vowell's remains despondent to the end. Where Hamburger lays out a semblance of a path forward, Vowell's outrage remains unmitigated, and she seems to feel no obligation to conclude with hopefulness. Indeed, Vowell imparts a distinctive sense of insecurity about the future.

Vowell's predilection for leaving us uneasy is certainly not confined to her narrative of the Inauguration. Many of her pithy essays leave us without a sense of closure. This structure is not arbitrary. It is more of an inclination—Vowell is inherently predisposed to leave us troubled. In "Democracy and Things Like That," Vowell reveals how the media took out of context a quotation from a venerated speech by Al Gore about gun violence and smeared him with it. She concludes not with a path forward or a reproach of the America media, but rather with a description of how a young student who heard the speech is now more skeptical of the media. Vowell's essay "The Strenuous Life" details a trip she and her sister took to a national park in North Dakota and ends with an unsettling description of how she feels "complacent" in her urban lifestyle, but without an impassioned plea to save our vast natural reserves or even some sort of epiphany (195). She consistently breaks the orthodox perception of how a cultural critic *should* end his or her essays—with a resounding call to action, or with at least a gesture towards something, *anything*, tangible we can hold on to. Vowell instead leaves us grasping at straws, uneasy and floundering.

In the cracks of Vowell's steadfast political beliefs lies a resonant and revelatory unease of her own: a deep-rooted sense of radical insecurity—a perpetual hyper-awareness of how arbitrary and transient the human condition is, and how powerless we are against disruptive events and death. In "The First Thanksgiving," Vowell describes the scene at the first Thanksgiving dinner her family has ever let her host. When her mother allows her to make the dressing, it hits Vowell that this means that she "is definitely, finally, totally going to die" ("Thanksgiving" 13). Vowell often uses this sort of whimsical humor and a lighthearted tone to defuse tense subjects and make the intolerable more palatable. Indeed, profundity generally underlies her drollness, and Vowell continues to come to terms with, and make meaning out of, this radical insecurity across much of her book. In her title essay, "The Partly Cloudy Patriot," she is struck by the fact that she is "overpaid to sit at a computer, eat Chinese takeout, and think things up in [her] pajamas," whereas her grandmother just fifty years ago "was picking cotton with bleeding fingers" ("Patriot" 163). It seems so arbitrary and, on a deeper level, fleeting—that at any moment, something could change or it could all be taken away. In the same essay, she mentions that, as a child of the Cold War, she still feels the "constant threat of random, sudden death" that comes from hiding under school desks (160). Radical insecurity seems to lurk perpetually in the corner of Vowell's consciousness, and it informs her essays.

Humans have crafted myriad responses to this existential dread, chief among them religion. But Vowell is an atheist, consistently critical of traditional religions—especially the "so-called god" of her parents ("Thanksgiving" 9). But the fact that she rejects conventional religions does not mean she is without *faith*. The *Oxford English Dictionary* defines faith as a "strong belief in the doctrines of a religion, based on spiritual conviction rather than proof" ("Faith"). Vowell answers her radical insecurity by turning the normative notion of faith on its head—instead of believing in a religion, she places her faith in an idea: *America*. This secular conception of faith is predicated upon understanding America not as a nation state or a collection of fifty smaller sovereign ties, but as a novel experiment unique in the history of man that, in the words of Abraham Lincoln, is "conceived in Liberty and dedicated to the proposition that all men are created equal" (qtd. in Vowell 2). And yet, in the 2000 New Hampshire primary, evangelical Christian and Republican presidential candidate Gary Bauer dismissed Vowell as one "who doesn't believe in God, doesn't believe in [the Declaration of Independence and the Constitution] because of [the presence of the] phrase 'endowed by their creator'" ("Congressman" 85). In response, Vowell writes, "I told him that, on the contrary, those documents for me have superseded God, that they are my Bible" (85). For Vowell, the principles of equality, liberty, and freedom transcend politics and resonate on a spiritual plane.

Her religion, like many, necessitates certain rituals and duties. Vowell believes a never-ending questioning of the government and societal norms to be one of the fundamental tenets of her faith. In "The Partly Cloudy Patriot," she scrutinizes the disturbing pressure she feels after September 11th to agree with every governmental policy, irrespective of how antithetical to American values she may find it. For her, the "ideal picture of citizenship [is] always . . . an argument," not a passive acceptance of the historical and political mythos of America ("Patriot" 169). Challenging this mythos—the idea of a perfect, infallible United States—is a recurrent preoccupation of Vowell's, and she understands it not as disloyalty but as fundamental to American patriotism. At first glance, Vowell's challenging *of* America seems to be directly opposed to her religious faith *in* America. However, as its definition reminds us, faith necessitates the suspension of disbelief. Vowell's faith in the abstract notion of America, a nation, in the words of her admired Lincoln, "dedicated to the proposition that all men are created equal," requires her to struggle with, rationalize, and ultimately not get discouraged by the darker chapters of our history: slavery, needless wars, and racism chief among them (qtd. in Vowell, "What He Said" 2). Indeed, this is what motivates her—by recognizing and studying the dichotomy between American ideals and American history, Vowell ostensibly identifies her purpose: to reconcile this disparity and improve the nation she so deeply loves. Vowell is able to overcome her unease about the insecurity of her way of life by positioning herself within a secular narrative of America—she believes she can be immortalized through advancing the cause of a more perfect union.

But Sarah Vowell's faith is unmistakedly jarred by the election of George W. Bush in 2000. This perceived crisis is a watershed moment for her. In her essays, she imparts the distinctive sense that she considers herself somehow separate from the vast majority of Americans. She writes that global warming is not a politically potent issue because "the public is not interested in wisdom and the public is not wise"; rather, "the public is actually reactive" ("Nerd" 102). Vowell does not identify with the *public*. "As a kid," she writes, "I never knew what to say to anyone" (91). In many ways, this insecurity of being fundamentally detached from the public is why Vowell identified with Al Gore. The man who would be so bold as to ask in his book, "'What happened to the climate in [the] Yucatán [in] 950?' . . . [tugged] at [Vowell's] nerdy soul" (100). But it was more than just nerdy camaraderie. Sarah Vowell saw *herself* in Gore. Her tears on Inauguration Day formed partly because she was angered that Bush won by a constitutional quirk, yes, but mostly because she felt that when America—the pillar of her faith—rejected Al Gore, it also rejected *her*.

Whereas other Americans may turn to religion in these moments of existential crisis, Vowell's faith provides no comfort. Normative religious faiths are all-encompassing—they answer questions about sin, death, friendship, sex, and love. Yet Sarah Vowell's faith does none of that. The Sixth Amendment guaranteeing a speedy trial is no consolation when you feel detached and rejected by the nation that for you has "superseded God" ("Congressman" 85). Even if she can overcome her radical insecurity, other fundamental questions remain. This uneasiness underlies many of Vowell's essays, even those with overtly political or historical subjects. From the 2001 Inauguration to her visit to the Salem Witch Museum, where she feels compelled to phone her psychiatrist to ask why she feels drawn to these "gruesome places," Vowell is deeply troubled by aspects of experience that her faith cannot explain ("Souvenir" 39). Indeed, it is this uneasiness that lingers with us in many of Vowell's essays.

When one returns to the documents of her faith, it becomes evident that the resonant unease Vowell imparts to us is neither accidental nor the ultimate purpose of her writing; rather, it is a means to an end. Whereas the Bible is an all-encompassing religious text, the Constitution is deliberately open-ended. The Founding Fathers never meant to resolve every dispute, but instead consciously created a living and breathing document. They wrote the Bill of Rights not as the final set of guidelines for American jurisprudence, but as its cornerstone—something to be built upon. Indeed, these documents limit themselves, and their omissions are very much deliberate. In contrast, most opinion essayists and cultural critics write with the explicit aim of elucidation, of forced inspiration. But Sarah Vowell breaks this normative understanding, and, due to the uneasiness she feels with her own faith, omits the resonant hopefulness that is so pervasive among other writers. Yet if she omits overt espousal of hope, she must have a deliberate rationale for writing—something else that motivates her essays.

Of all figures in American history, Abraham Lincoln inspires Vowell the most. "The teachers taught us to like Washington and to respect Jefferson. But Lincoln—him they taught us to love," she writes ("What He Said" 8). Vowell indeed appears to love Lincoln. She is especially struck by him not as a president or a politician, but as a writer. In "What He Said There," she humanizes him; breaking down the mythos around the "American Jesus," she feels "closer" to him (7). Vowell's fascination with Lincoln manifests itself most clearly with the recurrent motif of the Emancipation Proclamation, a document she believes to be the "perfect American artifact" ("Nerd" 168). Lincoln signed the Proclamation years before the Union had any authority to free the slaves in the Confederacy and before its "words [could] come true" (168). Its effect was unclear—no one knew whether it would prolong the war, what would happen to the slaves in the Union, or how the Confederates would react. Indeed, the Proclamation left its readers with a distinctive and resonant unease.

Moreover, its author was also uncertain about the document. Lincoln knew no better than anyone else what the Proclamation's future held. Vowell leaves us with the same insecurity that Lincoln imparted to his contemporaries with the Emancipation Proclamation. She is unsure about the answers her belief system leaves open-ended—an uneasiness that permeates many of her experiences, and that she freely imparts to us. Still, she does not feel obliged to contrive optimism or artificial hope to assuage our shared insecurity. Lincoln's Emancipation Proclamation perpetuated America's inexorable march even though—and perhaps precisely because—it neglects to offer the definitive final word, in faith that the document's inheritors will carry out its purpose. Sarah Vowell has faith that she, like Lincoln, can use the written word to fortify America's march toward a more perfect union, without saying precisely how to get there—and that is optimism enough for her.

WORKS CITED

"Faith." *Oxford Dictionaries*. Oxford UP, Apr. 2010. Web. 7 Dec. 2012.

Hamburger, Philip. "Visiting the Declaration." *The New Yorker*. 5 Feb. 2001: 32-33. Web. 7 Dec. 2012.

Vowell, Sarah. *The Partly Cloudy Patriot*. New York: Simon, 2002. Print.
    "California as an Island." 67-77.
    "Dear Dead Congressman." 79-85.
    "Democracy and Things Like That." 47-60.
    "God Will Give You Blood to Drink in a Souvenir Shot Glass." 31-42.
    "Rosa Parks, *C'est Moi*." 119-24.
    "The First Thanksgiving." 9-15.
    "The Nerd Voice." 87-117.
    "The Partly Cloudy Patriot." 155-72.
    "The Strenuous Life." 181-96.
    "What He Said There." 1-8.

Scars and Stories

IVING XU

In the wake of injury, the body heals: bleeding clots and new cells grow, reforming to recreate what was once whole, often so neatly that we forget we were ever broken. And yet the healing process isn't always a perfect one, sometimes leaving us to carry the lingering aches of injuries from long ago or the indelible etches of scars across our skin, raised reminders of past hurts and broken bones. Our scars then become stories, permanent tales of the experiences that left us fragmented and undone. Lawrence Weschler traces his hands across these scars in his collection of carefully crafted essays, *Vermeer in Bosnia: A Reader*, exploring the ways in which tragedy continues to affect us long after it should have been left behind.

Weschler finds that we carry the traumas of the past into the future, dredging them up both intentionally and unconsciously. As he sits in on the hearings of the Yugoslav War Crimes Tribunal, Weschler reflects on the continuing violence that has plagued Yugoslavia throughout time:

> Yugoslavia today has been turned back into one of those places where people not only seem incapable of forgetting the past but barely seem to be capable of thinking about anything else: the Serbs and Croats and Muslims now appear to be so deeply mired in a poisonous legacy of grievances, extending back fifty years, two hundred years—indeed, all the way back to the fourteenth century—that it's almost as if the living had been transformed into pale, wraithlike shades haunting the ghosts of the long-dead rather than the other way around. ("Bosnia" 23)

Digging up age-old graves, the people of the former Yugoslavia remain unwilling to let past conflicts and grievances pass. They revive even the dead to fight in their present-day civil wars. Intent on justifying their modern atrocities, they cling steadfastly to the tired ghosts of the past, anchoring them to this world even if to do so is to trap themselves in a "poisonous cycle" that hurts themselves as much as it does their opponents. By holding onto old injuries, they prevent themselves from ever putting the past to rest, and in so doing lose sight of what it means to live. Less consciously, the Serbians have also found themselves mirroring the past, a discovery recorded by Weschler in "Henry V at Srebrenica." He draws this connection after watching a rehearsal of Shakespeare's *Henry V*, which details the Battle of Agincourt and, most notably, King Henry's shocking orders, in defiance of all chivalric norms, to kill all of the French prisoners of war. As the scene unfolds, Weschler notes the similarities between the massacre at Agincourt in the 1400s and the more recent slaughter of Muslim prisoners at the hands of the Serbians in Srebrenica. In each scenario, the prospect of early victory, followed by an overextension of manpower and resources and a protracted battle, culminate in the killing of powerless prisoners. In both cases, the actions taken were defended as having been completely necessary. Events of the past resonate clearly into the future.

Spilling across time, tragedy leaves no individual untouched, affecting even those who come years later. In "The Son's Tale," Weschler interviews graphic novelist Art Spiegelman, whose parents' experiences during the Holocaust greatly influenced their children's lives for years afterwards. His parents were left "hollowed out and cratered" by their ordeal, creating for Spiegelman a home life "haunted, darkly freighted and overcharged with parental concern" (183, 188). His mother became overbearing to the point of obsession; after the war and the death of her first son, Spiegelman's brother, she "invest[s] her whole life" in Spiegelman (192). Unable to bear the separation when he leaves home, she commits suicide. At the same time, Spiegelman's relationship with his father becomes strained. Eventually the weight of his parents' tragedy proves to be too much for him to bear, leading to a nervous breakdown that precipitates Art's departure. The effects of the Holocaust are far-reaching, coming to not only define the survivors, but also trickling down to extend their poisonous legacy to the next generation.

Art Spiegelman achieves peace only after striving to comprehend the events of his family's history. As he retells their story in his graphic novel, *Maus*, Spiegelman sees his father, Vladek, in a new light: "but [being objective] also proved helpful—*is* proving helpful—in my coming to terms with my father. . . . there must have been a deeper sympathy for him which I wasn't even aware of as I was doing it, an understanding that I was getting in contact with. It's as if all his damn cantankerousness finally melted away" (197). Finally understanding his father to be "a survivor of hell, a mangled and warped survivor," Spiegelman sees and comes to terms with how deeply Auschwitz has pervaded his family's past, and his rage at his father slowly dissipates (196). Referring to Spiegelman's own young son, Weschler writes,

"Over a half century after the Holocaust, Vladek's line had at last produced a blessedly oblivious survivor," a testament to the end of his family's cycle of trauma (201).

As Spiegelman shows us, then, despite the long-reaching effects of our traumas, we do not have to resign ourselves to being products of the past. By working for a greater understanding of history and those who play a role in it, it is possible to reclaim the sense of agency lost in the face of oppressing and tragic circumstances. In his analysis of the work of poet Wislawa Szymborska, Weschler realizes the power that the act of comprehension may afford us as both writers and readers. Weschler examines the poem "Maybe All This" in light of Vermeer's *Lacemaker*, both of which concern the act of creation, and finds himself enraptured by a "double awareness" of Szymborska's existence as both all-powerful creator and humble subject: "as creator of the poem, Szymborska is of course simultaneously the Boss (as do we, too, the poem's readers, momentarily get to be, re-creating, recapitulating her epiphanic insight, seeing it clean for ourselves)" ("A Girl Intent" 404). Because the act of understanding involves the shaping of a reality for ourselves and the construction of our own knowledge of the world, it is also an act of creation that allows us to take on a more active role. Acknowledgement and understanding of circumstances that ensnare us also allow for conscious choices to break the temporal ties that bind us, further enabling us to move beyond the passivity thrust upon us by events.

This principle, this notion that history is not an inescapable force, and that our own conscious choices allow us to shape our legacy, is the underlying principle behind the Tribunal that Weschler bears witness to. In response to Weschler's questioning, lead prosecutor Richard Goldstone describes his envisioned mission for the Tribunal: "Specific individuals bear the major share of the responsibility, and it is they, not the group as a whole, who need to be held to account, through a fair and meticulously detailed presentation and evaluation of evidence, precisely . . . so that people are able to see how it is that specific individuals . . . [were] continually endeavoring to manipulate them" ("Bosnia" 24). An end to the cycle of vengeance and the subsequent creation of a more peaceful world comes only with an understanding of how tragedies occur.

But it is not enough to change our own perception of reality, to be the subjects of our own histories; we must rewrite our stories, but we must also recast our roles to truly transcend the circumstance into which we are born. Intent on changing the status quo, the subjects of Weschler's essays refuse to accept or fall into the role of victim that arises so readily in any tragedy. In "A

Parkinsonian Passion" Weschler interviews furniture-designer Ed Weinberger, who, in the face of his Parkinson's diagnosis, chooses to design several visually confusing pieces of furniture that, despite their stability, appear to be anything but stable. Weinberger describes his approach: "Going after what your mind can conceive or project but turns out to be physically impossible—that's an echt-Parkinsonian way of proceeding" (380). His designs are thus an act of subversion, a means of overturning the limitations of his debilitating disease through art and "an attempt to create for [himself] a life of [his] own, to assert that life, to safeguard it in the face of an otherwise overpowering condition" (398). Through his designs, he strives for exactly that which his illness has denied him, precision, in a blatant refusal to accept the limitations of his disease. Journalist Jerzy Urban, whom Weschler spotlights in "The Troll's Tale," adopts a similar mentality. Weschler observes: "One thing is clear: he cannot abide either playing the role of passive victim or being cast in it" (160). Despite his experiences as a child struggling to survive through the harrowing events of World War II (and the Holocaust as a Jew), Urban displays a remarkable "ability not only to survive but, time and again, to triumph" (155-56). In contrast to families like Spiegelman's, who remain mired in the past, unable to escape, Urban is defiant, fighting the constraints of his past and making his way to the top. Not only did he create his own history, independent of the tribulations of his childhood, he rose above his past experiences to quite literally direct the course of history at large, becoming a man in a position of power. Far from becoming pale ghosts, fading into the shadows of their pasts, these two men were defiant, creating for themselves lives that were vibrant and unapologetic, and above all, of their own choosing.

Appropriately, Weschler often lets his subjects do most of the talking. His minimal narration sets the scene or aids us in following the conversation. For the most part, however, his essays read more or less as monologues in which his subjects dominate the conversation and speak directly to us to tell their own stories in their own words. Weinberger's musings on tolerances, variances, and the golden ratio, for example, reveal a remarkably sharp mind that Weschler characterizes as "straining after greater and greater precision, toward an almost infinite perfection" ("Passion" 373). In Urban's often crude and profane remarks—"you know how it can be with girls who spend years cooped up with the nuns: inevitably they end up making the easiest lays"— we see a man who is irreverent and intractable, a man who is not afraid to say what he wants or do what he wants ("Troll" 154). As a result of Weschler's hands-off approach, his subjects are able to direct their own narratives and complicated histories. Their presences become clear to us. Both on the page and in our minds, they become real to us, and we are able to understand them on their own terms.

That's not to say, however, that Weschler as a writer is passive, or that he allows his subjects to do all of his work for him. Rather, he often works to orchestrate our experience of revelation through a deliberate juxtaposition of images. In "Vermeer in Bosnia," he sheds light on the work of the Tribunal by constructing a very specific visual metaphor, beginning with his introduction of Vermeer's *Head of a Young Girl*: "This is a woman who has just turned toward us and is already about to look away" (19). Interpreting the image as such, he understands the woman in the painting to be "autonomous, self-sufficient, suffuse with individual dignity and potential agency" (20). Having set up this image in our minds, Weschler later, at essay's end, describes Dusko Tadic, the man on trial at the Tribunal: "For a startling split second, he looked up at the camera. And then he looked away" (25). Weschler wants us to see that Tadic, like the young girl in Vemeer's painting, is autonomous and responsible for his own actions. Only by holding individuals accountable for their crimes can the tribunal hope, finally, to put an end to the violence that has for so long pervaded the nation. Weschler recognizes certain parallels and guides us through their every nuance and complexity, leading us to see, through a simple but haunting imaage, how blood feuds might finally end.

Weschler also draws attention to events and objects that are not necessarily connected. Through a juxtaposition of art, history, and biography, he evokes a new sense of understanding. His methods are reminiscent of another of his subjects, photographer David Hockney, whose primary preoccupation is creating works of art that are true to the ways that we actually see and perceive the world. Initially, Hockney forgoes photography as a medium, insisting that "your eye doesn't ever see that much in one glance. It's not true to life" ("True" 321). However, he finds a solution to his problem in his *joiners*, photocollages that piece together images of the same subject from different perspectives: "I realized that this sort of picture came closer to how we actually see—which is to say, not all at once but in discrete, separate glimpses, which we then build up into our continuous experience of the world" (326). Weschler's essays are, for us, joiners, assembling various glimpses of the world—Srebrenica through the lens of Henry V, the War Tribunal through the lens of the work of Johannes Vermeer—to present a more cohesive understanding of the world, one that we would be unable to see at first glance. Hockney also finds value in the complication his collages offer: "With five photos, for instance, you were forced to look five times. You couldn't help looking more carefully" (322). Complication commands our attention, forcing us to look closely until we uncover some sort of truth, until we achieve some level of understanding.

Weschler employs these careful juxtapositions to construct new narratives that focus not merely on how we are mired in the tragedies of the past but rather on how these tragedies are elements of a complex and often untold whole. Storytelling allows for the possibility of change and remaking; with each telling we choose to include or exclude certain evidence, thereby propagating different realities. The perception of Bosnia has lately been particularly bloody and violent. However, as Weschler is reminded as he speaks to a group of merchants of various backgrounds, there is another part of Bosnia's history that is often overlooked:

> Look . . . the thing you have to understand is that for eight hundred years around these parts, going all the way back to the Middle Ages . . . people around here have lived with each other *in peace*. Catholics, Muslims, Orthodox, Jews. In peace. No one anywhere else has been able to pull such a thing off. Sure, every once in a while some crooked politicians come along and muck everything up, but eventually they leave, and we're all still here. And people here know how to get along. ("Coda" 79)

Through the glimpses and snapshots presented in his essays, Weschler fills in our fragmented understanding of the world with the knowledge that other possibilities exist, forgotten amongst the more prominent stories of pain. Pulling together narratives that speak to the strength of the human spirit, Weschler demonstrates that these alternate histories are stories that we can and should tell. Ghosts can be banished and scars can begin to heal. Shadows and disfigurements need no longer remind us of horrors past but might instead testify to strength and survival, to the ways in which people can stand up in the face of conflict and oppression. Fashioning our words in the way Weschler has shown us, we can begin to create new stories of survival.

WORKS CITED

Weschler, Lawrence. *Vermeer in Bosnia: A Reader*. New York: Pantheon, 2004. Print.

"A Girl Intent: Wislawa Szymborska and the Lacemaker." 402-05.

"A Parkinsonian Passion: Ed Weinberger." 367-400.

"Coda: The Market on the Tuzla/Brcko Road." 77-79.

"Henry V at Srebrenica." 27-45.

"The Son's Tale: Art Spiegelman." 182-201.

"The Troll's Tale: Jerzy Urban." 151-81.

"True to Life: David Hockney's Photocollages." 319-52.

"Vermeer in Bosnia." 13-26.

Our Special Monsters

MEGAN STEINER

Euripides begins his tragic play *Medea* by painting a sympathetic picture of a woman scorned. Hiding within her home, "Medea burns with shame. Dishonored, she calls out . . . gives herself entirely up to a terrible despair" (24-30). She does not, however, remain a weeping victim for long. She subsequently appears on stage dry-eyed and furious at Jason, the husband who shamed her by taking a new wife. Medea vows by the gods that she must "set the balance right," must bring about justice in light of the injustice done to her (164). Justice, to Medea, is a matter of being "a scourge to [her] enemies, a benefactor to [her] friends" (888-89), and in her estimation of things, embodying this justice will certainly make her a heroine, "For those who act as I do, forever, their names live on in glory" (889-90). Jason is her enemy, and for wronging her she decides "foul murder is a fair return" (431-32). Action swiftly follows words, and with righteous glee she plots and carries out the gruesome murders of the new house of Jason—Princess Creusa and King Creon—the new family for which he abandoned hers. Medea stands a shining paragon of her brand of justice, a heroine who upholds tradition by helping friends and harming enemies. She certainly has harmed her enemies, but instead of casting her as heroine, this scene leaves us with the image of a Medusa-like woman, grinning maniacally as she stands over the corpses of her victims, her hands dripping with blood.

The tragedy is as yet incomplete, of course, as is Medea's revenge. She has resolved that the house of Jason must fall completely—that his name, his legacy, must be eradicated. She must kill her own sons. Medea falters in the face of such a heinous act, "the most unholy deed," and for a moment we catch a glimpse of the sad, lost woman from the beginning of the play, but this moment is fleeting (877). Medea ultimately commits filicide with the same steely resolve that led her to commit regicide, and the house of Jason is demolished. All that is left for Medea is to bask in the glory of her enemy's despair, and Jason does not disappoint; he is utterly devastated upon discovering that his sons are dead. He looks at Medea to see that she has become "not a woman, but a lioness, more savage than the sea-monster Scylla" (1469-70). Medea is undisturbed, and, if anything, Jason's hatred only deepens her satisfaction: "Call me a she-lion or a monster, as you like, for I have aimed and hit my mark—my barb forever lodged in your cleft heart" (1484-85). She has won! She is vindicated! She has harmed her enemy, set the balance right. She has brought justice. And Euripides shows that the gods do indeed stand behind her: Medea's exit from the play is a *deus ex machina*—an escape granted by the gods. Yet despite all this, as Medea flies off in her dragon-drawn chariot, the still-warm bodies of her sons at her feet, Jason denied "a father's right to touch their bodies," she still appears to her audience a cold-hearted monster on the wings of monsters (1538).

I want to cheer for the prototypical triumph of the woman scorned and for the justice she has achieved, as Euripides seems to suggest that we should in granting her a hero's departure, but instead, like Jason, all I can see is a "child-murdering monster" and the bodies left in her wake (1532). She is, theoretically, a heroine, at least according to the lengths to which she goes to achieve justice, yet the nature of her actions makes her seem a monster. Medea is a strange, startling paradox. Human nature is never black and white: we all fall within a murky, nebulous gray area to some degree, so I can accept the possibility of such a paradox personified. However, by the end of the play we see nothing human left in Euripides's creation, no trace of the weeping woman she once was. What happened to Medea's humanity?

Hundreds of years after Euripides created Medea, long after the last Greek tragedy was written, Mary Shelley created one of the most famous monsters of modern literature in her novel *Frankenstein*. Though Shelley's nameless monster is birthed in a laboratory and therefore inhuman by nature, he is far more than his epithet suggests; against all odds, her inhuman monster is a study in humanity. The monster, like Medea, is not always monstrous, but something has robbed him of his humanity. As the monster explains to Dr. Frankenstein, his creator, "I was benevolent and good; misery made me a fiend" (82). In an effort to prove this to the doctor, the man who despises him most, the monster tells his story, a tragedy not so unlike Medea's. From the moment he is sent from Frankenstein's laboratory, the creature's hideous form inspires the fear and hatred of mankind. He is forced to flee in the face of man's cruelty, seeking sanctuary in an abandoned hovel in the countryside. He observes the neighboring family, entranced by their daily lives—their struggles, their joys, and most of all their love. Their loving interactions amaze him: "I felt sensations of a peculiar and overpowering nature; they were a mixture of pain and pleasure. . . . I withdrew . . . unable to bear these emotions" (89). His feelings, which he cannot name, are a combination of longing, wistfulness, and loneliness. These are human emotions, yet this inhuman being possesses them. He is called a monster for his horrifying features, but these features are merely physical—his eloquence and sensitivity belie his deformity. He hopes that his protectors, as he has come to call this family, will show him the same compassion they show each other, but when he finally reveals himself, even these gentle humans attack him in horror. They see only a hideous giant and refuse him the chance to reveal the humanity beneath the superficial monstrosity. His hopes that he may find a place in this or any family are heartbreakingly shattered, and from his despair, for the first time, rises a monster. He recalls: "My protectors . . . had broken the only link that held me to the world. . . . the feelings of revenge and hatred filled my bosom" (118).

A broken, wounded animal, hopeless and friendless, he turns his rage upon Frankenstein, his creator and his arch-enemy. The monster is "determined to seek that justice which [he] vainly attempted to gain from any other being that wore the human form," a justice that takes the form of vengeance (119). Frankenstein must be punished for the injustice of casting his creation into a world that cannot and will not make room for him. Ultimately, the monster accepts the role that man's fear and revulsion have always forced upon him: that of "the fiend," the devil, the enemy of humankind (83). Like Medea, the monster finds justice in harming his enemy, and like Medea, he finds foul murder a fair return for all the harm done to him. The monster's first crime is the murder of Frankenstein's youngest brother. As he looks down at the body of the child, he triumphantly exclaims, "I too can create desolation" (122). I hear the exultation in his triumph, but it seems hollow. The ragged cries of the arch-fiend—the wretched angel cast from heaven to become Satan, king of hell—are audible in his cries. As the fiend triumphs, I imagine the benevolent creature he once was sobbing for the fate of the broken human at his feet, yet another human from whom he wanted nothing more than compassion and understanding, and in whom he found nothing but another rejection.

I ache for Shelley's arch-fiend, yet I cannot ache for Medea. I simply cannot hail her as the heroine Euripides so strives to create. But both monsters share a sense of justice, both have been hurt, and both have killed in cold blood; why, then, do I struggle so much with Medea and so little with Frankenstein's creation? Perhaps it is because Shelley depicts her monster's struggles more fully than does Euripides. She shows each blow that he is dealt. His pain is tangible as it chips away at his humanity, which is lost when despair and rage finally consume him. I get to see how the monster is born, and so empathize with him. Euripides denies us this understanding, this intimate view of the erosion of Medea's soul: one moment, she weeps and prays for death to "free [her] of [her] hateful life" (144), yet in the next she prays to see Jason and his wife "ground into grit" (168). The tragedy of the woman, Medea, is given only a moment's attention by Euripides, a mere means to an end: his heroine needs a reason to seek the vengeance—or justice—that is Euripides's primary concern. Yet to understand *what* Medea is, monster or heroine, we must understand *who* she is.

To his credit, Euripides does show us elements of Medea's humanity; the problem is that they are lost beneath the weight of the author's concern for justice. The details of Shelley's monster, though, help me to reconstruct the lost character of Medea. The monster's tragedy stems from his very nature— he wanders the earth alone, a foreigner among the human race. Medea, too, is a foreigner: "carried from a foreign land, orphaned by distance; I have . . . no family to offer refuge" (288-90). When Jason left her, he left her truly alone in a land not her own, making his betrayal all the more cruel. She notes the plight of an outsider: "judgment runs before knowledge. . . . they hate so easily and on the least of grounds . . . a foreigner must not resist the general will" (239-44). Shelley's monster agrees: "a fatal prejudice clouds their eyes . . . they behold only a detestable monster" (114). Medea is a target of prejudice—a "barbarian witch"—and her reputation and isolation compound her feeling of hopelessness at her plight (1518). And it is hopelessness that seems to be the final, most dangerous element in birthing a monster: it is only when Shelley's monster loses all hope of being accepted by men that he becomes bent on murderous vengeance against mankind. So, too, for Medea: it is only when she feels "[her] life is worthless anyway" that she resolves to "do this deed" and kill her children (878-79). It seems in both cases that utter despair, pure hopelessness, is the catalyst for the transformation. With nothing left to lose, seeing no joy in her future, vengeful fury against those who stripped her of her hope seems a logical last resort.

Provoked by thoughts of the creature within Shelley's fiend, an image flickers in my mind: I again see the scene of Medea murdering her children, but this time it is different. Though there is no trace of remorse in her stony face and her hands still drip with blood, I imagine the hopeless single mother sobbing again, locked away within the hardened monster, shrieking "What else could I have done?" And for a moment, I ache for Medea. Yet I cannot ignore the dead children at her feet for long—I cannot ignore the atrocity she has committed—and like Jason, I wonder, "Was a marriage reason enough to slay your sons?" (1493). Medea answers yes. Euripides casts this "yes" as heroism, as the enacting of justice at all costs, but I remain horrified by such a being, by such a justice. The Greek characters in the play acknowledge her as an abomination. They, like me, cannot fathom how "when you gaze upon your sons . . . you keep the ice of your resolve . . . and dry-eyed, kill them?" (950-56). Indeed, her acts have made her "hateful to all of humankind" (1451).

The Greek world would seem to hate Medea, and the human world rejects Shelley's monster; these two individuals are clearly refused by their respective societies. But what happens if the tables are turned? What of those individuals who hate—who indeed refuse—the entirety of human society? In "A Cover Letter to Molière's *Misanthrope*," Stanley Cavell considers the roots and the ramifications of misanthropy—a word, in fact, with Greek origins meaning hatred of the human. Cavell considers Molière's character Alceste, neither condemning nor praising his refusal to join the human race, remaining neutral as he strives to understand why Alceste's misanthropy evokes such strong reactions from those around him. Cavell believes that Alceste represents "purity to their purity, or to their sense of their purity lost—not as if corrupted exactly but as if misplaced, thus still present somehow" (98). Alceste possesses an innocence that is compelling because it has fallen out of sight of those participating in society. This innocence is not merely purity to Cavell, but a state of being unacquainted with evil, free from experience of wrong. Nor is it a mere trait—Cavell portrays innocence as a conscious being, one to be cast aside, surely, but "in a time and place of its own consent" (98). To consent to the world, one must first feel "that the world is good enough to want to live in"; misanthropy, then, is a visceral reaction to "the world as it is, [one] not wantable, or not acceptable" (99). The misanthrope says "no" to human society due to a feeling Cavell understands as "a mode of disgust, a repugnance at the idea that your life should partake of the world's" (99). Cavell's "disgust" seems a *repulsion*, a profound disappointment in the nature of the world that one has consented to. But the misanthrope proves there is a choice—*not* to do the expected, but to dissent, to dissociate, to be *openly disgusted*, and therein lies his power: "[those within society] think [he is] right . . . and cannot want to live without the thing [he means] to them" (101). That is, in a word, choice—Cavell "[extracts] hope from the very fact that we are capable of genuine disgust at the world," finds that perhaps "a consenting adult in a world of horrors" may dissent from being "a conspirator of that world" by spurning "the human capacity for *going along*" (102-03).

There are indeed moments when Cavell's possibility comes to pass. Medea's act of filicide sees the Greek world *stop going along*: they unanimously cry out, "do not do this awful deed; Medea, we beseech you!" and then simply, "No!" (943-44). In the modern world, too, such cries of disgust tend to echo everywhere in times of war—protests, newspapers, dinner table discussions, so loud that they can drive us mad. Indeed, Cavell himself has fallen victim to the madness of wartime society. He recalls that as World War II raged on, he dealt with the overwhelming din by dissociating—understandably, he clung to sanity by retreating into his own mind—and contributed to a "society [that] cannot hear its own screams" (104). Medea clearly cannot hear modern society's screams, and she is undeterred by the screams of Greek society, but dissent does not make monsters; rather, it unmasks them. Perhaps, then, her unthinkable actions become possible only when she can no longer hear the screams of her own conscience.

Cavell, like Euripides and Shelley, writes about his own brand of monster, though these are unfortunately monsters of history, not fiction. He believes Nazis to be "those who have lost the capacity for being horrified by what they do," who have lost the capacity for genuine disgust at themselves and their world (103). This loss of the capacity for "horror at the human" is what makes them "our special monsters . . . monsters of adaptability . . . [who turn] this human capacity for adapting into a mockery of itself, a mockery of being human" (103). Perhaps, because they are more real than boogeymen or devils or Shelley's monster, terrible men become our special monsters: they shed light on the very real human capacity to *be* a horror.

As a Jew raised on my grandmother's stories of the Holocaust and all of my ancestors who died at the hands of the Nazis, I find Cavell's stark representation at once startling and unsettling. Nazis are human beings who did monstrous things, whose hands are bloodied by genocide, who prove that there is danger, horrific danger, in losing the human capacity for "horror at the human," and I cannot help but see Medea in this description, and in so doing, finally realize why she disgusts me so (103). I can see why I find myself agreeing with Jason, Euripides's ostensible villain, and the Greek Chorus. We, as her audience, are made complicit with this woman who has lost the capacity for horror, who has lost the thing that makes her human and become a mockery of humanity. According to Cavell, being her consenting audience, accepting Euripides's insistence that something we feel to be horrific is instead just, we would be guilty of "complicitous tyranny over ourselves" (102). After her crimes are complete, Medea is characterized as a "Fury" (1371), "abhorrent to the gods" (1383), "not a woman, but a lioness, more savage than the sea-monster Scylla" (1469-70); none of the characters who have been an audience to her "justice" can bear to call her a member of the human race. And Euripides, by hailing this monster a heroine, demands that we, his audience, abandon our own feelings of horror to take up the banner of Medea's justice—a justice with no room for fundamental human concerns. There is, however, danger in fulfilling this request: we risk surrendering our own humanity to a human notion of justice, just as Medea has. To crown Medea a heroine, to call her actions just, is to justify monstrosity in the name of what is "right"; isn't that what the Nazis did? It would require me to set aside my disgust and hush my instinctual screams of horror, to give in to "the human capacity for going along," so to Euripides I must ultimately say "No!" (Cavell 103).

In telling his story, Shelley's monster wonders at "the barbarity of man" (88). In his own words, "For a long time I could not conceive how one man could go forth to murder his fellow. . . . Was man, indeed, at once so powerful, so virtuous . . . yet so vicious and base?" (160). His status as an outsider observing human nature grants him the asset of perspective. In a different yet similar way, I am granted this same asset as a reader, as are all readers (including my own). In reading these works and writing this paper, I exercise this privilege and come to picture another bizarre scene. I see all of my monsters—the world's monsters—seated together around a table years after the height of their crimes. With each of them stands the author who wrote them into existence, or in Cavell's case, who brought them into the light of observation. First I see Shelley and her monster. He is as hideous as ever, holding the locket torn from the neck of his first victim—Frankenstein's brother—with his head in his hands. His rage spent itself long ago, and all that remains is the abyss of loneliness. Shelley crouches next to him, puts her hand atop his, conveying the affection and compassion that he so desperately wishes for. From the monster reemerges the creature; though no longer innocent, he reaches towards hope. I smile. Next comes the Nazi. My grandmother's family portraits, dozens of them, each depicting another branch of my family tree mercilessly pruned, are piled in front of him. Cavell stands behind him, bending close to the Nazi's ear, and begins to scream. His screams perhaps offer a cleansing revulsion, redemption for his dissociation from the world back when Nazism was at its monstrous height. The Nazi seems distant, catatonic. I believe that his fate was presciently revealed by Euripides's Chorus: "Such killers are pursued by horrors in the shape of their worst crimes" (1385-87). I leave the Nazi subject to Cavell's screams, but not before adding my voice to his own. And finally, I come to Medea. I've described my evolving image of her too many times; I am overwhelmed by her presence already.

I turn to face Euripides, then, for it is he with whom I have truly been struggling. He looks on at Medea impassively, not proudly as I had expected, and then turns to me. I am about to launch into a diatribe on how horribly wrong he was to create such a dangerous "heroine," when he bids me pause. He says, pointing me to a question posed by the Chorus near the end of *Medea*, "But now that *this* has happened, what horror cannot be imagined, what will set the limits of our fault?" (Euripides 1416-18). I am briefly puzzled, and Cavell ceases screaming to call me over. He reminds me of a moment in his essay, during his discussion of human adaptability, in which he asks, "Who does not see that there must be *some* limit to this?" (Cavell 103). Medea springs to mind, and I tell him so. Cavell shakes his head with a smile and Shelley beckons to me. She points out the moment at which her creature cries out, "Oh, praise the eternal justice of man!" (82). She winks as though she has just let me in on a secret, but it remains secret from me. So I return to Euripides, mouth open to protest, but he stops me again. He puts a hand on my shoulder, adopts a conspiratorial smirk, and then he is gone. My imaginary summit dissipates, but the final thoughts linger. Of course, even after his departure, Euripides continues to confound me; I am still left with more questions than answers.

Perhaps the answer is in the very existence of my questions. Perhaps Euripides knew his heroine would be unacceptable—maybe he made her that way, to bring us to question where we will set the limits to our faults. Perhaps Cavell tries to show us that *we, humans*, must set these limits ourselves based upon our intellects, making full, conscious use of our humanity. And perhaps Shelley offers the insight that the justice of man mustn't be eternal. Humans and our justice must evolve, must question, must be questioned. It seems the task falls to humanity—as a race, but especially as a condition—to set it right.

WORKS CITED

Cavell, Stanley. "A Cover Letter to Molière's *Misanthrope*." *Themes Out of School: Effects and Causes.* Chicago: The U of Chicago P, 1984. 97-105. Print.

Euripides. *Euripides, 1: Medea, Hecuba, Andromache, The Bacchae.* Eds. David R. Slavitt and Palmer Bovie. Trans. Eleanor Wilner et al. Philadelphia: U of Pennsylvania P, 1998. Print.

Shelley, Mary. *Frankenstein.* New York: Penguin, 2000. Print.

Facebook the Orgy-Porgy

WARREN ERSLY

"Ford, we are twelve; oh make us one
Like drops within the Social River;
Oh, make us now together run
As swiftly as thy shining Flivver
Come, Greater Being, Social Friend,
Annihilating Twelve-in-One!
We long to die, for when we end,
Our larger life has but begun.
Feel how the Greater Being comes!
Rejoice and, in rejoicings, die!
Melt in the music of the drums!
For I am you and you are I.
Orgy-porgy, Ford and fun,
Kiss the girls and make them One.
Boys at one with girls at peace;
Orgy-porgy gives release."

(Brave New World 54-56)

Such is the disturbing refrain of *Brave New World*'s twisted, drug-fueled ritual of the Orgy-porgy, depicted by Aldous Huxley in his 1931 science fiction classic. The Orgy-porgy (among other social functions in *Brave New World*) is symptomatic of a culture completely controlled by the pursuit of pleasure and reward. All things risky, unpleasant, complicated, or dangerous have been erased and replaced with hyper-social communal rituals such as the quasi-religious and erotic Orgy-porgy, frivolous games like Centrifugal Bumblepuppy, a mind-altering upper known as *soma*, and sensual distractions like the Feelies, films that stimulate all five of the senses.

The characters that inhabit *Brave New World* are afraid of being alone, are motivated only by their consumerism, and have never felt real pain or taken real risks. Their world is dominated solely by "pleasant vices," and in the words of Mustapha Mond, *Brave New World*'s twisted propaganda minister, "You can't have a lasting civilization without plenty of pleasant vices" (161). The people of Huxley's *Brave New World* are enslaved not by an iron fist, but a velvet glove. Their constant and instant access to pleasure has made them sedate, easily controlled, weak, and unable to think for themselves. *Brave New World* shows us the darker side of a technological utopia and poses hard questions: is there such a thing as too much happiness? What are the merits and demerits of risk, danger, pain and suffering? And in a social environment defined strictly by reward and pleasure, can true reward and pleasure even exist?

Garry Kasparov is no stranger to such things as risk, reward, and pleasure. As one of the most famous chess players in history, he claimed his status as world champion in what is considered one of the all-time masterpiece games of chess history in 1985, and held on to his title until the year 2000. Yet Kasparov didn't just defend his title against fellow human chess players— during the late nineties and early two thousands, Kasparov was also the target of the thriving chess super computer industry. In his essay "The Chess Master and the Computer," Kasparov details his involvement in the world of chess supercomputing, outlining the many man versus machine chess experiments he participated in, eventually telling the story of his defeat at the hands of IBM's chess supercomputer *Deep Blue* in 1997.

Yet Kasparov's essay does not end with his defeat; if anything, that is where it all begins. He engages in a discussion on the sheer complexity of chess, and likens the possibilities of each game to the infinite possibilities of human thought itself; he then moves on to explore the implications of the effects of computers on the ancient game—how chess players practicing in conjunction with computer analysis are "free of prejudice and doctrine . . . [just] as free of dogma as the machines with which they train." Kasparov argues that computers have created a new normal in chess, upping the standard of skill it takes to be considered a master of the game and churning out an entire generation of human players who are just as good as, if not better than, the chess giants of yesteryear. Ultimately, Kasparov argues that with computer assistance, the chess player's "creativity [is] . . . paramount."

Despite his obvious admiration for the machines that beat him, Kasparov is quick to point out the new flaws he sees in the computerized culture of chess. He believes that chess computer developers have strayed from the original goal of developing machines that could learn the game as a human does. "Surely this would be a far more fruitful avenue of investigation than creating, as we are doing, ever-faster algorithms to run on ever-faster hardware," he writes, ultimately concluding that we are discarding our creativity in exchange for a steady supply of marketable products. He believes that our capacity for risk taking in science and industry is dwindling as a result of the "incrementalism and demands of the market." In sum, he laments the decrease in risk-taking behavior that he believes is a developing malady in society: as he writes, "we can't enjoy the rewards without taking the risks." In a very Huxleyan manner, Kasparov views the consumers of goods—particularly of tech products—as being both misled and content with a lack of progress. So long as what they purchase can entertain and distract them, they will be happy. The producers of goods, whom Kasparov chides in his essay, are aware of this trend and, as a result, put little effort into innovating when they develop new products. Kasparov believes that the joy the user experiences in interfacing with these goods is not true joy, but a kind of illusion—a hollow, cheap thrill, a riskless reward.

But Kasparov views the world from a chess player's perspective. His entire career is built on risk: big moves, calculated sacrifices, tactical tradeoffs, perilous self-exposure, secrecy, painful deliberation, and the constant, stressful awareness of victory teetering on the edge of defeat. Oddly enough, and certainly running counter to the nerdy and sheltered stereotype of the chess player, Kasparov lives a life on the edge. With a career defined by risk, perhaps he over-emphasizes, possibly even romanticizes, the act of risk taking. Kasparov sees man's proclivity to engage in risky behavior as evaporating in modern society given his definition of risk *as a chess player*. But do we all define what is risky in the same manner? And if not, doesn't that also change our perception and experience of reward?

An idea prevalent in Sherry Turkle's essay "Tethering" is that a sense of risk and exposure to risk are vital to one's identity. Turkle introduces the notion that in the digital age one's self-concept is becoming increasingly integrated with the technology that surrounds us and all the convenient new tools and toys it provides, including social networking, instant messaging, and constant access to email or other forms of digital media. But Turkle is quick to point out the dangers and shortcomings of this new reality: "[we live] on the Net, newly free in some ways, newly yoked and tethered in others" (221). In turn, this tethering "enable[s] us to store, display, perform, and manipulate aspects of identity" on an unprecedented scale (223). Thus, technology has given birth to a much more fluid and "free" concept of the self, allowing for greater sovereignty of expression and creativity in online social exchanges, which Turkle contends have become the norm. Additionally, because this sense of self now resides partly online, we have the ability to connect with friends and family anywhere, anytime. In this sense, we are "free," but as a result, we tend to avoid face-to-face interactions with new people and forego exposure to new experiences. Turkle argues that communities now exist on our phones and our laptops, instead of in our neighborhoods, schools, churches, or clubs. Physically, we find ourselves more isolated than ever, "yoked and tethered" to the objects of our digital addictions.

In addition, due to the ease with which the self can be digitally reconfigured and communicated to others, the risk-taking aspects of identity formation are diminished, and thus the vital rewards are too. Turkle considers this dilemma in terms of adolescence and the formation of identity, which she considers essential rites of passage, and technology's effects on this transitionary period. She writes:

> It is a rite of passage that communicates, 'You are on your own and responsible. If you are frightened, you have to experience those feelings.' The cell phone buffers this moment; the parent is 'on tap.' With the parent-on-tap, tethered children think differently about themselves. They are not quite alone . . . what is not being cultivated is the ability to be alone and to manage and contain [their] emotions. (224)

Turkle might respond to Kasparov by contending that it is not our *capacity* to take risks that is dwindling, but instead our very *exposure* to risk. Even when we are exposed to something traditionally considered risky (navigating the city at night, dealing with conflict) access to a support network is always available, always a touchscreen away. Dealing with risk, pain, loneliness, and danger, then, becomes much easier. Feelings can be quickly outsourced to others, stripping away the complex and unsettling aspects of an experience and spreading them about a social network for all to take note of; as a result, we are left with less to think about and less to feel. According to Turkle, technology has eroded how we experience risk, with neither science nor industry bearing the brunt of the damage; instead, the *individual* and his very sense of self suffer.

Both Kasparov and Turkle seem to grapple with the declining influence of risk on our decision-making. Kasparov discusses risk in light of his own experience playing against chess supercomputers, and with regard to technological innovation and the consumer market. To demonstrate his point, he poses the hypothetical question, "Why waste time and money experimenting with new and innovative ideas when we already know what works?" He encourages the development of new technology but fears its application; he believes that technology has made us *too conservative*, worrying that we will not use our advancing technology as a springboard for the development of new processes and new ideas, but that we will give into the market's endless stream of only-slightly-better-than-last-year's tech-products in the name of making money, avoiding failure, and keeping the masses happy. Turkle, in comparison, reflects upon the possible outcomes of the Internet and communications revolutions *not* in terms of human creativity and scientific advancement in a market culture, but instead in terms of human development in a so-called "always-on culture" dominated by the rapid dissemination of information, constant connectivity, and instant gratification (225). She asserts that the speed and frequency of communication influences how we think, forcing us to abandon our capability to ruminate on and properly digest information. She fears that new technology has made us *too interdependent*. So while we might seem to take risks in communicating with our friends, Turkle believes its not because we're unafraid but because we've become numb to the potential negative outcomes.

Both Kasparov and Turkle are concerned about technology's impact on our ability to detect and respond to risk. Each argues in some fashion that technology has had some sort of negative effect. Though I see validity in both authors' essays, I find myself asking: what about Huxley? What about the Orgy-porgies, Centrifugal Bumblepuppies, Feelies, and all the other "pleasant vices" of his *Brave New World*? Though both Kasparov and Turkle offer valid discussions of risk, perhaps risk is not what is at stake here. Perhaps it is not our capacity for risk-taking that has been distorted by the digital age, but instead our sense of what is rewarding, and to what degree.

Huxley could never have fully anticipated the advent of the Internet and web-based social networking. Despite this, the world of the web isn't a far cry from that of Huxley's *Brave New World*. Just as Turkle argues in "Tethering," online social interactions are dominated by the instant reception of reward and satisfaction, as *Brave New World* foreshadowed. The Internet has brought about an entirely new normal in which socializing online is just as important, if not more important, than its offline counterpart. Those who would oppose this march of progress are quickly becoming cultural relics, backwards in their ways and bitterly resistant to the changing tides of social life. Yet it is not hard to see why the Internet has become so pivotal in forming the modern social self; it is a brave new world that minimizes the risk involved in socializing and expression, and cranks up the feelings of reward to a maximum.

My generation lives online through social networking sites such as Facebook. Walls, message boards, and chat rooms are quickly becoming the new public meeting places where friends get together to catch up, reminisce, debate, share and discuss interests, and gossip, all via an eclectic mix of text, photos, videos, and content reproduced from other sources. With so much of public life now occurring on the web, it's easy to forget that social media giants like Facebook, Twitter, Google, and even Reddit (which is both famous and infamous for its free-spirited, user-created community and culture) are all corporate-style businesses, driven by the fundamental necessity to generate profit that undergirds even the smallest and simplest of companies. For a company like Facebook to keep its user base, and thus the cash it makes advertising to them, it must find new ways to draw the user in and keep him coming back for more. New features and tools are constantly added, tweaked, perfected, all to keep the experience feeling fresh and new for the long-time consumer of the product that is Facebook. Furthermore, Facebook works long and hard to keep competitors out of the market by siphoning off their user base, integrating and subsuming the competition such that a Facebook account may now be linked with a multitude of other online products such as Twitter, Stumbleupon, Instagram, Tumblr, and more. Through such appropriation these products no longer threaten Facebook, but provide yet another reason to use Facebook as a primary online social hub. We've staked a large part of our social lives, and thus important aspects of our identities, on but a few very large social media companies that profit from our continued consumption of their products. Thanks to businesses like Facebook, Google, and Apple, identity in the digital age has become just as lucrative a commodity as corn, coal, or crude.

So where does the concept of reward come into this discussion? In a culture dominated by quick and easy access to all sorts of media, sensationalism is the key. After all, how can any one thing hold our attention for any period of time when we have access to everything? In the fast paced digital-communications culture of the 21st century, companies sensationalize their products more than ever to attract potential consumers and retain current ones. Online social life seems to be centered on who can accumulate the most: who can get the most followers on Twitter, who can rack up the most likes on their status or picture, whose post on the thread has the most upvotes, who has the most original material posted to their blog. The socializing aspect of the web has taken the most superficial aspects of *irl* (a shorthand for "in real life," very well-known to those who frequent online message boards or blogs such as Reddit or Tumblr) and has elevated them to the nth degree. More and more time and effort are devoted to entertaining, showing off, propping up meticulously groomed online personae, and the one-way transmission of ideas, and less effort is devoted to actually communicating with others and learning about them. Just as in Huxley's dystopian England, everything online has been designed to quickly and effectively transmit a sense of reward, accomplishment, success, and pleasure. The marketers of social media have effectively convinced us that without their products, without more likes, more followers, more reblogs, more upvotes, more shares and posts and albums and videos and check-ins and tags, we will not be cool.

A sense of reward propels the success and popularity of the social media market. Anyone who has ever camped out, fixated in front of his computer, refreshing the page every five minutes awaiting the moment in which his clever status or photo from last night's party secures yet another like or comment, knows this intimately. Turkle hints at this very phenomenon in "Tethering" when she writes: "[The online self] measures success by calls made, e-mails answered, contacts reached. This self is calibrated on the basis of what technology proposes, by what it makes possible, by what it makes easy" (225). Though Turkle frames her discussion of web culture (and thus "tethered culture") primarily in terms of risk, emotional communication, and isolation versus connectivity, here she hints at the very same distortion of reward that is at the root of marketed Internet culture. Just as Turkle does, the Internet social media giants recognize that we measure our success, and as a result, the validity of our online identities, in part by what technology makes possible. Consequently, they've given us more features, tools, and routes by which we may achieve that sweet sense of online instant gratification. Social networking is all about feeling rewarded, special, and successful—*immediately*. But we must wonder whether, in a social environment where everything is interpreted as massively rewarding, satisfaction loses its value.

In one of the final scenes of *Brave New World*, John, a "savage" discovered outside the World Government's sphere of influence who has been inducted into Mustapha Mond's carefully constructed tyranny of pleasure, confronts the propaganda minister, deriding the sham of "pleasant vices" and arguing in favor of reintroducing to society the complexities of pain, God, poetry, danger, freedom, and sin. "Whether 'tis better in the mind to suffer the slings and arrows of outrageous fortune," he snidely asks, "or to take arms against a sea of troubles and by opposing end them. . . . But you don't do either. Neither suffer nor oppose. You just abolish the slings and arrows. It's too easy" (162). In a sense, John mounts the same offense as Kasparov and Turkle: namely, that danger, risk, death, and the possibility of failure are all necessary to advance and grow on both an individual and collective level. John cites the self-denial and humility caused by failure and risk taking as pillars of society, as the most important virtues that can define a man. He recognizes the absurdity of pure and constant reward, all the while acknowledging the necessity of *reward in moderation*. Huxley argues through John that failure builds character as much as reward, and that self-induced denial of pleasure and easy victories is necessary to strike a keen balance between the two. Perhaps Huxley, Kasparov, and Turkle would all agree that by denouncing and degrading risk, we are denying the very things that lend us our individual senses of self.

In response to John's attack, Mond reveals the darker side of reward: "Industrial civilization is only possible when there's no self-denial. Self-indulgence up to the very limits imposed by hygiene and economics. Otherwise the wheels stop turning" (161). He correlates indulgence with happiness, and happiness with social stability. And yet, the act of indulging does not always imply the attainment of happiness, as Kasparov notes when he writes, "We can't enjoy the rewards without taking the risks." It is quite possible that we must first know what it is like to be without something before we can truly enjoy it.

Yet the social networking culture of the 21st century has proven the contrary. Teens spend countless hours on websites like Facebook, Twitter, Instagram, and Tumblr; a "healthy" social life is now predicated on having a vibrant and prolific online personality, and one's social prowess is in part determined by how many people one can stay digitally connected to, and how frequently. This constant thirst for connection and recognition is what Aldous Huxley feared most when he penned *Brave New World*. He feared that we would become a culture ruled by all things trivial, too concerned with our own analogs of the Orgy-porgy (Facebook), the Centrifugal Bumblepuppy (Twitter), or the Feelies (Tumblr, Instagram, Reddit, and whatever else may be our vices) to deal with the real world. He was not worried about society caving in to traditional forms of totalitarianism by which men are so often painfully oppressed. He believed instead that men would be pleasantly oppressed, bound by their desires and their "infinite appetite for distractions" and pleasures (*Revisited* 35). Modern social networking has shown, more than ever, that Huxley's fear of a culture driven by this appetite for desire is not only possible, but even viewed as healthy by those who have given in and connected to the Greater Being—the Facebook that awaits.

WORKS CITED

Huxley, Aldous. *Brave New World*. Cutchogue: Buccaneer, 1946. Print.
—. *Brave New World: Revisited*. New York: Bantam, 1960. Print.
Kasparov, Garry. "The Chess Master and the Computer." Rev. of *Chess Metaphors: Artificial Intelligence and the Human Mind*, by Diego Rasskin-Gutman, trans. Deborah Klosky. *New York Review of Books* 11 Feb. 2010.

Web. 5 June 2013.

Turkle, Sherry. "Tethering." *Sensorium: Embodied Experience, Technology, and Contemporary Art.* Ed. Caroline A. Jones. Cambridge: MIT Press, 2006. 220-26. Print.

The Desideratum of Discourse: Lessons Learned from a Gay Sheep

WARREN ERSLY

What issue could be compelling enough to drive a host of prominent endocrinologists, bioethicists, animal rights enthusiasts, gay men and women, theologians, republicans, and democrats into a complete tizzy? Two words: gay sheep. In 2005, a member of the Oregon State football team was caught drunkenly speeding into the night with a sheep held captive in the flatbed of his truck. Upon the student's arrest, the police returned his ovine hostage to the university lab from which it was stolen. Perhaps a global scandal could have been avoided, were it not for the fateful words spoken by the lab attendant on its return: "That's one of our gay rams" (Dworkin).

Dr. Charles Roselli, a researcher at Oregon State, was, at the time, running a nationally funded lab devoted to decrypting the mysteries underlying mammalian sexual behavior. It was to him that the gay sheep—one of many— belonged. Dr. Roselli and his colleagues observed that roughly one in ten male sheep exhibit a "male-oriented" sexual leaning, characterized by their refusal to mount females and by their engagement in sexual activity with other males ("Volume" 478). Roselli's research, first brought to media attention by local Oregon news outlets, was eagerly picked up and circulated by national and global news companies. What ensued can only be described as a media flame-war with such participants as PETA, various gay rights activists, and, of all characters, Rush Limbaugh. How could anything generate such a far-reaching controversy? What, exactly, was Dr. Roselli working on?

In their 2004 study titled "The Volume of a Sexually Dimorphic Nucleus in the Ovine Medial Preoptic Area/Anterior Hypothalamus Varies with Sexual Partner Preference," Charles Roselli and his colleagues posited that a specific region of a sheep's brain dramatically influenced sexual behavior and, in rams, partner preference. Roselli observed that male-oriented partner preference among rams is rooted in neither dominance nor in flock hierarchy, nor is it the result of reduced or elevated hormone levels—adult male-oriented and female-oriented rams share equal basal concentrations of testosterone, and exhibit the same partner preference even after castration ("Volume" 478). Given this absence of social and hormonal factors, Roselli reasoned that there must be a neural mechanism responsible for the observed variations in the rams' sexual partner preferences. He hypothesized that "the medial preoptic area/anterior hypothalamus [also known as the sexually dimorphic nucleus], a region known to be critical for the expression of masculine sexual behavior in most mammalian species," is the neural mechanism responsible for the variations in the rams' sexualities ("Volume" 478).

Roselli used a series of tests to determine the sexual orientations of his rams before euthanizing all twenty-seven of his rams and ewes. Roselli and his colleagues then removed the sexually dimorphic nuclei (SDN) from the animals' brains, employing various staining techniques and protein assays to measure the size and density of the area hypothesized to be responsible for sexual partner preference. They noticed that the female-oriented rams had the largest SDNs, the ewes the smallest, and that those of the male-oriented sheep were of intermediate size relative to the female-oriented males and ewes ("Volume" 481). Despite this correlation, Roselli and his colleagues were quick to note in their conclusion that "it is impossible to predict the sexual partner preference of any individual on the basis of a single brain measurement. Nor do the present data allow us to determine whether the observed differences in the size of the [SDN] are the cause or consequence of an animal's sexual partner preference, or whether the size of the [SDN] is influenced by other unidentified variables" ("Volume" 482-83). Roselli and his colleagues also found that the ovine sexually dimorphic nucleus is highly receptive to both estrogen and androgens during fetal development ("Effect" 502) and that prenatal exposure to abnormal levels of testosterone may alter both its size and organization ("Ovine" 4450).

In 2006, critical coverage of Roselli's research was kicked around the local Oregon news circuit for some time, until it finally—and rather mysteriously—made its way to the London *Sunday Times*. According to that publication, not only did Roselli's research open up a Pandora's Box of scientifically rationalized homophobia, but Roselli himself was leading the secret charge against homosexuality, conducting his research so that he might eventually uncover the biological basis of homosexuality and eliminate it. The *Sunday Times* speculated that Roselli would someday develop a so-called "Hetero-Patch," "a 'straightening' procedure [such as] a hormone supplement for mothers-to-be, worn like a nicotine patch" (Cloud). The *Times* ultimately went on to put forward the notion that Roselli's research "could pave the way for breeding out homosexuality in humans" (Schwartz). This blatantly sensationalist commentary, though, was only the beginning. What started—and could have ended—as nothing more than a passingly interesting piece exploded into a global campaign once the *Times*' article caught the attention of the animal-rights organization, People for the Ethical Treatment of Animals (PETA).

PETA's campaign against Dr. Roselli officially began when their spokesperson, the openly gay tennis player Martina Navratilova, declared: "Homophobes are murdering gay sheep" (Cloud). Choosing to de-emphasize the animal research elements of Roselli's work, PETA's campaign instead opted to focus on the potentially homophobic aspects of Roselli's research insinuated by the *Sunday Times*. PETA kicked off its media war against Dr. Roselli by hurling accusations of "sexual eugenics" (Dworkin), backing up the *Times* by publishing a write-up on their website reaffirming that "Roselli has made it very clear that he intends to use the findings of his experiments to 'cure' humans next" ("Crosses"). PETA and its allies in the gay community based their claims regarding Roselli's intentions primarily on an early grant application that Roselli and his colleague Frederick Stormshak had submitted to the National Institute of Health. The grant application stated, "This research also has broader implications for understanding the development and control of sexual motivation and mate selection across the mammalian species, including humans" ("Crosses"). However, PETA failed to make two major distinctions in its interpretation of the grant application: that there are ideological and intentional leaps and bounds between "understanding" and "curing," and that the NIH, as an institute devoted to funding research with possible human applications and benefits, would not get behind Roselli's animal studies unless he could show that they relate to humans in some peripheral way ("Crosses"). PETA also decried the liberal use of the word "control" in Roselli's grant application, while Roselli and his colleagues contended that "the word 'control' was used in the scientific sense of understanding the body's internal controls, not in the sense of trying to control sexual orientation," and that their experiments were performed in the scientific spirit of discovery and understanding, with no ulterior motives (Newman qtd. in Schwartz).

PETA's battle against Roselli culminated in an email campaign in which PETA's supporters sent Roselli and various University of Oregon administrators upwards of 20,000 vitriolic messages, accusing them of being "worthless animal killer[s]" who "should be shot," begging them in a variety of ways to "please, die" (Schwartz). Yet it wasn't just PETA and various gay activists who threw themselves into the fray—based on the *Sunday Times* fringe speculations regarding the research, right-wing activists came roaring to Roselli's side, despite the fact that their support was neither wanted nor warranted. Spurned by the *Times*' baseless conjecturing of a "Hetero-Patch," Al Mohler, president of the Southern Baptist Theological Seminary, wrote on his blog, "If a biological basis [of homosexuality] is found, and if a prenatal test is then developed . . . we would support its use as we should unapologetically support the use of any appropriate means to avoid sexual temptation and the inevitable effects of sin" (Zylstra). To add insult to injury, Rush Limbaugh covered the media blitz on Roselli's work, concluding that "gay activists finally have a reason to oppose abortion" because homophobic mothers might abort their children if they could prenatally determine the child's sexuality (Cloud). It seemed that everyone wanted a piece of Roselli's research—taking the *Times*' speculations and running away with them, bending and contorting the facts in order to serve their own ideological agendas. By 2007, with a flock of critics ranging from republicans to gay activists, animal rights groups, bioethicists, journalists and theologians, the controversy surrounding Roselli's work seemed to have finally reached its critical mass.

And it had. The public opposition to Roselli and the University of Oregon quickly fell apart due to changing conditions. Accusations regarding the direction of Roselli's work became more and more extreme. Internal pressure from the gay community mounted as more and more gay supporters defected, and several prominent science bloggers and journalists worked frequently and fervently to cover the media firestorm, dispelling many of the myths and much of the hyperbole released on the part of PETA, thus turning public opinion in favor of Roselli and his work. Soon enough, the negative media that was originally directed at Roselli was redirected towards his opponents in PETA, the gay community, and various bioethics circles. Opposition soon dissipated, prompting PETA and the *Sunday Times* to pull their original criticisms of Roselli's work from the web.

With Dr. Roselli's arguments grounded in rational objectivity and PETA's in fear mongering and rancor, one may feel compelled to ask why there is such a stark divide in rhetorical approach. PETA's foreboding and cautionary language fully reveals their aversion to and apprehension of science. With such language as, "if we learn how to recognize gay brains in development, look out" ("Brokeback" 2), "the more we play God or try to improve on Mother Nature, the more damage we are doing" (Navratilova qtd. in Schwartz) and "resentment [of homosexuality] will give way to pity. We'll come to view homosexuality as a kind of infertility—a disability,"

("Brokeback" 2), it is evident that scare tactics, bleak futurism, and inflammatory prose dominate the articulation of PETA's case; whereas Roselli, his colleagues, and his supporters seem to stick to more objective presentation of the research, as well as exposure and refutation of the opposition's more absurd claims.

Perhaps the asymmetries in the opposing sides' approaches to this debate are the results of *mediacized* science—the compression of complex scientific research into digestible news tid-bits that are to be communicated and marketed in a highly competitive and fast-paced media environment. So long as Roselli and his colleagues were receiving funding from the NIH, it is most likely that public opinion would not be a huge factor in how they chose to conduct their research. Roselli naturally had to defend himself to ensure that the NIH would not cut his funding due to public outrage, as well as safeguard his scientific reputation, but he and his colleagues had much less to lose than their opponents in the media war. On the other hand, the *Sunday Times* had papers to sell, and PETA had funds to raise and donors to please. The volatility of their arguments reflects the fact that they had potential revenue on the line, whereas Roselli's stoic restatement of the research and its conclusions suggests lower monetary stakes. Emptypockets—an anonymous blogger who vigorously defended Roselli—perfectly summed up the degree of mediacizing in this debate when he blogged, "PETA picked Dr. Roselli because sheep are adorable, unlike mice or flies [on which sexual orientation research is also performed], and because gay-rights is a hot-button issue" and "a fuzzy lamb is a better fund-raiser than a rat" ("Crosses," "Wolf"). This conflict demonstrates that when science enters the realm of the media business, facts are vulnerable to being truncated and cherry-picked to suit the tastes and opinions of the audience.

Despite the fact that PETA's claims and supporting arguments may have been affected by a deliberate stretching of the truth and mediacizing, their sincerity is not diminished. PETA and its allies in the gay community had every right to be concerned about the direction and possible implications of Roselli's research. The concern that any scientist could abusively tamper with the sexual aspects of identity is a legitimate one. Though it does not necessarily validate PETA's extreme reaction, it does give them grounds to be scared. However, this concern infers that mechanism and motive are separable, something PETA and its supporters failed to recognize. They feared that the only thing that could possibly be driving Roselli's quest to *understand* the mechanisms behind sexual behavior was a motive to *correct* sexual behavior; in their minds, scientific research on such a controversial topic could not be done simply for the sake of discovery—everyone must have a motive.

In late 2007, after the public debate had died down, William Saletan of *Slate* magazine—who covered the controversy extensively—published a post-debate analysis and reflection entitled "Wool and Graze: Gay Sheep Revisited," in which he noted the tricky pitfall of thought that motive presents. "You can't infer Roselli's motives, nor can you predict the motives of people who might exploit, in a later technological program, the mechanisms he's clarifying," for "scientists such as Roselli don't focus on achieving a preferred outcome. They focus on learning mechanisms" ("Wool"). Saletan goes on to argue that one is always justified in being worried about scientific research that one believes to be "going too far," but that research without a visibly vile motive has no reason to be stopped—even if the public disapproves. It seems as if the resolution to this conflict lies in conceding to one of the two opposing camps: PETA's position (stop all sheep research now) or Saletan's (all science must go on). However, Emptypockets offers us a middle ground:

> Which experiments are worth it? The answer is not just up to the scientist —vertebrate research is heavily regulated, with lengthy approval processes from the government, the state, and the university. In many places, your experiments need to be approved not just by administrators and fellow scientists, but also by members of the community, regular people without scientific training who are put there to make sure that your experiments not only make scientific sense but also make common sense, that they are consistent with what your neighbors would find reasonable. ("Crosses")

Emptypockets presents a balanced approach to conducting scientific research, one in which neither the public at large nor specific interests groups have complete control over the scientific approval process. Science, he points out, is much like democracy with its checks and balances. Organizations like PETA are just one voice among many in the republic of science, one check in a much larger, self-regulating community. Yet PETA failed to recognize the extent of its role in the scientific process; by failing to approach the debate from a position of *informed democracy* and instead favoring a position of *moral superiority*, PETA did not communicate rationally or realistically with its opponents and the public.

Morality is not always at odds with rationality, but as Steven Pinker points out in his essay, "The Moral Instinct," it certainly can be. Pinker argues in favor of exploring the science and psychology that form the basis of our moral conceptions. Just as Roselli argues that research into the biology of sexuality fosters tolerance towards homosexuality ("Wool"), Pinker posits that "the science of the moral sense can instead be seen as a way to strengthen. . . [and clarify] what morality is and how it should steer our actions," thus fostering an analogous sense of moral tolerance (Pinker). In his discussion of alternative and divided conceptions of morality, Pinker accurately depicts the moral underpinnings of PETA's bellicose reaction to Roselli's work. He writes:

> The moral sense, we are learning, is as vulnerable to illusions as the other senses. It is apt to confuse morality per se with purity, status and conformity. It tends to reframe practical problems as moral crusades and thus see their solution in punitive aggression. It imposes taboos that make certain ideas indiscussible. And it has the nasty habit of always putting the self on the side of the angels. (Pinker)

Purity, status, conformity, avoidance of harm, fairness, and community are all elements influencing the concepts of morality that Pinker points out. He notes that some people have a moral sense that is more in tune with some of these elements than that of others; thus, there are varying forms of morality. Controversies such as the Roselli debate stem from differences in morality. Communication breakdowns occur when these varying moral conceptions fail to level with one another, dissolving discourse and instead taking the form of "moral crusades."

Pinker also points out that the point of all public discourse is mutual agreement, consensus-making, and "practical problem solving." However, the conduct of the participants in this debate—perhaps with the exception of Dr. Roselli—clearly demonstrates that they weren't at all out to solve any problems, let alone agree on a preferred course of action. PETA's aggressive email campaign and the high degree of simplified, rhetoric-rich media coverage suggest a lack of communication between Roselli's supporters and those of PETA. The latter group, though, reasonably concerned over the direction of Roselli's research, unreasonably did nothing to create any sort of informed dialogue with their opponents. Instead, they held this debate in the court of public opinion, employing harsh and bombastic prose to bully both the public and their opponents into accepting their position unequivocally. A lack of communication and moral leveling in conjunction with a stripped down, media-centric approach to debate resulted in the partial collapse of democratic discourse.

Science is unpredictable. The unforeseen applications of new research can lead us down unexpected and unexplored paths. Motivated by a fear of the unknown, many choose to shy away from the complication and uncertainty that science presents. By dismissing PETA's reaction to Dr. Roselli's research, one risks falling into naïveté by failing to recognize the potential dangers of science. However, by blindly acquiescing to the organization's strict ideology and moral crusading, one also risks denying and even fearing the more progressive elements of science. Rarely does a debate demonstrate science, media, and morality intersecting so clearly. In order to successfully navigate these crossroads, one mustn't commit oneself solely to any one of these three perspectives, but instead should remain able and willing to negotiate in active discourse and dialogue among them. Even if Roselli's gay sheep fail to teach us the mysteries and complexities of sexuality, at least we can say we learned a thing or two about the desideratum of discourse.

WORKS CITED

Cloud, John. "Yep, They're Gay." *Time Magazine* 26 Jan. 2007. Web. 28 Nov. 2012.

Dworkin, Andy. "The Politics of Gay Sheep." *The Star* 6 Feb. 2007. Web. 28 Nov. 2012.

emptypockets. "PETA Crosses the Line." *The Next Hurrah* N.p., 5 Sept. 2006. Web. 28 Nov. 2012.

—. "A Wolf in Gay Sheep's Clothing: Corruption at the London Times." *The Next Hurrah* N.p., 4 Jan. 2007. Web. 28 Nov. 2012.

Pinker, Steven. "The Moral Instinct." *The New York Times Magazine*. N. pag., 13 Jan. 2008. Web. 3 Dec. 2012.

Roselli, Charles E., Henry Stadelman, Reed Reeve, Cecily V. Bishop, and Fred Stormshak. "The Ovine Sexually Dimorphic Nucleus of the Medial Preoptic Area Is Organized Prenatally by Testosterone." *Endocrinology* 148.9 (2007): 450-457. Chevy Chase, MD: The Endocrine Society. 1 Sep. 2007. Web. 28 Nov. 2012.

Rosselli, Charles E., Kay Larkin, John A. Resko, John N. Stellflug, and Fred Stormshak. "The Volume of a Sexually Dimorphic Nucleus in the Ovine Medial Preoptic Area/Anterior Hypothalamus Varies with Sexual Partner Preference." *Endocrinology* 145.2 (2003): 478-83. Chevy Chase, MD: The Endocrine Society. 2 Oct. 2003. Web. 26 Nov. 2012.

Roselli, Charles E., J.M. Schrunk, H.L. Stadelman, John A. Resko, and Fred Stormshak. "The Effect of Aromatase Inhibition on the Sexual

Differentiation of the Sheep Brain." *Endocrine* 29.3 (2006): 501-11. PubMed. 26 June 2006. Web. 28 Nov. 2012.

Saletan, William. "Brokeback Mutton: Gay Sheep and Human Destiny." *Slate Magazine*. N. pag., 2 Feb. 2007. Web. 28 Nov. 2012.

—. "Gay Sheep Revisited." *Slate Magazine*. N. pag., 8 Feb. 2007. Web. 28 Nov. 2012.

Schwartz, John. "Of Gay Sheep, Modern Science And the Perils of Bad Publicity." *The New York Times* 25 Jan. 2007. Web. 26 Nov. 2012.

Zylstra, Sarah E. "Re-engineering Temptation." *Christianity Today*. N. pag., 9 Apr. 2007. Web. 28 Nov. 2012.

The Road to Bourgeois

JIAWEI HE

My seven-year-old cousin always shows off his armory of toys when I pay a visit to my uncle's. The spacious storage room under the stairs becomes his arsenal, occupied by his army of colorful gadgets, some big, some small, some newly enrolled, some long retired. It is the place where he, the commander, spends most of his time (other than kindergarten or bed.) Adult that I am, I can hardly summon enough enthusiasm to pick up the toys, divide them into opposing forces, and direct a fictional war between them. Rather than detecting the soul my cousin imagines inside every figure (the Lego warriors, a Japanese superhero named the Ultraman, various different kinds of monsters, Gundam model robots), I can only smell the undesirable odor of plastic and guess how much each trinket has cost his parents. I can only think to teach him that a crane is used for construction rather than for war and to help him work out a jigsaw puzzle, actions I hope will make him smarter. He then inevitably labels me a boring playmate, and I join in conversation with my relatives who have also lost interest in such toys.

An adult is not supposed to play with toys. Toys, in the eyes of adults, are a naïve and monotonous use of time (my relatives label most of them "gigantic superheroes"). Toys have no life in them—they are mass-produced, common, and some of the ones in my brother's collection still carry price tags. The French critic Roland Barthes would go so far as to attribute a "bourgeois status" to my cousin's beloved soldiers, as he does in his essay "Toys" (690). "Bourgeois," a word used mostly in sociology to indicate the middle class or, more broadly, the negative effects of capitalism, is unprecedentedly applied by Barthes to toys, highlighting an intrinsic characteristic of toys that is closely related to the whole of society. "Selfishly materialistic or conventionally respectable and unimaginative" is the exact meaning of the word (*OED*). Current toys seem unimaginative to Barthes because they are highly "socialized, constituted by the myths or the techniques of modern adult life" (689). They are also too functional. Their main characters are often restricted to certain occupations, and the scenarios in which they are set are basically real life situations. Thus, the toys "*literally* prefigure the world of adult functions," establishing a "microcosm" of adult life so "there are, prepared for [children], actions without adventure, without wonder, without joy" (689). My cousin, then, serves as a perfect "victim": shrunken athletic equipment (for mini-golf, mini-basketball, and soccer), model cartoon cars, toy guns and play-house gadgets occupy most of his play space. Indeed, toy-makers no longer have to think to engage children—all they have to do is make real life objects into cuter and smaller models. Toys have in a sense become nothing but a tool for pre-school education: behind the toys are "selfishly materialistic" manufacturers and designers. Most toys nowadays are not even bred or borne from joy, as their creators do not sketch outlines or find optimum materials with the intention of making children enjoy the final products; instead, they are producing products under the huge influence of marketing and toy designers' own dreams to make profits off children.

I was wandering in the signature toy store in Times Square the other day, intending to relax and recollect a sense of childhood happiness. I found all the toys sorted in several sections. Most were based on bestseller cartoon characters or enduringly popular superheroes. The smile on Wendy from "Toy Story" looked routine, even hypocritical. What I saw in the organized, colorful, derivative toys, as I've seen in my cousin's armory, is how toy factories and companies hardly make an effort to entertain their potential customers. They lack "the spirit of do-it-yourself" because most of the product models come directly from Hollywood studios and favored cartoonists (Barthes 689).

I did, however, have a flashback to my own childhood when I was lingering around the section of toy guns. When I was a kid, my parents didn't buy many toys for me because they said toys were meaningless and a waste of money. One of my few priceless memories is of a black plastic toy gun that my grandmother bought as a Children's Day gift. With that toy, I would often imagine myself as a righteous policeman and amusingly aim toward a dog and say, "Don't move!" I once took it to a kindergarten festival and was regarded as the most popular participant in the "Toy Exchange" session. Even as I grew up, whenever I bumped into the gun, covered in dust, in my bedroom, I always had to smile at how funny I'd been back then. I wanted to experience at that Times Square store the same enthusiasm for my coveted gun that I had felt as a child in the small toyshop. This was my ultimate goal in that enormous store, but I failed to achieve it. I've grown up. I am not able to appreciate toys anymore. I am not supposed to play with them, and my former joy has long subsided.

But as a kid, even if I had learned the word "bourgeois," I would never have related it to toys. They provided me with so much fun that I still view them as the most loyal playmates of my childhood. Now, as an adult entering the store, I can only think of such words as "fancy," "commercial," and "uncreative." I had always up to this point identified myself as a schoolboy, the son of my parents and a person who loved to play. I felt lost between those racks, troubled that such an identity had always been just a vague illusion, and that I'd already changed drastically in this last decade of my life, somehow and somewhere, undesirably and inevitably. In a sense, it was unavoidable that I wouldn't even realize the changes while I was actually changing—I didn't *choose* to change.

The essayist Bernard Cooper describes such "inevitable" transition in his essay "Labyrinthine" when he discusses the different roles labyrinths have played in his life (347). At first he was so preoccupied with mazes that "[he] had to stop and rethink [his] strategy, squinting until some unobstructed path became clear," and he found enjoyment in labyrinths since "even when trapped in the hallways of the maze, [he] felt an embracing safety" (345). He then began to find imagined mazes in everyday objects, in "the mahogany coffee table," "the fabric of [his] parents' blanket," "veins of the marble heart," and so on (345). Cooper grew so invested in mazes, in fact, that they became for him like Barthes's "invented forms," which Barthes himself seems to regard as "very rare" nowadays, and which help a child become a "creator" rather than just a "user" (689). Moreover, Cooper starts to make mazes on his own with passion and a sense of accomplishment, solidifying them as the signature of his childhood, a choice that would likely be praised by Barthes in the zealous "spirit of do-it-yourself" (689).

However, no matter how passionate he once was, as soon as Cooper grew up, his attitude toward mazes altered. Mazes had served as the fountain of imagination and fun in his childhood, but the labyrinth quickly became the portrait of his life journey. As he grows out of juvenile naïveté and into middle-aged anxiety, Cooper gradually gets lost in the labyrinth of adult life: "Recollecting the past becomes as unreliable as forecasting the future" and there soon comes "the endless succession of burdens and concerns" (346). A labyrinth finally becomes something "as slippery as thought, as perplexing as the truth, as long and convoluted as a life" (347). He has, with maturity, lost his childhood joy with labyrinths and is not likely to preoccupy himself with, find, or create with any more.

Everybody has toys as significant as mazes were to Cooper. For me, it was the toy gun; for my young cousin, it might be one of his model superheroes.

However, at a certain point in life, everyone has to undergo an inevitable transition, a transition in which former passion is replaced with disinterest, in which childishness is replaced with social conventions and loss of imagination, in which uniqueness is lost and you become "bourgeois."

Such a transition comes silently and unconsciously. When I was a kid, all my relatives would converse at reunion dinners and say that I was so creative and lovely, and that as a smart boy I was likely to have a prestigious occupation—as a novelist, a scientist, a musician. I would, however, arrogantly choose to leave the table, impolitely, without saying thanks, and enjoy cartoons alone. As I grew into school age, all the dialogue suddenly turned to grades: how I should strive more for a higher rank in class, how outstanding my peers and my relatives' friends' children were. No matter how full, no matter how little I liked the conversation, I felt obliged to stay at the table out of either etiquette or respect. As I grew up, I became one of the boring conversation starters, enthusiastically instructing my younger cousins to do better in school, based on my own experience (only to receive their silence and gray faces). I talked about the features of adult "bourgeois society"—social networking, business projects, celebrities in town, how to make money. In what seemed only a moment, I had passed the watershed moment into adulthood, becoming a garrulous teacher instead of a naughty, inquisitive child without even realizing it. Somehow, my childish arrogance had been replaced by mediocrity and humbleness.

The transition, even if unwanted, is certainly predetermined. It seems that there are certain genes one might inherit: in childhood they are not expressed, but as one grows up, such age-dependent genes are gradually expressed. I do happen to have such genes, and they started to shape me as a person when I was still of school age. Once in a while someone would say that I was becoming more like my father, the man I understood least in my childhood. I couldn't, for instance, understand why he was not interested in anything I loved. We did no sports together, let alone watch movies or play games. We had a great generation gap between us. He was such a workaholic that I couldn't see if there was anything done for fun in his routine life. Now, years later, I have begun to understand his job and his personality, and gradually feel compassion for him. After all I have the same genes. I have become a "studyholic" and stopped playing games. I have abandoned my few childhood toys. I instantaneously react with "Junk food!" when my friends have burgers and fries for dinner. My former passionate and sunny outlook has been replaced with responsibility and diligence.

It is not a genetic mutation that creates new traits and new species, but regular gene expression inherited from older generations. I see the shadow of Cooper on myself too: when he proudly showed his masterpieces, his "do-it-yourself mazes," to his parents as a child, their indifference and disinterest overwhelmed him. "It was inconceivable to [him] that someone wouldn't want to enter a maze, wouldn't lapse into the trance it required, wouldn't sacrifice the time to find a solution"; but thirty years later, he understood his parents refusal: "Why would anyone choose to get mired in a maze when the days encase us, loopy and confusing?" (346). His latent genes were finally expressed, and he mourns, "Mother, Father . . . I suppose it was inevitable that, gazing down at this piece of paper, I'd feel your weary expressions on my face" (347).

In the labyrinth called growing up, one will always get lost when one's brain begins to mature. One is encouraged and even forced to have an objective and a destination: at the center of the labyrinth lies a notable college diploma, a powerful position in a company, or a grandiose mansion. A genuine sense of direction, however, is somehow missing. Calculations take the place of critical thoughts. Hectic schedules and designated tracks make one operate like a machine, following the prescribed path into bourgeois society. One becomes, like French toys, "entirely socialized," and the sense of inventiveness and creativity disappears (Barthes 689).

To attempt to escape this aimless, sweeping current, to get out of the vortex of adulthood, I tried to go back to nature. A few weeks ago I visited the Monet's Garden exhibition at the New York Botanical Garden at a close friend's invitation. I wanted to find an asylum, a refuge from the hectic city lifestyle, and I certainly managed it. An hour's ride away from downtown, true nature exists, a place to purify a New Yorker's bourgeois mind.

Different from the primal beauty of an African preservation zoo, the small pond there represents the elegant beauty of nature; it not only impresses me with the splendor of its scenery, but also provides a sense of kindness that keeps me lingering. Blooming water lilies of various colors coexist in the pond despite the looming midtown skyscrapers. The contrast of color is obvious: even with the deep blue water reflecting the gloomy sky, big shining green leaves holding various species of water lilies arrest my vision—the yellow ones are sacred, the white are pure, the pink are vibrant, the purple are noble. Their vibrancy is not stained by the mud beneath, nor affected by the dim sky.

The garden has left me not merely with a sense of a functionally green planet, but with real nature—beautiful, primitive, and pure. It made me put to rest all the stresses of my adult life. This kind of serenity and return to the natural state of things is exactly what I needed to put things in perspective, the kind of scene that promotes "art for art's sake," that inspires masters like Monet to create glorious pieces like his triptych *Water Lilies*, one of the most outstanding of all impressionist works. As Monet himself claimed, it was his garden and pond in Giverny that inspired him most throughout his life, because they provided him with a shelter outside bourgeois life (MoMA). Barthes also found nature to be the epitome of real life, indicated by his admiration of wood; as a toy material, he hails it for the "natural warmth of its touch" and claims "it is a familiar and poetic substance" (690).

Nevertheless, nature is a rather scarce commodity, and our connections to it are always fleeting. Wood used to be a predominant part of human manufacturing in a time when people were not as materialistic as they are now. It is, however, being fast replaced by artificial chemicals as demand for different products always increases. Barthes describes the undesirable transition of materials by pointing out that "many [toys] are now molded from complicated mixtures; the plastic material of which they are made has an appearance at once gross and hygienic, it destroys all the pleasure, the sweetness, the humanity of touch" (690). Regardless of wood's "firmness and its softness," its "warmth," it's being inevitably replaced by plastic; no matter how clean and sacred water lilies are, flower-buyers prefer roses and lavenders; no matter how beautiful Monet's Garden is, it's still only a place for a one-time weekend outing (690). The illumination of and perspective on life that nature provides is impressive but ultimately ephemeral. Visitors at the garden walked past the lily pond and kept walking into the labyrinths of their own lives: I was one such visitor. On the train back to campus, it occurred to me that the garden served as an asylum from complication, but only an asylum. It was not an exit from the labyrinth of maturity; that maze is so enclosed and its twists and turns are so convoluted that few find the way out. I eventually returned to the real world, to where it seems I belong, and walked the uneven paths in the populous, winding puzzle that is New York City.

The road to the bourgeois life is so smooth and silent that one hardly realizes what's happening. Like a timed software program, the road of growing up is planned and determined by parents, by society, and by genes. As the memories fade away, the destinations become distant and unclear. Everyone endeavors to be a high-hearted water lily, rising from the mud and standing out elegantly, but is eventually subsumed by the crowd and the raging current of life. Many turn out to be dandelions in the wind, fallen leaves in a vortex, or pebbles in quicksand—lost in the everlasting progression, in the overwhelming labyrinth. This is a mandatory lesson about growing up. This is the bitter transition that is the road to becoming bourgeois.

WORKS CITED

Barthes, Roland. "Toys." *Occasions for Writing: Evidence, Idea, Essay*. Ed. Robert DiYanni and Pat C. Hoy II. Boston: Wadsworth, 2008. 689-90. Print.

"Bourgeois." Entry 1, Def. B2. *OED Online*. Oxford University Press, 2012. Web. 23 Oct. 2012.

Cooper, Bernard. "Labyrinthine." *Occasions for Writing: Evidence, Idea, Essay*. Ed. Robert DiYanni and Pat C. Hoy II. Boston: Wadsworth, 2008. 345-47. Print.

Monet, Claude. *Water Lilies*. 1914-26. Museum of Modern Art, New York. *MoMA Online*. Web. 23 Oct. 2012.

Remembrance of Selves Past

HUI MIN LEE

> Words and images are incomplete class notes from the world, a way of catching reminders. Of course they are only traces.
> —Jim W. Corder, "Aching for a Self"

With every word we write, we believe that "our character could be in the text . . . that we do exist [and] that we can be in our words" (140-41). Jim W. Corder, in his essay "Aching for a Self," proposes that we produce in our writings "evidence" of our existence; we translate our experiences into written form and sometimes between different languages in order to share ourselves with our readers and, in the process, to re-affirm our presence in the world (141). Corder believes that "if we tell our stories carefully to one another," "fully, painstakingly," sharing the intimate details of our lives, we might allow others to see us in our "local habitations" and recognize our existence there (142). But he is also disturbed by the fact that we can never fully convey ourselves via language, a system of symbols by which we try to capture shared experience. Corder turns to John Kouwenhoven, who tells us that any speaker of English knows what the word 'grass' refers to because that word "suggests an identity" we are familiar with: such symbolic language universalizes our personal experience, but still the intricate *details* of unique experiences, the "different looks, feels, tastes, and smells" of the objects in reference remain open to personal interpretations (qtd. in Corder 142). Our understandings of words differ, and mistranslations are inevitable. Given the limitations of language and the difficulty of translating sensations and images into words, it seems impossible to render completely our experiences and "compose [ourselves] for another," even if we do it "carefully" and "painstakingly" (141,142).

Eva Hoffman grapples with leaving a trace of her childhood experience encoded in her essay, "Lost in Translation," an autobiographical account of her immigration from Poland to Canada. Onboard the *Batory*, a World War ll ship that is poised to take her away from Krakow, her hometown, the thirteen-year-old Hoffman is overcome with *tesknota* when she takes in "the crowd that has gathered on the shore to see the ship's departure . . . the waving hands, the exclamations" (176). Even though she knows that her family is heading towards a land of "freedom," she yearns to remain in war-torn Krakow, to be a part of the crowd that is waving goodbye (177). Hoffman describes her feelings toward this departure using a Polish word instead of the English "nostalgia": such refusal to translate, she explains, compensates for the inadequacy of her new language. Attachment to her native Polish language reveals what all bilinguals know intimately: not all thoughts and emotions can be translated. Had she just used "nostalgia" to explain her sentiments, the "tonalities of sadness and longing" of the Polish word would have been missing (176). With *tesknota* she clarifies her emotions, but only to herself. Non-Polish readers will not know the full meaning encapsulated in this word and its culture. Even as she attempts to explain the word, we can sense that the emotion aroused by *tesknota* is lost to us, the inexperienced.

Hoffman's inability to translate her emotions from her native language to English is shared by Russian author Vladimir Nabokov. In one of his collected interviews, Nabokov, an immigrant to both Germany and America and a masterful writer of English, observed that the different linguistic codes we use to represent our experience often lead to "unavoidable blunders . . . [which] could lend [themselves] to hideous mistranslation" (37-38). The ineffable emotional knowledge attached to words and linguistic structures shared by a community who all speak the same language is often unavailable to outsiders who lack access to that language and culture. Perhaps Hoffman's refusal to use an English word to describe her feelings arises not because a semantic translation does not exist, but rather because she senses in *tesknota* a connotation unavailable in English.

To Nabokov, mistranslations seem unidirectional: unlike the loss of emotions that accompanies his translation of written texts from Russian to English, his "descriptions of tender emotions" in English "slip very delicately into lyrical Russian" (53). Nabokov explains that he is able to represent his emotions and thoughts well to himself in Russian because it is his "natural language," the one that he grew up with, the one his heart speaks (15). But perhaps the accuracy of this translation from English to Russian is obvious only to Nabokov. A reader whose "natural language" is English and who is as proficient in Russian as Nabokov was in English may compare Nabokov's original text in English to its Russian version and still see a mistranslation, a difference in "tender emotions." Nabokov's experience leads us to wonder whether the significant loss of meaning that seems to accompany translations can affect the ability of readers to understand the author's unique experience. Is the loss greater for fellow speakers and readers than it is for the writer, who at least knows his own intent? Such an attachment to Polish, her "natural language," allows Hoffman to represent her emotions more faithfully, after all, in the word *tesknota*. Yet, even when Hoffman uses her "natural language," it seems as though something is still lost.

The usage of *tesknota* offers a clue to the particular, individual sense of loss that Hoffman is grappling with, but it does not allow her to represent entirely or re-experience what she has lost. On the surface, Hoffman's "youthful sorrow" seems to be brought on by her departure from Krakow (176). She confronts the absence of her hometown: she misses "the sun-baked villages where [her family] had taken summer vacations" and the "conversations and escapades with friends" (176). She had loved these experiences "as one loves a person" (176). The intensity of her attachment makes us wonder why, if she truly misses Krakow, she could not return to her hometown when it becomes possible after she grows up. Yet she does not, and neither does Nabokov return to his: having left Russia as a young child, he never went back, because he was aware that the Russia he was missing had disappeared. It was no longer the place he had once known. The physical Russia had changed along with its political and social landscape. His return would not bring him to a place that still stirred in him the "tender emotions." Instead, "all the Russia [he] need[s] is always with [him]: literature, language and [his] own Russian childhood" (9-10). Likewise, even if Hoffman had returned to Krakow, it would no longer have been the same place as when she had left. The "paradise" and "sun-baked villages" would have been replaced by an environment filled with "memories of wartime suffering" (177, 176).

"Lost in Translation" reveals, however, that the Krakow Hoffman misses is not really lost. It remains etched in her mind—after all, she is able to recall the most minute details of her bedroom in the last paragraph of her essay: she still remembers the "goose-feather quilt covered in hand-embroidered silk" that she "snuggled under" (177). Her childhood memory also includes more than just the visual details of the room: she recalls her bodily experiences, the "bracing but not overly fast swaying" motion of a tramway ride and the "hum of the tramway" she heard from her room (177). She remembers the time when "the world . . . flow[ed] so gently into [her] head," when "being awake [was] so sweet" (177). To us it may seem that it is not the physical Krakow she misses but rather the sensations her body experienced in her childhood bedroom. We begin to understand that moving to Canada meant more to her than a departure from Krakow, more than a loss of her native tongue; it meant being "pried out of [her] childhood, [her] pleasures [and her] safety" (177).

In "Aria: A Memoir of a Bilingual Childhood," Richard Rodriguez attempts to understand this act of translation. For him, though, it takes shape in the process of maturing from childhood to adulthood. Rodriguez nostalgically describes the childhood bodily sensations that he misses and the intimacy he had within his close-knit family, a closeness disrupted as much by growing up as by the English language he was required to speak outside his home. As a Mexican child growing up in America, he had heard speech as sounds instead of words with meanings. He describes himself as a "listening child," less concerned with what people say than with the tonalities of the language they speak (502). "The very different sounds of Spanish and English" have very different meanings for him: Spanish is a "private language," one that is exclusively used at home, and English is a "public" one used by "*los gringos*" (502, 503). The sound of Spanish, his "natural language," serves as a "pleasing, soothing [and] consoling reminder" that he belongs to his family "*like no one outside*" (502, 503). This intimacy he finds with his family, based on a shared language, among other things, fills his childhood with "laughter" and "pleasures" of home (504).

Rodriguez's unadulterated happiness, however, lasts only until he realizes the need to commit to English in order to communicate in public. Maturing from *Ricardo* to Richard, he gains a new identity—a public one—which gives him "confidence" and allows him to accept the fact that he is "an American citizen" (505, 506). Yet, in so doing, he gradually forsakes his "natural language" and his private identity. To his family he becomes one of "*los gringos*." Rodriguez believes that his "childhood start[s] to end" when he accepts the idea that he is entitled to use English (508). But along with this empowerment, he loses that "special feeling of closeness at home" that used to be protected by Spanish, the "ghetto language that deepened and strengthened [his] feeling of separateness" from the public (506, 504).

Hoffman's childhood "paradise" also predates her introduction to the language of strife and "wartime suffering" outside her home (177). Her happiness is compromised by the knowledge gained by growing up. In the last paragraph of her essay, she transports herself back to a four-year-old state and allows us to see the object of her *tesknota*, her Eden, an innocence which gave her a "sense of utter contentment" and "sufficiency" (177). Even though her country was destroyed by war, she felt that "being awake [was] so sweet" because she was unaware, sheltered by her parents and detached from the world by her innocence (177). She loses her child-like state of mind, however, when she is introduced to the language of racist prejudices and the "daily struggle for existence" (177). She becomes aware of the anti-Semitism in Krakow and the alienation her family faces. Her Edenic environment keeps her from knowing "that [her] happiness [was] taking place in a country recently destroyed by war," and she is overcome by the reality of wartime suffering and "dark political rumblings" (177).

As Hoffman begins to recognize that Krakow is not as ideal as she thought it to be, and as Rodriguez begins to understand the need to adopt the public language as his main language, the respective worlds that Rodriguez and Hoffman experienced as children—bubbles, temporary and fragile—pop. The unconditional sense of safety and sufficiency that once filled their childhoods fades away, and they experience sorrow and despair, for they find themselves unable to return to that ideal, idyllic state. Like Rodriguez, who admits to missing his "magical world" of childhood infused with the sounds of Spanish, and Nabokov, who has lived a life without "settling down anywhere" because "nothing short of a replica of [his] childhood surroundings would have satisfied [him]," Hoffman tries to regain her paradise by writing it into being (Rodriguez 503; Nabokov 27).

The last paragraph in Hoffman's essay reads as a self-serving one. She documents her experience with such intense focus on her own pleasure that we see the image of her bedroom as her attempt to re-experience her childhood, not an invitation for us to step into the enclosure of her private Eden. Similarly, Rodriguez tries to use the narrative element in his essay to help himself return to his childhood by constructing on the page the wonderful moments he shared with his family when Spanish was their exclusive language. Paradoxically, the closest he comes to this return is when his narrative is disrupted by strong nostalgic sensation—"so deep was the pleasure!" (504). He feels compelled to record this eruption even though this is not a moment we, the readers, can share with him. We can follow his narrative, but we are unable to feel the 'deep pleasure' brought on by a spontaneous experience that is only his. The intensity of his embodied experience seems impossible to weave into the story, and he has to settle for an interjection, bracketed away from the rest of the narrative it intrudes on. Hoffman's and Rodriguez's attempts to freeze their memories into "rhetoric" inevitably bring them face to face with the impossibility of communicating in any language the intense bodily sensations they remember (Corder 141). Hoffman's hesitation in her last paragraph vividly demonstrates the limits of language to convey emotions: while recounting her childhood experience, she is "fill[ed] with a feeling of sufficiency" but is unable to explain the reason. Eventually she settles for "just because I'm conscious" (Hoffman 177).

Perhaps it is impossible because the memories that each tries to put into writing are pre-verbal, emotions and images experienced without words. As children, we struggle to master the language that we speak before we can form coherent autobiographical memories. Because Rodriguez used to hear languages as sounds instead of words, his childhood memories favor sounds, images and emotions. Hoffman's childhood memories had been stored as images of her bedroom instead of as verbal descriptions. As Hoffman attempts to re-create the image of her bedroom, she is engaging in a pre-verbal kind of translation (Hoffman 177). But then language gets in the way and Hoffman and Rodriguez are denied any unmitigated return to the childhood they desire.

Their return to the past may forever remain out of reach. Our narrated memories are always re-shaped by new experiences. According to psychologist Dr. Elizabeth Loftus, an expert on human memory, the act of remembering is actually a re-creation and re-interpretation of a given experience in light of present circumstances. We fashion and re-fashion our memories to keep them in line with our current knowledge in order to make our selves seem coherent ("Memory"). This process makes memory "a current record, encumbered, of another time that was also encumbered," further distancing us from the very sensations that accompany the original memory (Corder 142). Despite her best effort to translate the image in her mind into the words of her essay, Hoffman is unable to perfectly transport herself back to the innocent and ideal state that she yearns for. Her present-day consciousness and knowledge intrude upon the sensation she is trying to recall. She feels compelled to include the fact that "[her] happiness is taking place in a country *recently destroyed by war*" (italics mine; Hoffman 177). Her adult voice also breaks through the idyllic bedtime scene that she tries to re-experience as a child. Both Hoffman and Rodriguez attempt to return to their past via their pre-verbal memories, but their childhood experience seems to escape as they reach for words.

According to Nabokov, pre-verbal memories are "absolutely permanent" (12). They are "immortal" and can be re-experienced even if we do not write them down (12). He believes that all we actually need to access these pre-verbal memories is a trigger: a sound, a smell, a taste, an image. This idea is not new. In *Remembrance of Things Past*, Marcel Proust shows the possibility of returning to the past using the "exquisite pleasure" and "all-powerful joy" that "invade[s] [his] senses" when he eats a morsel of a madeleine with a spoonful of tea (48). Initially, he does not understand the sensation that he is feeling, but "suddenly the memory reveal[s] itself" (50). Uncannily, "the whole of Combray and its surroundings . . . [springs] into being, town and gardens alike, from [his] cup of tea" (51). This taste of madeleine triggers Proust's attachment to a pre-verbal memory so strong that it remained forever imprinted in his mind. So did the Spanish voices allow Rodriguez to "[recall] the golden age of [his] childhood" (Rodriguez 508). For Hoffman, the occasional "hum of the tramway" and the "slowly moving shadows on the ceiling made by the gently blowing curtains" allowed for the re-experience of the safety and contentment from childhood, and "the freshness of the flowers" and "black fir trees" remind Nabokov of "the park on [his] country estate in Russia" (Hoffman 177; Nabokov 12). It seems that the best way to re-experience our loved memories is thus not through language but through our own physical bodies.

Yet we continue to translate our memories and experiences into words, because stories seem to be the best way to keep our memories alive. Stories allow readers to know the authors' individual experiences, and they serve as "evidence of their lives" (Corder 141). Our writings do not allow us or our readers to fully re-experience past sensations, but they allow us to leave a trace of ourselves in this world. We still write because we "long to be absolutely present to the world, acknowledged, known, and cherished" (139). However, with Corder we may have to accept that words can only help us document an approximation of our emotionally charged memories, and they will never be able to convey our true experiences to others. Pre-verbal memories are not stories that people can insert themselves into, and they do not allow themselves to be shared with others. Language may give us knowledge and public identity, but it estranges us from that unique blissful state that we yearn for. Nevertheless, we should continue to translate our experiences into writing as we attempt to transcend the confines of our own bodies and minds to seek companionship and commonality with others.

Language allows us to communicate and to be "members of the crowd," but our interpretations and understanding of language remain unique and personal (Rodriguez 508). Our thoughts, pre-verbal memories, and embodied experiences make us distinct, and by keeping them to ourselves we can preserve our sense of a unique self. This need for self-preservation also requires us to look beyond the present. The stories we write, the traces of ourselves that we leave in the world, may not be merely for others to remember us by. To Nabokov, an author's "best audience is the person he sees in his shaving mirror every morning" (18). The story is perhaps for the author himself.

Written narratives—journal entries, memoirs, essays—remind us of our past and future selves, even if the words fail to capture the emotional imprints of our memories. All we need is a trigger. When asked what language he considered most beautiful, Nabokov responded, "My head says English, my heart, Russian, my ear, French" (49). Indeed, language is often allied with our sensory organs, and our senses are the best triggers to our memories. When our stories are enlivened by senses, the blissful state of knowing who we once were comes within our reach. Our "inability to accept that we . . . someday . . . will [vanish] without a trace, unremembered and unredeemed," as Karsten Harries puts it, spurs us to write in the present for our future selves (qtd. in Corder 140). Other selves will remember us, and our treasured memories and experiences will live on. With our texts, we allow ourselves to remain unique and ever-present in the world.

WORKS CITED

Corder, Jim W. "Aching for a Self." *Occasions for Writing: Evidence, Idea, Essay*. Ed. Robert DiYanni and Pat C. Hoy II. Boston: Wadsworth, 2008. 139-44. Print.

Hoffman, Eva. "Lost in Translation." *Occasions for Writing: Evidence, Idea, Essay*. Ed. Robert DiYanni and Pat C. Hoy II. Boston: Wadsworth, 2008. 176-77. Print.

"Memory and Forgetting." *Radiolab*. June 2007. Web. 1 Dec. 2012.

Nabokov, Vladimir. *Strong Opinions*. New York: Vintage, 1990. Print.

Proust, Marcel. *Swann's Way*. Trans. C. K. Scott Moncrieff and Terrence Kilmartin. New York: Vintage, 1989. Print.

Rodriguez, Richard. "Aria: A Memoir of a Bilingual Childhood." *Occasions for Writing: Evidence, Idea, Essay*. Ed. Robert DiYanni and Pat C. Hoy II. Boston: Wadsworth, 2008. 501-08. Print.

On Sharing

AYSE SENGOR

In his article "At Galleries, Cameras Find a Mixed Welcome," Fred Bernstein interviews a director at the Louvre who was greatly disturbed when a group of tourists rudely pushed her aside to take pictures of the painting she was admiring. According to the director, these tourists photographed every single painting, not even taking a minute to *see* the art apart from the lenses of their cameras. The tourists behaved as if cameras were "extensions of their senses" (qtd. in Bernstein).

People, more now than ever, depend on image-making technologies to capture whatever they consider noteworthy. It seems that our desire to photograph the *Mona Lisa* has surpassed our desire to *see* it. Yet, as art critic Karen Rosenberg writes in her article on image-sharing and social media, the mere "act of snapping a picture is no longer enough to confirm reality and enhance experience" ("Everyone's Lives"). We are only satisfied when *others* acknowledge our photos and thus the richness of our lives. We solicit such acknowledgement by constant sharing, and the new social media sensation Instagram is one of the many platforms on which we convey idealized versions of reality, including ourselves. We often believe that the images we see on Instagram represent reality, and we forget that someone else framed this particular slice of life and filtered it to share in the context of some narrative. We choose to accept the copied versions even if we are aware of how easily and carelessly they are produced. John Berger warns us about the dangers of staying at such "*copying* distance" in his essay "Steps Toward a Small Theory of the Visible" (108). Berger suggests that if we forgo direct involvement with art or life, if we fail to see truly, we may end up ceding the intensity of our experience to those who have the power to arrange our perception for us (107, 110).

Theorists and planners arrange perception and establish the criteria for sharing. Walker Percy calls them the "class of privileged knowers" in his essay "The Loss of the Creature" (756). According to Percy, the planners of experience foist their own vision of the visible world on the untrained eyes of lay consumers who are "content to receive an experience just as it has been presented" (756). As a result, at the hands of planners, the experience of the consumer becomes mediated in a limiting way. Percy explains that the way we are educated especially affects the way we perceive and engage with the world. When a biology student dissects a dogfish, the fact that the singular fish is now called a "specimen" immediately devalues the unique existence of this particular dogfish (758). The student's recognition of the fish does not depend on any kind of confrontation with the reality of the creature in front of him. As far as the student is concerned, there is nothing to confront: the whole experience and its outcomes are already determined by his professor. Later in life, when thinking about his school years, the student will forget about the dogfish. It never truly existed in the first place. He will merely remember the mediated, pre-planned "experience" of an experiment in a laboratory, just as tourists at the Louvre, whose engagement with *Mona Lisa* is limited to sharing filtered versions on social media, will remember not the magic of the painting, but the mere fact that they once saw it (758). Automatic, superficial sharing also robs the sharers of the awareness that they are only seeing the *Mona Lisa* through the eyes of the planners—not only the museum curators in this case, but also Kevin Systrom and Mike Krieger (inventors of Instagram) and the infamous Mark Zuckerberg. As Zadie Smith suggests, it is their visions of reality we share on Facebook or Instagram. We promote curtailed versions of unique moments that initially should have belonged to *us*.

Smith provides insight into Zuckerberg's phenomenal influence over millions of people who have built a virtual second life around Facebook, his groundbreaking invention. In her essay, "Generation Why," Smith presents Zuckerberg as a person who seems to be the epitome of Percy's planner, for every single aspect of his invention is a reflection of himself. According to Smith, Facebook is "blue, because it turns out Zuckerberg is red-green color-blind"; it is "preoccupied with personal trivia, because Mark Zuckerberg thinks the exchange of personal trivia is what 'friendship' *is*." Yet 500 million of us willingly check our Facebook accounts every day and partake in this "Mark Zuckerberg Production." We're deceitfully satisfied as we seek human contact by sharing and accessing superficial information about unfamiliar people we call our *friends* because Facebook entices us to do so. This illusion of keeping in touch with our acquaintances and even our actual friends and family transforms our relationships into streams of frivolous data. We opt for fleeting instances of digital connection rather than the intensity of intellectual engagements and real conversations. We cling to technology and social media because they eliminate the risks and faults of physical existence. We can edit the texts we are about to send, we can retouch our photos until they are flawless before sharing them on Instagram—we are slowly losing touch with "our messy feelings, our desires, our fears" (Smith). We talk in *comments* and feel in *likes*. Eventually, we are reduced to our profiles and ironically, unavoidably, "become like Facebook: falsely jolly, fake-friendly, self-promoting [and] slickly disingenuous" (Smith).

But it might not be technology alone that distances us from deeper engagements with reality. The *Mona Lisa* experience can still be far from genuine if we don't realize that the curators plan every small detail before exhibiting the world's most famous, enigmatic smile. *They* determine the exact spot for hanging; *they* decide on the distance visitors must maintain while observing the artwork. The only way to escape partially is to become aware of their influence, and see through their mediation. But such clarity of perception requires a very specific kind of sight. In "Steps" John Berger worries that technological mediation distorts our ability to see. With cameras even in our cellphones, "appearances [are] registered, and transmitted with lightning speed," and as images multiply, physical appearances become increasingly volatile and lifeless (106). Berger believes we can overcome the reductive influence of technology through the process of collaboration with the visible. He wants us to see the world as good painters see their models, through an act of emotional connection that allows us to capture the essence of the objects hidden beneath transient appearances. This process requires us and the artist to establish a degree of intimacy that would allow us to *receive* whatever the model or object can give. Given the degree of engagement, collaboration is "seldom based on good will: more usually on desire, rage, fear, pity or longing"—negative and frustrating emotions that are part of the condition of our existence (109). Like Percy, who insists on confrontation as a prerequisite to genuine engagement with the reality of our experience, Berger calls us to establish a dialogue in which we try to discover the unsettling as well as the pleasurable emotional aspects of our object. However, as Smith notes, if we want to avoid the anxiety produced by such feelings, in our contemporary culture we can. We carry our relationships to the virtual world where we can have tighter control over them. For instance, after a couple ends a relationship, their home pages typically fill up with status messages intended to demonstrate their contentment after the breakup, and their flawless profile pictures not-so-subtly imply, "This is what you're missing." The digital environment gives these people space to carry on an ersatz conversation on computer screens and smartphones, so they can avoid the genuine yet embarrassing outbursts of real emotions inevitable in face-to-face encounters.

The broad consequences of this lack of engagement may not be as trivial as those of a romantic breakup. Sometimes the price for lack of genuine engagement can be oppression that—if not recognized for what it is—may never be overcome. In "On Seeing England for the First Time," Jamaica Kincaid, an author born in the small British colony of Antigua, examines the consequences of colonial oppression. As colonized citizens of Antigua, Kincaid and her family had been forced by the colonial power to substitute the reality of their impoverished lives for images that allowed them to feign participation in British culture. While Kincaid's father cannot escape the British identity imposed upon him, Kincaid achieves freedom through a long and arduous process of continuous engagement with the often discomfiting truth of her existence. Kincaid's father hopes to claim a place in the colonial power structure by wearing a British-style hat not suitable for the climate he lives in. He internalizes the British ideologies and hopes that imitating what he considers a superior culture might entitle him to the riches of the empire. Kincaid, however, analyzes her place under colonial rule more critically and realizes that she cannot draw similarities between her life and the life of a Briton. British customs, like the breakfast that makes her feel sleepy, seem unsuitable for island living, and "[her] dresses did not rustle in the evening air" as they would have had she she walked with the heroines of Jane Austen's novels (723). The British lifestyle is a fairytale far from reality. Its characters are prosperous and powerful, and when Kincaid turns her gaze towards her own surroundings, the magic suddenly gives way to the painful picture of the economic and psychological burden carried by the colonized people. "The reality of my life," Kincaid explains, "was conquests, subjugation, humiliation, enforced amnesia" (723). For Kincaid and her countrymen and women, the unrealistic idea of England, constructed by their teachers—the planners—resulted in an alternate understanding of the empire, an understanding that would form the basis of their sense of reality, their sense of the meaningful and the meaningless and, most important, their sense of identity and place in the world. But, unlike her father, Kincaid can identify the ways in which colonial oppression infringes upon her freedom of mind, and she fights to regain her intellectual independence.

To reclaim her identity from the destructive forces of colonial rule, Kincaid shares a specific vision of her experience with us. Her essay is a public counterattack against years of subjugation. She establishes the true conditions of her existence through candid portrayals of colonial hypocrisy and an analysis of her compatriots' misplaced respect for their oppressive rulers. She is not afraid to confront the realities of her oppression and bravely invites us to collaborate with the rage and disappointment that arise from her own sense of truth. Kincaid's conceptual work not only cultivates *her* identity but also enhances *our* perception of the ways oppression works on her and us. We react to her words, and we are fascinated by her honesty. Kincaid's captivating awareness makes us wonder how much *we* are aware of *our* surroundings. She prompts us to discover what we are not *seeing*: the reality hidden, perhaps, beneath layers of oppressive mythologies. The colonizing myths filter and share a perfected reality, just as Facebook and Instagram distort our sense of reality. But Kincaid's intellectual engagement and honest sharing now solicit a genuine response through confrontation and collaboration. Her cognitive process allows her to diagnose, analyze, and act against a lifelong oppression; if we follow in her footsteps, we too could begin to *see* beyond our own myths.

It is highly unlikely that we will stop using cameras, social media, and other technology, but we are not necessarily doomed to surrender real human interaction to superficial and virtual contact. It is up to us to reclaim what awaits us on the other side of our cameras and to see our existence for what it is instead of doctoring it with mind-altering technologies. We can still be active online, entertaining ourselves with instantaneous and superficial sharing, while keeping in mind that the key to meaningful discovery lies in *critical* sharing, engaging with our world in an often unsettling but honest way. Confrontation and collaboration give us a chance to experience real human contact, and restore *contact* to its original root—*tact*, touch—so that we can expand beyond our digital profiles and touch, or even collide with, others as we seek ultimately to restore our sight.

WORKS CITED

Berger, John. "Steps Toward a Small Theory of the Visible." *Occasions for Writing: Evidence, Idea, Essay*. Ed. Robert DiYanni and Pat C. Hoy II. 106-10. Print.

Bernstein, Fred A. "At Galleries, Cameras Find a Mixed Welcome." *New York Times* 14 Mar. 2012. Web. 11 Feb. 2013.

Kincaid, Jamaica. "On Seeing England for the First Time." *Occasions for Writing: Evidence, Idea, Essay*. Ed. Robert DiYanni and Pat C. Hoy II. 720-26. Print.

Percy, Walker. "The Loss of the Creature." *Occasions for Writing: Evidence, Idea, Essay*. Ed. Robert DiYanni and Pat C. Hoy II. 751-61. Print.

Rosenberg, Karen. "Everyone's Lives, in Pictures." *New York Times* 21 Apr. 2012. Web. 11 Feb. 2013.

Smith, Zadie. "Generation Why?" *New York Review of Books* 25 Nov. 2010. Web. 12 May 2013.

The Dread Beast Boredom

EVAN BOBELLA

It's easy to think of life as a collection of moments. More than that, it's comforting. A series of crests and troughs, patchwork highs and lows, temporary and powerful instantiations, visitations, of angels and demons: these are how we like to imagine our lives, because in this way we can lend them shape and significance. It is not so difficult, after all, to compose something of great import if one starts only with pieces of the greatest value, to be left with a divine and deep vision of the world if this vision is constructed piecemeal from cherry-picked, twinkling occasions of profundity and clarity.

Unfortunately, this is no longer how the world works, if it ever was.

There are also, and have always been, creeping molds, ceaselessly crashing waves, three meals a day, stretches of empty silence, empty conversations, meaningless social pleasantries, feelings of others to be navigated, bathroom breaks to be had, flowers to be pruned, the rising and setting sun, wind and sun and snow and rain, things to be collected and sorted and looked after, and on and on and on forever. The modern age has added to these the burdens of ticking clocks, countless idle hours spent in gardens and cars and offices, rituals of cleanliness and preparation, forms and bills to be completed, household chores ever piling up, shopping trips, pets to be cared for, entertainment to be consumed, bureaucracy to be navigated, endless cycles of mindless practice at instruments and athletic games and academic endeavors, haircuts, hygiene, mirrors and making beds and phoning friends. These are what truly shape the passing of days, which suspend us, weightless, an all-surrounding ether, a nourishing and smothering amniotic medium within which we toil and struggle and discover and create. It is really only by the mastery and tacit understanding of this invisible and inescapable milieu of necessary functions that we are free to ascend, to strive, to leave our mark and reach those heights to which we all aspire, to create lives of substance and value that match the vision we have of what it means to be a human being.

Many forget this: David Foster Wallace did not. His final, unfinished masterwork, the posthumously published *The Pale King*, is a testament to it. It is both a dirge and a comically self-aware, triumphant, glorifying celebration of the oft-reviled American IRS worker who, amidst his proverbial-level scraping and toiling, his boulder-like persistence and commitment to greasing the hidden gears of modern life that things might function as they are designed, sits, ultimately "unborable," beneath sodium-yellow lights in football-field sized offices in utter silence, flipping pages at his custom Tingle desk, closer to the unknowable, ineffable truths of the world than any who might think to lay claim to them (440). The tedium breeds revelation in the way recognizing one's own mortality begets perspective, and it becomes apparent in Wallace's explorations that not only do illustrious and powerful moments constitute only a fraction of what it is to exist, they actively obscure the beauty and the resonant depth of what it is to be a human amongst the quotidian minutiae that swirl endlessly about us all.

The Past

Time, though, has changed things: our conflict is new, and different from that of the past. Critic and essayist John Berger puts it thusly in his essay "Steps Towards a Small Theory of the Visible":

> Until recently, history, all the accounts people gave of their lives, all proverbs, fables, parables, confronted the same thing: the everlasting, fearsome, and occasionally beautiful, struggle of living with Necessity, which is the enigma of existence—that which followed from the Creation, and which subsequently has always continued to sharpen the human spirit. Necessity produces both tragedy and comedy. It is what you kiss or bang your head against.
>
> Today, in the system's spectacle, it exists no more. Consequently no experience is communicated. All that is left to share is the spectacle, the game that nobody plays and everybody can watch. As has never happened before, people have to try to place their own existence and their own pains single-handed in the vast arena of time and the universe. (12-13)

The truth of this fulmination is undeniable. The reverberations of the mythic, of the ancient stories and rituals that underpin all we know, those passed down through ages from the Greeks, the Egyptians, the Norse, do not sing of the small in the way Wallace wishes to; they are concerned always with the big battles, and the obvious ones. They stave off darkness and try to apply meaning to a savage and cruel world. Humanity has, for most of its brief existence, after all, contended with disease, hunger, the unknowable and literal beasts of the forests and the night, death and destruction and pain and the ends of things, as these things were real, and they were everywhere; the quotidian has for most of history been defined by struggle, and thus capital-N Necessity; if anything, the banal was there as reassurance in rare moments of repose when life was safe and comfortable enough for reflection. Our ancestors didn't have the time or the energy for the dithering that now occupies the human species, for the conflict that defines our collective existential angst and dread: but now that we, by a function of civil society, removed from life-affirming struggle, have introduced to our pantheon that dread beast boredom, how do we reconcile our own struggles, our own estrangements and bizarre toiling, with this long and fruitful legacy of man versus nature? Hercules did not grapple with malaise and purposeless depression, nor did Perseus when he slew Medusa, nor even Orpheus when he descended into Hades, and yet in the current age it is as if, by our own abstraction from the world, we have manufactured an entirely new host of antagonizing forces, or at least called them up from the obscure corners of being, and now must contend with the threat they represent.

A Return to the Earth

Perhaps one of the most intuitive solutions contemporary culture has put forth to deal with this problem has been to reconnect and reconvene with the natural, to forgo the unwelcome pressures and monsters of industrialized life and instead commune with the unsullied profundity that resides in the rocks, the trees, the fibers of the world that surrounds us. After all, this closeness has been the guiding light for our predecessors, has worked admirably for so many generations before us, and it makes a certain amount of sense to presume that a return to it might have benefits even now. Even Wallace admits there is a certain kind of power in nature: *The Pale King*'s exposition is built, after all, upon "electric sounds of insects at their business. Ale-colored sunshine and pale sky and whorls of cirrus so high they cast no shadow. Insects all business all the time. Quartz and chert and schist and chondrite iron scabs in granite. Very old land. Look around you. The horizon trembling, shapeless. We are all of us brothers" (5).

E. M. Forster, though, an author to whom the exploration of the primal and basic side of mankind was of the utmost interest, tackles this proposition directly in *A Passage to India*, a novel which, although ostensibly concerned with reconciling the highfalutin imperialism of the British Empire in the nation of India in the 20th century, grapples, in an earthy and direct way, with the power of the Earth and how we might interact with it: at its core it is an experiment in what results from the collision of the modern mind with the natural world. Indeed, one of its most conceptually important scenes involves an excursion of two English high society ladies, Mrs. Moore and Adela Quested (the former a world-weary and cynical older woman who hopes in the so-called primitive and foreign nation of India to find something of depth and significance that might redeem the world she knows, the latter a flighty and optimistic young thing who nevertheless hopes for the same, for a reprieve from her betrothal to a British official and all the stuffy implications of her married life), who, in a bid to enjoy what they refer to as "the *real* India" (a phrase undeniably pregnant given the current discourse and which, in their vocabulary, refers to the local, unpolluted life of the natives), descend into the confined blackness of the Marabar Caves, a series of smooth tunnels in the Indian foothills renowned for their remarkable acoustic and photic properties (22).

What they encounter, however, is complex and and uncompromising: the echoic "ou-boum" that issues from the caves is powerful and sobering, surely, but perhaps not in the reassuring, transcendent way that the women had hoped it might be (163). Mrs. Moore later reflects on her encounter with that sound and comes to realize that she would rather be quit of life than deal with all that the Earth has to say in its manifold and reverberating voice about the affairs of man:

> How indeed is it possible for one human being to be sorry for all the sadness that meets him on the face of the earth, for the pain that is endured not only by men, but by animals and plants, and perhaps by the stones? The soul is tired in a moment, and in fear of losing the little she does understand, she retreats to the permanent lines which habit or chance have dictated, and suffers there. (275)

Adela, on the other hand, a prototypically silly young girl lost in the throes of epic romanticism, blind in many meaningful ways to that skullduggery and ceaseless friction of her new Near Eastern home which plague Mrs. Moore and cause her death, is led to this particular circumstance by her innocent pathological need for spiritual vindication, for a way to make her passage to India worth it, to step outside her stifling and stymieing upper-class existence, and so is more vulnerable: it is no surprise, then, when she is overwhelmed by the concentrated and focused reverberation of being, the pin-point excitation of the minute and the unmagnificent in the Marabar Caves that is the ouboom. The sound leads her to suffer a psychotic break in which she accuses Aziz, an Indian doctor and her guide, of attempted rape, an allegation which sparks cultural warfare and the drama that is the rest of the novel.

Perhaps, then, in Forster's estimation of things, the Earth is not ready for our return, or at least we in our present state, swaddled as we are in modern convenience and cursed as we are by all the knowledge this swaddling affords us, are unready for the truths it might have to offer us. When finally at novel's end Aziz and Fielding (the aforementioned Indian doctor and a British professor teaching in India), characters who might stand as personifications of enlightened and friendly Eastern and Western culture, try to join in friendship, to bridge the old world of man (with all its Necessity and all its danger) and the new world (with its dread beast boredom and its confining drudgery), Forster tells us that the Earth and the hills and the rivers say, "'No, not yet,' and the sky [says], 'No, not there'" (362).

Indeed, in Rainer Maria Rilke's view of things, the Earth is, although beautiful and all-consuming, intrinsically in its beauty and depth too much for the fragile human constitution that has become so removed from it, which has so differentiated itself from the rest of the animal kingdom and lost the gift for convening with it openly and honestly and purely:

> We, though: never, not for a single day, do we
> have that pure space ahead of us into which flowers
> endlessly open. What we have is World
> and always World and never Nowhere-Without-Not:
> that pure unguarded element one breathes
> and *knows* endlessly and never craves. (47)

How, then, could we hope to connect with the purity we see in the Earth and in its other creatures if we're lacking in the vocabulary of need and Necessity that allows simpler animals to derive its treasures? Perhaps it was foolhardy for Mrs. Moore and Ms. Quested to seek their justification in natural grandeur; perhaps it is not viable for man to try to hew from the rocks and convene with the sky and the river and Earth, for perhaps this is just an attempt at escape, to force open the encapsulating order that surrounds, and perhaps to do so, to try to so brazenly subvert the structures we are born into, enticing as the potential payoffs might be, is suicide. Although Forster holds the natural as the ideal, he also realized in his way that its power is too absolute, is too different from the human, no matter how captivating it might be. Berger again, in "Opening the Gate": "The result [of seeing through the interstices of the human order] is unsettling: there is more solitude, more pain, more dereliction. At the same time, there is an expectancy which I have not experienced since childhood, since I talked to dogs, listened to their secrets and kept them to myself" (6).

Artistic Transmutation

Virginia Woolf was no stranger to the burdens of polite modern society, high born and ensconced as she was in turn-of-the-century Britain with many responsibilities and social obligations. In *To the Lighthouse*, however, a story that appears to be about the day-to-day goings-on of a family on vacation but proves to be a treatise on the distillation of glory and life-affirming creation in the idle moments of repose and reflection—the tender and quiet moments on the beach playing ducks and drakes or lying supine on the grass in the warm sun, moments that prop up reality like the unseen flow of time—Woolf provides for us another powerful tool, art, that we might potentially use in the aid of breaking the dread beast boredom.

Mrs. Ramsay, the novel's matriarch, who is a pervasive and ethereal force patterned after Woolf's mother and perhaps the impetus behind the novel's conception, is a conductor, an expert at bending the passage of the concrete world into an elastic and meaningful thing. Even as she clings uncompromisingly to domesticity and order, even as she organizes elaborate dinners with Boeuf en Daube laboriously prepared days in advance and admonishes all of her children and guests to behave cordially and prepare their hair and clothes and brooches just so, "she had a sense of being past everything, through everything, out of everything, as she helped the soup, as if there was an eddy—there—and one could be in it, or one could be out of it, and she was out of it" (83). Mrs. Ramsay is simultaneously in the thick of things and removed, an observer, a shaper, a lender of energy and attention: she grants strength to her brilliant but flagging husband by reminding him of the import in small moments, fills the minds of her guests, even the erstwhile and unhappy Charles Tansley, with contemplation and self-examination, rallies her children about her in reverence and thanksgiving so that as they grow into the sober world of adulthood without her and dip their minds into the repetitive and endless nature of their world they might have her memory and the stately compunction and grace with which she carried herself at all times to guide them. She lets no one forget the roots that keep them tethered to the world around their house in the Hebrides and to one another, and any sort of understanding (or then, Understanding) they gain is a function of this grounding, of this manipulation of elements, of this playing with the rules of the game, so to speak, that all involved might have a chance of achieving purpose and depth instead of living their lives by rote.

The true embodiment of this ideal, though, is Lily Briscoe, a girlish woman with mawkish artistic inclinations who summers with the Ramsays and who bears the brunt of the novel's thematic exploration. Indeed, she might in some ways personify Woolf herself: consider her crisis in the novel, wherein she tries, confusedly, often in vain, to manifest something of value on a canvas, to understand the secret of Mrs. Ramsay's beauty in the language of paint and parallel lines and the way that matriarchal dignity unifies the sulking Charles Tansley, the obdurate Mr. Ramsay, the air-headed Paul Rayley and Minta Doyle, the way it transmogrifies their wayward proclivities and critical self-chastisements into concerted, beautiful scenic memories that reek of purpose and meaning, even and especially when they are boring and picayune. In this struggle we can see the parallel work of an author who must wrangle with the disparate and unrelated tendrils of energy and consequence and implacable daily progress that twist forever about us to create some erogenous, erotic release of purpose and form such that others might see and be enriched by the act of its making. Surely when done right it is a sight to behold, one that leaves the mind positively throbbing with manifold readings and interpretations, each one of value. Rilke, again in the *Elegies*, asks "Earth! Invisible! / What, if not transformation, is your urgent charge?" and it would seem that for Lily and for Woolf transformation from experience into art, the reduction and capture of energy into the organizing shape of words or paint, is all (57).

Why might this kind of creation work where communion with the Earth might fail? In the nature of her pursuit, after all, Lily is the same as Adela Quested, a hopeful and helpless young woman lost in the gravity of her adoration for an older woman and so too in the inescapable natural powers of the world around her, believing there to be forces beyond her and outside her which bend things to their will and which, if she can commune with them, might give meaning to her own life. The difference between the two, then, is that Lily is critically aware of the ways of the slow and uncompromising world. Instead of succumbing to the weight of her realization and losing her grip on the world as Adela did when she encountered hard truth (for Lily, instead of an "ou-boum," this truth is the death of Mrs. Ramsay), Lily manages to achieve some sense of higher meaning. It matters not that her painting "would be hung in the attics . . . ; it would be destroyed," for at the end of her creating, she stands in a sort of defiance and resolute supremacy against being itself, against the implacable, creeping glacier of rules and manners and moments which form her life at the vacation house but which all conspired, too, to give her just this moment (Woolf 208). She finally, but not without the aid of much time passing and the pervasive, far-reaching spirit of the illustrious Mrs. Ramsay reminding her always of the beauty in the inescapable, by way of resignation of ego and the handing over of her heart to the care of time itself, to the struggles and the myriad unsexy capitulations one must make to ensure domestic and daily harmony, manages to capture with her brush something worth keeping, some pearl of transcendence far different from the ones she originally sought to obtain, and much more valuable for it, and at the end decides, "I have had my vision" (209).

The New Hero for the New Mythic

This visionary act is the genius of Wallace, then; he has recognized this new world, has lived deep within the depths of strangling academic upper-middle-class life, has seen the lineage of myth and Necessity we've turned our back on, but so too realizes that we cannot merely return to a state of nature, cannot merely digress from the rails of daily habit as they draw us inexorably onward, cannot dismount from the dread beast boredom without its violent and disastrous bucking. He knows too that the secret to transcendence lies to some degree in creation as Woolf shows us in *To the Lighthouse*, but that it cannot end there, for although Lily succeeds in her endeavor, we are also told of the difficulties in the novel's second section where the natural world intrudes into the sphere of man:

> [T]ouched by human penitence and all its toil, divine goodness had parted the curtain and displayed behind it, single, distinct, the hare erect; the wave falling; the boat rocking, which, did we deserve them, should be ours always. But alas, divine goodness, twitching the cord, draws the curtain; it does not please him; he covers his treasures in a drench of hail, and so breaks them, so confuses them that it seems impossible that their calm should ever return or that we should ever compose from their fragments a perfect whole or read in the littered pieces the clear words of truth. For our penitence deserves a glimpse only; our toil respite only. (127-28)

What is the answer, then? What is the prescribed course of action to handle boredom that Wallace dangles in front of us like a carrot, to take it all in hand and force some new meaning into a world neutered of its cogency and force by repetition and banality and manners?

By way of an answer, we might look one final time at *To the Lighthouse*; specifically, at the character of Augustus Carmichael, a bearded man, opium-dulled, who floats like a ghost through the Ramsay's summer home in a decidedly Zen-like, contemplative capacity. He is a watcher and scribbler of poems, and so in some ways akin to Lily in her need to be creative. But he is also immune to her fears, to the quailing she feels at the enormity of things, seemingly content to immerse himself in each and every sliding second that he might wring from them some verse or just sit contented on the grass outside the house. True, Woolf never grants us access to his thoughts as she does with other characters, and we see him always only through the eyes of someone else, but through this lens we come to understand him as naturally predisposed to the fruitful nature of acquiescence, as it were, as imbued with quasi-divine potential to supersede the boundaries of his devotion to drudgery, and then so to stand as a shining example of peace and transcendence—happy and confident in the passage of time and in the fiddling of the everyday. He has perhaps a passing antipathy for Mrs. Ramsay, for the fervor of her reorganization and the desperation of her creation, but is nevertheless in harmony with it all, a new sort of heroic figure for a new mythic landscape.

"Heroism," then—perhaps that's the answer. A new, particular type of heroism that's about outlasting and suffering and supporting to create. In *The Pale King*, everyday life is clearly painted as villainous, or, at the very least, as an obstacle to be overcome, a challenge to be risen to, to be smote and cast down and brought to heel much as the monsters of old myth; only now the heroic virtues are different than they once were. Take Wallace's own words:

> [An economics professor to his accounting students on the last day of his class:] This may be the first time you've heard the truth put plainly, starkly. Effacement. Sacrifice. Service. To give oneself to the care of others' money—this is effacement, perdurance, sacrifice, honor, doughtiness, valor. Hear this or not, as you will. Learn it now, or later—the world has time. Routine, repetition, tedium, monotony, ephemeracy, inconsequence, abstraction, disorder, boredom, angst, ennui—these are the true hero's enemies, and make no mistake, they are fearsome indeed. For they are real. (233)

Every character in *The Pale King* is, in some way or another, an example of this new heroic ideal. Each is an outwardly unremarkable IRS worker whose life is related in crushing, extensive detail, all his past foibles and failures and the underwhelming experiences related to the reader, so we realize just how unremarkable he is. Yet each has some bizarre secret power or curse. Shane Drinion, a near-autistic savant of contemplation who is capable of preternatural levitation in moments of extreme fixation and focus, such that "one night someone comes into the office and sees Drinion floating upside down over his desk with his eyes glued to a complex [tax] return" (487). Leonard Stecyk, who is so doggedly, supernaturally kind and optimistic that his grade school principal "fantasizes about sinking a meat hook into [his] bright-eyed little face and dragging the boy face-down behind his Volkswagen Beetle over the rough new streets of suburban Grand Rapids" (34). Claude Sylvanshine, whose whimsical last name refers to an optical illusion wherein the wax that exists on the leaves of certain types of trees reflects light in the heat of summer so that to an observer they seemed white and covered in snow, beautiful and impossible and contrary, and who is a "fact psychic," a person to whom data of all sorts ("That the 1938 featherweight WBA champ had mild scoliosis in the region T10-12," "The average molecular weight of peat," "the name of his [fourth grade] homeroom teacher's husband's first love's childhood cat who'd lost one side's whiskers in a mishap near the coal stove in Ashtabula OH," and so on) come randomly and unbidden and to very little usable effect (121-22).

Each is beset by some strange malady, given to unfathomable pressures and fears of shortcoming for their strangeness on top of the (paradoxically) already crushing normalcy of their lives, and yet each stands confident, resolute, "unborable" in the face of it all, and each, even as a sort of challenge to reality itself, decides to join the IRS and hunker down in the trenches of the battle against mind-numbing, fatally boring facts, the unyielding progression of day after day, return after return, moment after interminable moment, such that he can show the world there is a new way out, a new way to saddle the dread beast boredom and make it work for humanity, a way to best the inky and insidious malaise that waits in every room and empty alleyway and train car, and in *this* way transmute it. This new hero's struggle is not only for the creation of something worth having, not only for the glorifying and remembrance of the power of the Earth, but even for sanity and purpose in a world of incoherence and informational chaos. This is selflessness in the deepest sense of the word, this is the new standard of striving, this is the new mechanism humanity needs, his new Hercules, despite the fact that even at novel's end each is gray and tight-lipped and suffers under the weight of the world.

WORKS CITED

Berger, John. *The Shape of a Pocket*. New York: Vintage, 2003. Print.
Forster, E. M. *A Passage to India*. San Diego: Harcourt, 1984. Print.
Rilke, Rainer Maria. *Duino Elegies*. Trans. Edward A. Snow. New York: North Point, 2000. Print.

Wallace, David Foster. *The Pale King*. New York: Back Bay, 2012. Print.

Woolf, Virginia. *To the Lighthouse*. Orlando: Harcourt, 1981. Print.

The Mythical Touchy-Touch

ALYSSA BÖEHLE

Strange all this difference should be,
Twixt Tweedle-dum and Tweedle-dee!
—John Byrom (1692-1763)

At fifteen I am touched by a Horror who takes my Human Touch away.

To my riddled mind, my friends' nudges, my parents' hugs all appear to be sexual advances, sexual threats, and I react by keeping my physical body removed from communication. The years of physical self-exile collect under my skin, while calluses fail to form the way they do upon regularized human touch. In its preserved state, my skin becomes raw, thin like an embryo's, painfully sensitive to the brine of sea breeze, to the grains of sand on the shore.

My sister, her boyfriend, and I are at the Jersey Shore. The September seawater feels warmer than the air, sort of stupid in its hope for the return of summer. And though the waves seem all riled up in a rage, it is the fluid wind and invisible moon that set today's storm into motion.

My sister and her boyfriend look like two lame poles lodged between the cream-capped waves, appearing and disappearing without moving, but surely warm from the blood of each other's bodies. I watch them from the shore, where my hands coat balls of ocean-wet sand with the powdery dry sand upon which I sit.

They are twenty, in love and fascinated with each other, and I am eighteen, in mania and memory of a ritual my sister and I performed as kids. We would make these sand cannonballs for throwing, not at people but at the Atlantic. "Give us *Wawa Waves!*" we would scream while catapulting the balls into the tide, the name *Wawa* stolen from the South Jersey mini-market where we'd get ICEEs and milk. This ritual, we thought, would make the sea rise and swell into a surge more suitable for bodysurfing, for riding the waves as human torpedoes. We'd tumble with the current, crashing onto shore, slapped by jellyfish and slimy seaweed on the way. I never minded these touches, not me.

I could barrage the couple, but I aim instead for the waves. I will not admit to myself how jealous I am of the lovers, their ability to bear each other's bodies without pain.

The waves stay the same. Accompanied by no one, I enter the ocean.

Rainer Maria Rilke might applaud my descent into the sea, an unaccompanied dance, an affair with the water. In *Duino Elegies*, he tells us of a "Land of Lament," a place where we must go alone to realize our disconnection from the Earth. We cannot gain entrance there with a lover, or an ersatz mother to protect us from the urging, primal world within. We must open ourselves to the Earth as our singular, monogamous partner.

And so I do. I have my way with the ocean. The seaweed lodges itself between my thighs, my breasts; my hypersensitive, untouched body takes in the saltwater of the ocean.

And it seems so noble to reject infatuation and save my sensual attention for the body of the Earth. But it also becomes too easy to separate *human bodies* from the body of the earth, humans with bodies that were once and will again be dirt of the body of the earth. It becomes easy to keep repeating, "I will not touch" and thus "I will not love" until it seems like a fine affirmation, a chant of the holy. I forget the fear behind the words, why I needed them in the first place: to cope. The words, the chant, the repetition, the ritual cease to be mine. They become too general, too removed from the specific origin of private hurt they were meant for. But they preoccupy me.

Virginia Woolf tells us in "A Sketch of the Past" of how her half-brother inspects her private parts, awakening in her "instincts already acquired by thousands of ancestors in the past," specifically how "this seems to show that a feeling about certain parts of the body; how they must not be touched; how it is wrong to allow them to be touched; must be instinctive" (69). Her point is not touch but instinct, and yet I cannot help fixating on touch. The ocean touches me, and I seem to be fine. And theoretically speaking, these parts are *allowed* to be touched. Otherwise, recreational sex would disappear from the human and dolphin populations. My sister and her boyfriend would spend less time in the bedroom, a place where it seems touch is good. So the problem is not in allowance but in perception, which can make all human touch *seem* taboo.

The problem of touch dwells in sight, in the sight of the same darkness Persephone sees when Hades steals her from the earth and rapes her in the Underworld. He literally takes the ground from beneath her feet in a feat of blindness and disequilibrium, creating a chaos of the senses. This chaos feels a lot like being submerged underwater in the matte twilight of a September afternoon.

At eighteen I unconsciously reenact the Horror by stepping into the Angry Atlantic.

I almost forget that in my somersault beneath the sea, I still need a sense of gravity. I need to distinguish up from down, I need to shoot through the waves that want me drowned. My skull, my knees scrape the bottom of the ocean floor, and my mind realizes that my body cannot bear the physicality any more. They, my body and mind, work like awkward, mad scientists, separately trying to find a solution to the Problem of Touch. They work at the expense of an instinct that tells me the riddle must be solved soon, the pain of All Touch must be stopped before it grows and grows into something forever unsolvable.

At seventeen I am obsessed with the riddle of body and mind.

I find a way to bridge the two, my love of bodies and my fear of human touch. Energy healing, healing bodies bridge the two. I heal the slow vibrations in peoples' slowed down bodies, helping them quicken, helping their seven main energy centers turn and churn the way healthy wheels do. I learn symbols at Reiki seminars. I learn Sanskrit symbols that I picture in my mind's eye. I draw them in my head while I let my hands hover over other peoples' slowed bodies. We never touch. When I'm seventeen I find a boy who wants to believe, so I lift my hovering hands over his body, and intuit a knot near his heart. *Why?*

"My mother died two months ago," he says.

I do the best I can to unknot the knot, but I know I can't. It's a riddle his body will never solve. I know, he knows, but we hope he can cope with its presence. We talk about circuses and aliens to downplay the strange exchange, until my mom walks in, my mom who introduced me to Reiki and ritual. Later when he leaves, she asks me, "Did you guys have sex?"

No. He's a boy. He's a being. He's a being caught in a conversation with the ghost of his mother, and I'm a being searching for the ghost of my body. We are two bodies, riddled by the unearthly, unable to let our live flesh touch, nonetheless express the libido beneath.

Carl Jung, master of the archetypal, says in his compendium *Symbols of Transformation*, "If it is not possible for the libido to strive forwards, to lead a life that willingly accepts all dangers and ultimate decay, then it strikes back along the other road and sinks into its own depths, working down to the old intimation of the immortality of all that lives, to the old longing for rebirth"

(398). Libido, he suggests, is not a singularly sexual force but a more general lust for life. It is a force that comes like instinct from our ancestors from ages back, from a well of riddled voices and messages, a collection of calls that can pull us back into the Underworld.

The boy and I do not yet know that we lie in risk of lingering in the realm of the dead too long; that we, like Woolf, may be giving our ancestors too much voice, too valid a claim on our earthly lives. We meet and seduce each other at our crossroads, at our thresholds, our *limen*. We meet within the liminal, the limbo between two worlds where the dead and the living touch, the Underworld and the earth, where we build a provisional home and work out that which has been taken from us in our earthly realm. It is a place where we must waver while waiting for the new, the post-liminal, where we the wounded emerge healed and transformed, better for the process we've been through.

But it is so easy to get too comfortable, to forget to move forwards into the post-liminal. As Jung tells us, the seeds of libdo can be planted, can grow into the wrong direction, pulling the living too far into the comforting depths of the *limen*. According to myth, those who linger in the liminal for too long become tricksters, deceivers, sphinx-tongued hybrids neither dead nor living. Tricksters take on the forms, the faces of others, and pretend to provide entertainment, diversion, relief from pain with their two-faced nature, their playful games. The boy and I fool each other into pleasure.

For a moment, I cradle the boy with a mother's touch.

For a moment, the boy looks at me without desire.

Neither of us means to deceive, but the communion can only be provisional.

We are stuck in the liminal, in the limbo where libido lies festering, "betwixt and between" neurosis and transformation. Imagine our crossroads, imagine a room. You are in the middle of a white room. A colossal stretch of hot rolled steel sits below your feet, pressed to the ground. It is rectangular, like a river dock. Above you, flattened onto the ceiling, hangs suspended another massive steel rectangle, rotated at an angle perpendicular to the slab of steel you stand on. The sculpture is inspired by a Christian cross, yet it forms a severed plus sign, a *pagan* cross, lines cushioned from each other by a thick layer of space.

You are standing in the room that houses Richard Serra's installation *Delineator*. Your mind quickens in the presence of the huge, menacing steel plates, exhorting your eyes to dart up and down in frantic nystagmus—a series of swift eye movements that cause the pupil to flash back and forth as in the experience of watching a train or traffic flitting by. You can track this speedy side-to-side or up-and-down eye movement (as in the case of *Delineator*, a *still* object). You can track the shifting black of your pupils and trace a sinusoidal wave; you can trace the shape of a sound wave; you'll find yourself tracing a song in the face of a visual image, engaging in a logical contradiction, your senses of sight and sound shivering against each other.

Such synesthesia is not just an affliction reserved for the few; it is perceptual sex, *friction*, for the sensitive masses. Sex means pleasure, birth, and multiplication, as problematic a topic in science as it is in my mind. Even just sticking to sight, we can see paradoxical union in the problem of light. The amount of light that enters your eye is the product of the amount of light emitted from the original light source multiplied by the light reflected from the object's surface. The two factors cannot be disentangled, cannot be delineated from each other the same way the boy and his mother cannot be disentangled, the way my love for bodies and my fearful ghost of a body cannot be disentangled. The factors' identities remain invisible, and yet they conspire to create the perceivable phenomenon that is light. You can feel their combined effect, the entanglement of two disparate senses. You can feel the image, you can see the grain of the light and feel the physical photons scraping through the layers of your brain like grains of sand to form a picture. This mental fuck is touch, too, a touch that leaves its residue.

The boy and I entangle ourselves in a nonsexual way that appears quite sexy to my mother. She sees something on our faces, the pleasure of touch, the weird meeting of libidos caught in transition. She sees, on our earthly faces, what I see when I watch my sister and her boyfriend in the sea. I do not know what goes on beneath their skin. But I know that body and mind are not two, because the ocean tells me that I must cease being a trickster, I must stop confusing sky from ground in order to breathe. I must put the argumentative scientists of body and mind to rest in order, literally, to survive. This necessity for oneness shows me that even the lovers have riddled perceptions; the lovers who intertwine their bodies will leave a psychic riddle in the liminal, a riddle of confused libidos to be solved in time, in an unfamiliar realm.

Perhaps the only difference is that I am already familiar with the Underworld and the disorienting forces it insists upon shooting throughout my body, a nausea I can remember.

Nausea comes from the disagreement between the senses: sight says the world looks like this, and balance says the world feels like that. Balance is the sixth sense, making the perception of spirits the seventh, according to my Old Country parents. Balance is the crazy force in our body that measures our relationship to the gravitational pull of the earth. It is the force that tells our brains, *Flip upside-down-picture of the world coming into your eyes right-side-up!* so that the earth does not look upside down. But sometimes balance and vision do not, cannot agree. They tilt away from each other by degrees. This is the subtle nausea of the liminal.

But underneath the stormy sea, my senses are in such chaos that I can barely keep track of my dislocation. I feel no epiphany, no nausea. In *Delineator*, however, floor and ground play tricks even when they seem plain. Who can say if the steel plate on the ground serves as a floorboard, when it is the plate on the ceiling that appears tarnished with footprints? A weathered ceiling, a spotless floor. We get a riddle born of logical contradiction, an opposition of certainties welded into the space we, the privileged viewers, inhabit as we stand between the plates, and space and perception play with our bodies, our sense of direction. The subtle shivering of my sight, my nystagmus and my balance, my orientation, inspire that nagging nausea.

The nausea tells me to leave the crossroads I have been standing at for the past five years and *grasp*, not touch, the world for support while my sealegs adjust to the ground, the hard post-liminal ground. It tells me to stop overanalyzing the difference between sexual touch and platonic touch, but just to touch, *please* just touch, because all is libido. I must stop riddling over the unsolvable fear of being a hybrid, a trickster, too monstrous to engage with the world, when perhaps the boy and I may serve our ancestors better, may serve all of us better, by accepting our entanglement, our strange libidos—explaining them in words and symbols the earth can understand.

WORKS CITED

Byrom, John. *The Poems of John Byrom*. 1894. Ed. Adolphus William Ward. Vol. 29. Manchester: Charles E. Simms. 37. Print.

Jung, Carl. *Symbols of Transformation*. Trans. R.F.C. Hull. Princeton: Princeton UP, 1956. Print.

Rilke, Rainer M. *Duino Elegies*. Trans. Edward Snow. New York: North Point, 2000. Print.

Serra, Richard. *Delineator*. 1974. Steel. Metropolitan Museum of Art, New York.

Woolf, Virginia. "A Sketch of the Past." *Moments of Being: A Collection of Autobiographical Writing*. 2nd ed. Ed. Jeanne Schulkind. Orlando: Harcourt, 1985. 61-160. Print.

The Naked Narrative

KATIE EILER

Spaces tell us how to inhabit them. A feeling of openness, a sudden cohesion of lines into corners, a smell: these are things that say at every threshold "you are welcome" or "walk carefully," often both. This sense is a combination of the intuitive and the learned: for example, most grand holy places have high ceilings, vaults suggesting the infinite bound in mortar, but only other people can tell us the way to genuflect correctly or the name of the captive god. The architect of a labyrinth wants you to feel a certain suspense, experience the space as you would the movements of a song, bar building upon bar and twist upon twist. The acts and rituals carried out in a space are bound by what the walls and floors tell the people in it. Although seemingly simple, this shifting nature defies reduction; to understand a space is to grapple with its history and even its subjectivity, the way the corners shift and the distances alter as you move about a room.

So let's walk into a locker room. Uncomfortable? Good; the space invites self-consciousness. Locker rooms in general are places with ceilings high enough to discourage coziness but not high enough to nudge us towards transcendence. They are white and stark; they smell of Clorox and mildew. There are rows and columns of lockers standing at Roman attention. Everything is easily wiped; sitting is discouraged; it's a place to be exited from, and quickly, a place designed for steam but not for warmth. I would mark these features down to school budget cuts, but even well-funded adult gyms and public pool changing rooms follow this pattern. It's a practical room for a practical goal: getting many people clean and presentable enough to rejoin humanity. This simple process, though, is loaded with tension and significance.

Why is the character of this specific space such a big deal? It's just a changing room. We don't have to analyze it. I, at least, am decidedly under its spell. I *hated* changing for gym. I was deeply and truly not comfortable soaping up with my peers. As far back as I can remember, public exposure was something that's always held a particular terror for me.

This fascination is valuable, though: a spade is never just a spade when it comes to humanity. You can't talk about the body, or about dirtiness, without talking about morality and normality. The metaphors have become ingrained—cleanliness is next to godliness, to be clean is to be good, to be acceptable. It is ritualistic—water allows one to enter into a compact with the community, whether it be through a baptism or the ducking of freshman in the fountain by upperclassmen. Getting clean together is a way to codify standards of hygiene and self-perception. How much a society thinks about cleanliness, and what they think about it, speaks volumes.

Consider a 1915 ad for Sunlight Soap: a gallant fighting man aims his gun over the lip of a trench wall, crates of soap around him. Above him hangs the message "The CLEANEST fighter in the World—the British Tommy!" In the background, a soldier washes his face in a bucket. The audience for this ad was most likely made up of those who had family in the war, and they were likely desperate for the strength and cleanliness promised by Sunlight Soap, by smiling tommies lathering up in buckets. Waging war requires a notion of being on the right side, of order amidst chaos. Those concepts had to be preserved in order for the warring nation to stay together psychologically. The war was being, in this image, quite literally sanitized, and it *worked*. The brand is still going strong under Unilever.

Soaps, though, for all that they do to make us touchable and clean and nice-smelling, somehow subtract from our corporeality. In soap commercials nothing is ever being washed *off*—the soap isn't there to remove something but to augment or replace what is already there: the smell of skin, the smell of a person. The ads are flirty, winking at us, promising us an unseen smeller and toucher, but that conspiratorial nature is all somehow neutralized, defanged. The soapy, perfumed body is covered and denied as well as cleaned.

The word "touchable" occurs in nearly all personal hygiene advertisements, from those of the cutting-edge, cheekily subversive new companies to the painfully wholesome campaigns of Proctor & Gamble. It hints at the erotic and the connective. But while scent is a wonderful sense to play and accessorize with, much like the colors and textures of our clothes, and while these things can be delightful to ourselves and others, the way they are sexy is to actual sex as wrapping paper is to a Christmas present. It all comes off when you get to the good stuff. When you get to the body-as-it-is. When scientists do studies on chemical attraction, they don't use Chanel No. 5 or Axe—they use sweat.

All this subtext lives in and so defines the space of a locker room, and so too any space concerned with the human body. It doesn't end there, though;

this sanitized way of thinking about the body is complicated by what Vivona and Gomillon call "the social fiction of neutrality" in their article "Situational Morality of Bathroom Nudity" (134). They discuss a perfect sample case for this sanitization of concepts: a tiny college bathroom in a women's dorm used by many people at the same time. Interestingly, it is a space that was intended to be a large private bathroom and thus to be free of the communal trappings of a public locker room—several of the new girls describe being reprimanded for locking the door, not knowing that it was a shared space. The architecture betrayed them and lulled them into a false sense of privacy, and so made them believe they could remain neutral and alone there, made accepting the space as a public one even more jarring than usual.

How do people reconcile with the reality of public bathing in an era of great privacy and modesty? What allows them to strip off and soap up in front of acquaintances with a more or less untroubled heart, to remain neutral and unashamed, especially if they usually balk at the idea of revealing their body to another person? One of the young women interviewed by Vivona and Gomillon distilled it beautifully:

> If I think of the person as a body and not as an exposed person, there's no embarrassment. . . . If you think of it as a body, it's an impersonal thing, an object, and there aren't really personal objectives or thoughts involved. If you see the person as an exposed person, however . . . your thoughts could be personal. This could be embarrassing because you could make the other person uncomfortable. . . . I suppose that questions of some kind of sexual interest could be raised in that case. (133)

For public bathing to be safe or neutral, she implies that you have to think of the other person's body, and your own, as just objects. To do otherwise would be, the woman insinuates, bordering on the sexual and the taboo. In fact, the pains taken not to seem gay are something that the interviewees mention repeatedly: "it would be embarrassing for both of you if they saw you looking at them . . . it might imply a homosexual interest" (133). One suggests, "maybe you're more interested than you're supposed to be" (133).

All these women, to my knowledge, are straight, and yet the specter of homosexuality looms over and defines all their interactions just as the specter of "dirty war" loomed over advertising and public thought in 1918. These women are trying to *disprove* something, not prove a positive: they don't obsess over acting straight, but over acting *not gay*.

Locker rooms, then, are spaces with an inherent tension of identity. The struggle of reconciling other human bodies with our perceptions of sexuality and of ourselves defines much of the behavior therein, and is particularly relevant to the non-straight or non-straight-passing people. Whenever people joke about finding gay people in such a space, they always point to the men who slap each other's asses and the girls who help each other unhook bras. But that's not a come-on, that's a theatrical reassurance of straightness. Look in the corner. See the girl who can change shirts in thirty seconds without showing a single strip of skin, one shirt nested inside the other, the boy who sits on the very end of the bench to tie his shoes so he won't accidentally get flashed. There they are, those for whom public nakedness is dangerous, has an extra layer of meaning. There I am, sliding my uniform shorts on under a skirt I wore explicitly for that purpose.

This desire for secrecy being perceived as a sign of inversion or weakness isn't new. When I was eight, surrounded by books of Greek mythology in my backyard, Hercules taught me that the strength of the body and of the mind are one; Cartesian dualism was to his culture and era an alien concept lurking in a distant future. The brave fight and train naked. They have nothing to hide. To the ancients, the concept of desiring bodily privacy would be downright antisocial. The public baths of the ancient Mediterranean and North Africa were designed to be bustling social centers. They were comprised of a succession of low-ceilinged, boxy rooms lined with benches and shelves for lounging, decorated with mosaics and graffiti slandering opposing chariot teams—warm, communal spaces. A place of leisure open to senators and slaves. Business meetings were conducted there; friends talked for hours; two or three generations would mill about at once, shouting and laughing (Bowman). I was fascinated.

Of course, the Greeks also fucked each other. Achilles mourned Patroclus, Sappho pined for Anactoria. I picked up on that early; I was looking for it.

Queers have a complicated relationship to history. We try to coax the future towards us by manipulating the baits of the past. We grasp at lines of poems, hidden glances in black-and-white photos. If we existed then, it means we're allowed to exist now. We have a precedent.

Ancient Greece has become a safe haven for a lot of gay people over the centuries. A historical example that helps explain and vindicate the pervasive shame and estrangement in modern locker rooms. Victorians and Edwardians sometimes even referred to sodomy as "the Greek sin"—it is also from this time and place that we get the term "Sapphic." This longing, for the normalcy of homosexuality of the past, is the subject of Tom Stoppard's play *The Invention of Love*, a work about Victorian poet A.E. Housman's lifelong desire for his friend Moses Jackson. Housman, confronted by Jackson about the rumors one day, initially denies them but then says:

> Theseus and Pirithous . . . They loved each other, as men loved each other in the heroic age, in virtue . . . Virtue! What happened to it? It had a good run—centuries!—it was still virtue in Socrates to admire a beautiful youth, virtue to be beautiful and admired. . . . Well, not any more, eh, Mo? Virtue is what women have to lose, the rest is vice. (76)

In the 50s and 60s, partly to reclaim the Greek ideal, gay bathhouses emerged in major cities. They functioned, too, as sort of reclamation and joyful subversion of the concept of moral and physical cleanness, of the ritual of public bathing. No place for us in the locker rooms? Fine. We have our own place.

Except—isn't the recreating of the "Greek ideal," the clutching at history, just another form of sanitizing? The thing about the Greeks is that, no matter who they wrote their love poetry to, they, like every culture, had a group of sexual outsiders whom they mocked and found hideous. In *The Clouds*, a comedy by Aristophanes, any sign of gender nonconformity or same-age relationships between people of the same sex is roundly mocked; characters talk with disgust of the boys these days "prancing" and "simper[ing] softly to [their] lover[s]" (978-79). And yet somehow the myth of past equality persists; the need for that story is still there.

Denial, the "sanitizing" of the world or the false performance of an ingrained cultural narrative, is a process that is personal for everyone but that nevertheless hinges upon the mass reaction and interpretation of the culture. The body collective of repeating tropes and ideas about cleanliness and sexuality, or really any issue, needs to be recognized and shared by society as a whole to become entrenched in us as individuals. I see it as kind of a collective social immune response: the symptoms of a cold arise as the body's way to defend against a real threat. Autoimmune disorders, however, come about because your body mistakenly believes its fighting a bigger viral threat than it actually is. A defense response is a part of having a body in a world filled with germs; overreaction, though, can be deadly. The girls in the bathing study, faced with the reality of peeing next to a bathing, naked near-stranger, used denial as a tool to give them a little peace and dignity. But this freedom, to so regularly deny the humanity of others, and so too the validity of your own body, is a dangerous one. It becomes an automatic response. It follows you. I once caught myself getting changed under my towel alone in my bedroom.

Consider the insidious dangers of transcending the body, of slipping out to some ascetic place and looking down at your hands as you would a rake or a fork. It was something I needed to do to get along in groups. Straight people do this too, of course, but I and those like me take the performativity to a different level. We stretch it to the point of breaking—but you can see some interesting patterns in the fault lines of an ill-made mask.

Take the effects of my paranoia. When I was eight, I hid the fact that I had pneumonia for three months. I focused incessantly on not coughing, and then on coughing quietly when that proved impossible. I hid a stash of cough drops. I ignored the choked, bubbling feeling growing in my lungs, the crackling noise when I breathed in. Whenever anyone mentioned it, I said that it felt like it was going away.

These activities took up a staggering amount of time and effort, but I really didn't allow myself to notice the progression of the illness. I thought of it as something to be hidden, if I thought of it at all, but I never considered it as something that could truly hurt me. So I turned the rattling into just another noise, no more or less important to me than the sound of the air conditioner or the hum of the freeway. Then I almost drowned on my own bodily fluids.

And so a cultivated social response used only for practical means—the proverbial "cold"—develops into a full-blown autoimmune response. The body attacks itself, perceiving its own white blood cells, its own sexuality, as an external threat, and nearly dies for it. This happens in large-scale social movements too—see the panicked Red Scare directly after WWII in America, or the widespread rioting during the post-Civil War Reconstruction. A society can't just turn off a wartime mentality like a light switch. Neither can individual people.

Fiction, myth, denial, and lying are all facets of the same extremely powerful construct—I suppose you could call this thing "crafted untruth," or a "shared lie." Humans are narrative creatures; we *think* using stories. We embellish, idolize, and drift naturally towards the picturesque and the "correct"—sometimes to our salvation, sometimes to our destruction.

But the dangerous thing about the natural tendency to perform narratives is that our lives go on even after the climaxes. We cannot simply end the process of fiction and denial; it would be equivalent to ending our humanity. Ending a cultural era would necessarily leave a terrible lacuna within us: it's dangerous to think that we know ourselves entirely, or that we have reached some sort of mountaintop of self-knowledge. Every person contains at least one entire city—a multifaceted, half-grown, half-built structure populated with endless versions of themselves. Ill-lit bars full of decanted desires; huge libraries of books they'll never write; every citizen a different self. A place like this cannot be glanced at and known; its narrative is never simply "over." Paradigms can shift, but they cannot simply be destroyed.

Our relationships to the stories we tell are not one-dimensional. I think there is another thing to take from the ancient Greeks and the tendency of some homosexuals to latch on to their myths and their history: the story of descent into the underworld. Usually it begins with the hero being set to a task: he must go under and walk among the dead before being allowed back into the world. For all that I've pointed to in the idealization of the Greeks as problematic and based on fuzzy historical rigor, the LGBTQ community picked these stories for a reason, and it's not just about the sex. There are obvious parallels with going through the sort of "initiation ritual" that closeting has become in the past few decades: both are trials usually completed in early adulthood; both are shared experiences of travel difficult to describe to outsiders. But there is also a connection to and respect for the past in both cases. Odysseus meets his hero Achilles in hell. Orpheus attempts but fails to save Eurydice and goes back to the world alone, full of new songs (D'Aulaires 104).

The incorporeality of this type of myth, the disconnectedness of such a descent made in order to connect, is the natural complement to the other strand of myth leading to the bathhouses, that of fiercely joyful Maenads and beautiful temple acolytes, of exuberance and joy and celebration of the flesh (D'Aulaires 66). It's impossible to connect to one without feeling the echo of the other, but in today's society we seem determined to miss the connection. How did the function of public bathing spaces shift so radically? It has to do with cleanliness as a component of our sense of morality, I think. We have metaphor in our blood. Ancient morality and modern morality differ *enormously*; although we hold many of the same things to be sins—murder, incest, cowardice, disloyalty, theft, and yes, queerness—we have entirely different ways of quantifying culpability and guilt. Morality has become internal. Honor used to be defined by how you related to the community—now I change under my towel, flinch at my own dishonorable thoughts. What is there to flinch at? I didn't *do* anything. We have become creatures of motive and guilt rather than of acts and public shame, sojourners into the underworld where all is shadow and disquiet. We have created gods who can look into our hearts. Aphrodite could bite a heart, bewitch it, control it, destroy it, but never *read* it. We have invented souls that detach from the body, nations that detach from the land; we are couched more in concept than in action or being. And that can create a need for a different brand of story.

That's not to say that the ancients lacked the capability to imagine the body and spirit as separate; they just saw no need to. There was no real compartmentalization of a sense of the divine—ritual was constant, fluid, physical; it permeated society. Temples were extensions of a casual and constant exchange with the gods—places to organize divinity, not *contain* it. There was no reason to trap gods in structures; they existed primarily in the physical realm. We, *humanity*, existed in the physical realm. Olympus was a tall mountain and Hades the endpoint of a deep, deep cave. Who are we to live above the body, to make our baths into bastions of a strange order, instead of just extensions of the way of things?

What subverted this way of thinking? God, what didn't? Falling empires, fracturing group identities, diaspora upon diaspora. The concept of original sin, of individuals fighting lifelong battles against themselves, as part of the self as evil and not just unruly or mischievous. Human society shifts, complicates, and necessitates different forms of denial, so of course things change— but at root, I think, is a complicated reminder of a desire to reach out. If we are narrative creatures, we need others to hear the story.

Performance artist Regina José Galindo's piece "Alud" ("Landslide") reveals the urgency, the primal nature of cleanliness, of what it means to a community and its sense of physical health. The artist lies on a metal table used for washing corpses—asleep, or at least insensate. She is naked and absolutely caked with mud. It mats her hair; it is in the whorls of her ears. The audience stands along the walls, watching. They notice the towels and showerhead near her—they move forward. As Galindo says in her statement about the piece: "La posición pasiva del público como observadores reemplazado por la acción de participar y limpiar el cuerpo, motivados, quizás, por cierta empatía hacia ese individuo desconocido, escondido detrás del lodo" 'The public's passive position as observer is replaced by the action of participating and cleansing the body, motivated, perhaps, by some empathy for the unknown individual, hidden behind the mud' (Galindo; my translation). A man in a plaid shirt bends over her, gently wiping at her cheek. An older woman and a younger one, clearly mother and daughter, roll her onto her side to wash her back. Someone lifts her leg to hose down the back of her thigh; anonymous hands rinse and run through her hair. Soon a pack of people surround her, joined together in basic human kindness. The indignity of being handled by strangers is transformed by the inherent dignity of what they are doing: restoring her humanity, taking responsibility for it. Removing that which has made her an object, like one of the dead, the audience surpasses the awkward dehumanization of the locker room. There are only human bodies here.

We are programmed to touch, to check in with others. The mental gymnastics of modern public bathing are a moving-away from the actual fact of the act; the process has become unbearable to us. And so we tell ourselves stories. We distance ourselves from the body. We engage in denial, in a shared lie. But stories told skillfully, like the immersive narrative of "Alud," can also bring us back, remind us of what we're actually *doing* in our daily rituals. They can bring the deliberately suppressed thoughts to the surface. Jeffrey Eugenides' *Middlesex* was such a story for me. The description of protagonist Calliope changing for gym was like a slap in the face of compassion and understanding. I didn't even *think* about the intricate maneuvers I would take to get undressed until I saw them reflected back at me in print, and suddenly I didn't feel alone in Hades.

Such recognition of oneself, is in its essence an escape from time and space, a transcendence of the self through identification. Having the ghosts of Calliope and the Grecians around me made the locker room bearable; it transformed the space, broadened its walls, put it in a wider context.

I don't mean to sound like a drama queen: "oh closeting was just literally *hell!*" I had it easy. I know people who didn't. At least I was in the hell of the Greeks, which is different from the Christian hell: it's *quieter*. The people punish themselves there, no demons necessary. They roll their own personal rocks up hills over and over; they reach up for the fruit they planted in life. Consider Persephone: she spends half the year underground, half above. Her descent and ascent are never *done*—it is a state of being, a perpetual cycle.

So how do we keep ourselves from sleepwalking into toxic patterns of denial and replacing one sanitized version of the world with another, over and over again? Part of the answer is that we can't. We may as well try to stop ourselves from having allergies—this is just a way that a body reacts. But, accepting this inevitability, we must discover ways to identify patterns and narrative inclinations within ourselves and examine them for their value or their rottenness. We must become responsible storytellers of our own lives—lucid dreamers, aware of all the dreams that came before and helped shape the spaces we are in. Look around yourself; what are you drawn to? What spaces do you avoid, and why? Who are your gods, and are they proud of you? Know these things. Learn how to live with the beauty of the human penchant for narrative, the inexorable pull towards the creation of stories, in an open-eyed way. Look at your life as a story amidst stories. It is one.

WORKS CITED

Aristophanes. *Clouds*. Trans. Jeffrey Henderson. Newburyport: Focus, 1992. Print.

Bowman, Alan K. *Egypt after the Pharaohs: 332 BC-AD 642*. Berkeley: University of California, 1986. Print.

D'Aulaire, Ingiri and Edgar Parin. *D'Aulaires' Book of Greek Myths*. New York: Delacorte, 1992. Print.

Eugenides, Jeffrey. *Middlesex*. New York: Farrar, 2002. Print.

Galindo, Regina José, perf. *Alud*. Thessaloniki Performance Festival, Thessaloniki, 2011. Web. 10 June 2013.

Stoppard, Tom. *The Invention of Love*. New York: Grove, 1998. Print.

Sunlight Soap. Advertisement. *The War Budget* 30 Dec. 1915: ii. *Wikimedia Commons*. Web. 10 June 2013.

Vivona, Charles M. and Merillee Gormillion. "Situational Morality of Bathroom Nudity." *The Journal of Sex Research* 8.2 (1972): 128-35. *JSTOR*. Web. 14 June 2013.

Soul and Soil

GEORGIA HALLIDAY

samgrahah: he who holds everything together

The Lord of the Universe and Professor Godbole stand at "opposite ends of the same strip of carpet" (*Passage* 283). The room is full of "coloured rags, iridescent balls, chandeliers of opaque pink glass, and murky photographs framed crookedly"; of effigies; of mild-featured Hindu men; schoolboys; jasmine garlands; musics, multiple and indeterminate; an altar covered in rose leaves, golden tablets, silver dishes; a banana tree (283). God will be born at midnight—although he was born hundreds of years ago—although he will never be born. Sri Krishna, the Lord of the Universe, just like the music that fills the air with vibrations from choirs, cymbals, hand drums, a harmonium, the thumping of an electric generator, a Europeanized band playing a waltz in the courtyard, and elderly Brahmans singing a hymn, is multiple and indeterminate. The poets of the State have written inscriptions and hung them about the room "where they could not be read" (285). But evidently someone has read them, because we are shortly informed that one of them is in English "to indicate His universality," and that a mistake on the part of the draughtsman has resulted in the inscription reading "God si love" (285). We are then treated to this sentence, set apart in its own paragraph:

"God si love. Is this the first message of India?"

And then the choir starts to sing again: "Tukaram, tukaram, thou art my father and mother and everybody" and mothers squabble over the children and the band in the courtyard plays "Nights of Gladness" and someone breaks cordon in an effort to get closer to the silver icon of Sri Krishna and Professor Godbole attempts to untangle his pince-nez from the jasmine garland around his neck (283).

But wait.

Who *said* that?

Look around the rafters, behind the columns, through the pink glass sparkling in the glow from the electric lights. From whence that voice, who asked about the "first message of India"? Was it Godbole? No, his attention was elsewhere; and anyway he has demonstrated that he cares little for messages, for India as a nation, as a unity, as a voice. Was it the congregation? They reportedly can't see the inscription tacked to the stucco, and wouldn't understand the English in any case.

Sri Krishna, was it You who spoke? You who read the inscription that "could not be read" and wondered what message India was sending to the outside world? Did You, three years ago and hundreds of miles west of here, in the bungalow of a red-nosed imperialist, hear an old lady insist passionately to her son that "God . . . is . . . love," carry those words on the breeze of Your divine will to the scribe who so charmingly transposes letters (51)? You must have done it on purpose, Lord, for how else could the words have migrated so far, found a new purpose long after the death of the old woman who spoke them? You brought her along as well, for she enters Godbole's mind in the middle of the ceremony, though he met her only once years ago, sang her a song about a milkmaid who desires Your divine love. You pushed the old lady to the forefront of the Brahman's mind, so that he might "[impel] her by his spiritual force to that place where completeness can be found" (286).

What are we to make of this intrusion of the voice of the Lord of the Universe in this story, E. M. Forster's *A Passage to India*? More than editorializing at odd moments, the deity even appears to be interfering with the plot, transposing a mantra, a woman's face, the memory of a lone wasp on a stone, across time and space, across hundreds of miles, hundreds of pages. The "temple" of Forster's final section is tied to the "mosque" of the first through His sorcery; we are granted coherence and unity by His divine grace.

visvabaahuh: he whose hand is in everything

Sri Krishna has showed His hand here, during the ceremony of His birth. But we can find traces of His presence, or someone like Him, omniscient and omnipotent, throughout the novel; this lofty voice even speaks the very first words of the very first chapter. Before the earthy joy of chapter two, of the young doctor Aziz gallivanting around town on his bicycle and engaging in breathless verbal sparring matches with his friends, we are shown a grand view of Chandrapore from a vantage point far too close to the sky to make out anything clearly on the ground. We are assured of the supremacy of the sky, who "settles everything—not only climates and seasons but when the earth shall be beautiful. . . . But when the sky chooses, glory can rain into the

Chandrapore bazaars or a benediction pass from horizon to horizon" (9). Chapters often end by drawing sharply away from the human players and someone makes an ominous observation of the natural world, warning us (as the sky is not only omniscient but prescient too) of the impending crisis that builds throughout the first section: Mrs. Moore's coo to a sleeping wasp "float[s] out, to swell the night's uneasiness" (35); "Never tranquil, never perfectly dark, the night wore itself away, distinguished from other nights by two or three blasts of wind, which seemed to fall perpendicularly out of the sky and to bounce back into it, hard and compact, leaving no freshness behind them: the hot weather was approaching" (100). At the end of the novel, we hear the voice of the Earth instead, as it drives up obstacles to sever the friendship between Aziz and his English companion Fielding:

> [T]he earth didn't want it, sending up rocks through which riders must pass single file; the temples, the tank, the jail, the palace, the birds, the carrion, the Guest House, that came into view as they issued from the gap and saw Mau beneath: they didn't want it, and they said in their hundred voices, "No, not yet," and the sky said, "No, not there." (322)

It must be more, then, than just the Hindu god who sees all this, from the stirring of a single leaf to the oncoming tempest, who speaks for the Earth and the sky. *A Passage to India*, after all, contains a virtual pantheon: in addition to the eternal rebirths of Sri Krishna in the temple, we have the ninety-nine names of Allah written in black on a white marble frieze in an empty mosque, Mrs. Moore's "poor little talkative Christianity," and the nihilistic "ou-boum" from the Marabar caves (149-50). While searching for the last word among all these divinities, we might forget the gaze that encompasses them all.

Forster's all-knowing narrator, who sees things as small as a wasp or a tin-tack and things as grand as human oppression, seems to rule over everything, even the Gods, even the Caves. This voice is a deity, more powerful or at least more active and agile than Allah, than Christ, than Sri Krishna, than "ou-boum." Sri Krishna, after all, is not a supreme being, even in Hinduism; he is an avatar, a manifestation of one of the great gods, Vishnu, He of a thousand names. Still of the same essence, but with a more narrow purpose, avatars descend to Earth to accomplish some divine end, and dissolve back into their supreme deities when they are no longer needed. Third-person narrators in fiction act in much the same way: they are inseparable from the ultimate Creator, but with a more specific function, earth-bound, page-bound, and are thus easier to find, to analyze, to assign intentions and opinions to, than the elusive Author-god.

To begin *Passage* looking down out of the sky makes any mortal who arrives on the scene thereafter shrink to nearly the size of the wasp; characters become diminuitive and easily manipulated by Sri Krishna's divine blue hands. In such a malleable world, we are not quite so bound by realism; though set in historical India, the world of the novel simultaneously exists in the universe of all the holy texts that are strewn throughout, and the allegorical logic borrowed from Moses and Rama smooths over some of Forster's more fanciful narrative devices. The fact that he as author has won our trust enough to allow such intrusion makes him all the more powerful. In the world of the novel, the narrator, this avatar of the Great God Forster, is responsible for creating coherence and sowing discord, for making sense and leaving us baffled, for sending rocks up from the Earth and judgment down from the sky.

al-muntaqim: the avenger

But Forster isn't the only one who populates the world with a pantheon of narrator-demigods. All authors of fiction are Creators who ultimately control the lives of their characters, and it's so standard for third-person narrators to have divine knowledge that we even incorporate religious terms into the literary vocabulary, referring to them as "omniscient." Forster is only remarkable in the way he allows his avatar-narrator to reveal itself to us instead of vanishing into the page, becoming transparent. Often, a narrating voice is so unobtrusive that we forget its role as mediator and become convinced that we have an unfettered, objective view of the characters. Forster won't let us fall into that trap: the narrator in *Passage* is ostentatiously divine, displaying his power and reach for all to see. If he is visible, if he has a personality, he becomes a character. Characters, no matter how disembodied, are at least partially human. And with humanity comes subjectivity, and fallibility, characteristics rampant in pagan times but taken out of many modern, sterilized religious discourses. In polytheistic traditions, as of the Greeks or the early Hindus, devoid of mysticism and abstraction, Gods were essentially human beings with access to vast amounts of power that they could barely control, and they played games with humans the way Forster plays with Godbole, Mrs. Moore, Aziz, and Adela. Those gods were jealous, intemperate, passionate, and vengeful. Forster's narrator is not just any deity but a pagan one, an Old Testament God, a Titan.

The old gods spoke not through parables but through tempests and minotaurs. Their messengers were not soft-spoken itinerant teachers but raving oracles who predicted death and destruction more often than salvation. In *Mrs. Dalloway* and *Sula*, Virginia Woolf and Toni Morrison both exercise their ancient divine will through the garbled mouthpiece of a mad prophet. Their characters, Septimus and Shadrack, whom today we would know as sufferers of PTSD, are largely ignored by their peers, but their declarations, brief and assured—"Always" (Morrison 62) and "Men must not cut down trees" (Woolf 24)—ring true and resound over the relatively petty clamor of the societies around them. The title character in each novel finds meaning in her prophet's madness in the end: Clarissa Dalloway hears of Septimus's suicide and discovers her own salvation; Sula, dying young and painfully, is reassured by a memory from decades ago, an incoherent rambling of Shadrack's that she now interprets as a promise of peace, a "sleep of water always" (149).

hiranyagarbhah: he who dwells in the womb of the world

Morrison's narrator is earthy, like Forster's. *Sula* begins and ends not with Sula herself but with the rocky soil out of which she grew and into which she is returned: the Bottom, a facetious name for the black community in the nearly un-farmable highlands around Medallion, Ohio. Morrison gives us the hills long before she fills them with people, and we are reminded of what James Hillman tells us, in "Peaks and Vales," that mountains are archetypes of the spirit, the seeking, driving part of the human mind, that peak-related experiences convey "godlikeness and God-nearness . . . absolutism and intensity," purity, coldness, virginity (114). Vales, meanwhile, are the domain of the soul, fertile and feminine, "regarded as the scene of the mortal, the earthly, the lowly" (115). But Morrison takes this imagery and literally flips it, naming the high ground the "Bottom," meaning, supposedly, the bottom of Heaven. The soil still doesn't grow crops very well, but its fertility is unmatched when it comes to producing characters, vivid, emphatic, and bizarre. Morrison's peaks are full of women, matriarchies as firmly embedded in the soil as the roots of the trees, while the men come and go, weightless. The only man who leaves any kind of imprint is Shadrack, the first character we meet, who wakes up in a hospital in the second chapter a year after the end of the First World War. Despite his obvious instability, he is released, and Morrison guides her prophet home to the hills of Medallion to preach from the Mount.

These two tragic figures have more than a hint of Christ about them, especially Septimus, who quite early in the novel becomes convinced that he is "taken from life to death, the Lord come to renew society" (25). Shadrack, in an attempt to conquer the unpredictability of death, institutes National Suicide Day, one day a year devoted to death, so that "everybody could get it out of the way and the rest of the year would be safe and free" (14). It's not just authors, though, who beget Christlike characters; the allegory entices any artist who wants to tell a story of transformation, including the Avett Brothers in their album *The Carpenter*. The first song, "The Once and Future Carpenter," begins with a banjo riff, twangy and winding. The lyrics tell of a drifter who was once a carpenter but abandoned his trade and "took to the highway / a poet young and hungry." If the title of the song isn't enough to make us think of the life (and return) of Jesus, the last moment of the song provides the eucharist in pure musical form: the earthy banjo riff has been transformed into a sparkling, celestial piano.

What are we to make of these literary Titans, who grow characters from the fertile earth of their inverted valleys, send prophets to warn us of ruin and beget sons to die for our sins, shout down from the clouds with voices so clear and distinct we can't help but notice them? What drove these authors to display their divinity so openly, to reside in the peaks of "godlikeness and God-nearness" that dwarf their characters in comparison? Why attempt to speak with the voice of God?

YHWH: I am that I am

"Miss, they write Allah!"

A small boy, one of my sixth-grade students, comes running across the soccer field, holding wide a sheet of newspaper covered in curling, stylized script. The newsprint is cheap and translucent, and even the expensive advertisements only print in three colors: black, green, and red.

"They write Allah," the child repeats. He points at the place where the swirling green and black lines loop into the word *mash'allah—as God wills*.

"We cannot throw away," he says, his large black eyes peering worriedly over the top of the paper. He gestures at the other students who are gathering the scattered papers from the brilliant green astroturf, the closest thing to grass we can get out here in the desert, and stuffing them into a gray plastic trash bin. "We must . . . fire it?" He makes a gesture like flicking a lighter.

"Okay," I say. I take the paper from him.

I remember in fifth grade history class when Maddy Sall taught me to write "G-d" so that I could throw away my papers with a clear conscience. I wasn't Jewish, and she didn't think I was. If you'd asked me at the time I probably would have told you that I didn't believe in God, in the same way that I didn't believe in Santa Claus. But I picked up the habit in the way that children assimilate all myths, parables, dogmas, and fantasy stories into one great indeterminate mass of superstitious feeling, and for a time wrote "G-d," thinking it mattered with the same lukewarm faith that kept me waiting for my letter from Hogwarts that summer.

In Nicole Krauss's *The History of Love*, a little boy called Bird learns the same thing, that you cannot throw away anything that contains the secret name of God (the Tetragrammaton), and because he's angry that his mother threw away everything that belonged to his dead father, he scribbles the four Hebrew letters on everything he can get his hands on, desperately clinging to what remains, using God's name as an invocation to make everything around him indispensable, and thus eternal. When the boy goes away, I fold the newspaper and throw it away with the others.

al-hafiz: the preserver

Are we all Bird? Our creations are fragile, perishable, destined to rust. And if they fade, mold, crumble, if they are discarded and forgotten, what becomes of us, their creators? Are we stuffed into a bin and abandoned like cheap green-and-black newsprint? If our little friezes of natural perfection, the small handful of times each of us is able to take the painfully ephemeral beauty of nature and make it into something permanent, something with form, something that fights the vast indifference of the universe (the ouboum); if even that permanence can be once again lost, destroyed, forgotten, discarded—have we not lost? So we sign, instead of our own name, the name of God, in the hope that the divine letters will ensure permanence, our immortality.

But it can't be quite so simple, because Bird becomes so obsessed with mystic Judaism that he begins to believe himself to be the Messiah, jumps off a building and breaks his arm because he wants so badly to fly and believes so much that he can. Another character, a long-suffering elderly Polish Jew, sees him throwing stones into a fountain one day, and guesses that "probably he believe[s] he wasn't made for this world. I wanted to say to him, *if not you, who*?" (Krauss 222).

asankhyeyah: he who has numberless names and forms

For we must not become so wrapped up in our own divinity that we forget that we were made for this world, for life; that we, and our pagan Gods, grew from the soil. Bird forgot that before the Messiah can ascend to Heaven, he must walk among the salt of the earth, be a drifter, a poet, a carpenter. Another of Forster's avatars writes in "Cnidus" of a cold, dark, muddy pilgrimage across a forgotten Greek island to visit a crumbling temple to Demeter, who "alone among gods has true immortality" (176). Millennia after the fall of that ancient civilization, the Earth goddess survives because she is the progenitor of the others; she is all we need. In "Winkelmann," Walter Pater argues that, regardless of era or culture, out of the "soil" of human nature grows a "universal pagan sentiment" that transcends any higher religious philosophy placed atop it (201). This sentiment is "the broad foundation, in mere human nature, of all religions as they exist for the greatest number" (200). It is "ineradicable, like some persistent vegetable growth," much like the slums of Chandrapore with all its "inhabitants of mud moving" and its outline persisting "like some low and indestructible form of life" (Pater 201; Forster 7). From the fertile soil of our human nature, the valley of the soul, we raise temples to Demeter, and then our rituals and art decorate them; other shrines follow, other gods, stories, songs, poems, mantras, novels, prophets. For as Forster shows us with his pantheon, we have as many names for God as we have uses for him, in Arabic, in Sanskrit, in Hebrew: 99 names of Allah, 1,000 names of Vishnu, and 7 names of God over Israel. And though they look down from the clouds, each came from the Earth, just as we did.

visva-retaah: the seed of the universe

In "February Seven" and "Through My Prayers," *The Carpenter* lifts us to Heaven on gently strummed strings, celestial piano and pentatonic melodies of harps eternal, as allusions to death and ascension surround us: "And as the last of breath was drawn from me / the light broke in and brought me to my feet." In the penultimate song "Paul Newman vs. The Demons" we have also been to Hell, incongruously full of screeching guitar feedback, stiff-armed cymbal crashes, and wailing backup vocals. And now we are back on Earth for the last track, "Life." Without ever pronouncing the word "life," the singer gently extols it: "One comes of it, love it, love it / Let go of it, love comes from it / We're not of this world for long." The melody neither soars nor dives, but steps up and skips down, alternating regularly, keeping us firmly planted in the soil of the soul. *If not us, who?*

Forster, Woolf, and Morrison, despite their lofty, powerful narrators, build their worlds out of color, texture, and character, keeping the world close at hand, drawing the life force of their novels from it. "Keep it, use it, build it, move it," advise the Avett Brothers, still gently stepping and skipping up and down the hills of the Bottom, of the Marabar (*The Carpenter* "Life").

We still might try to fly, like Bird, to make a racket as we crash to the ground, just to prove that we exist: "Watch us fly as loud as we can," sing the Avetts, defiantly (*The Carpenter* "Life"). But in the end we know that no matter how fervently we believe in the power of the name of G-d, someone still might throw that newspaper away. The name remains, though, not in Heaven but here on Earth, for whenever we might need it, to borrow when we need to write a novel and want to begin from on high, looking down out of the sky.

The stepping and skipping ceases, the melody wavers and settles on a single note, a C#, the third, the sweetest of all, halfway between the celestial floating fifth and the bedrock root of the chord, and the Carpenter sings: "Oh, you and I know all too well / about the hell and paradise / Right here on earth."

WORKS CITED

The Avett Brothers. *The Carpenter*. Republic, 2012. CD.

Forster, E. M. *A Passage to India*. San Diego: Harcourt, 1924. Print.

—. "Cnidus." *Abinger Harvest*. London: Edward Arnold, 1936. Print.

Hillman, James. *A Blue Fire*. New York: Harper, 1989. Print.

Krauss, Nicole. *A History of Love*. New York: Norton, 2005. Print.

Krishnananda. "Sri Vishnu Sahasaranama Strotam: Sanskrit, Transliteration, and English Translation." *The Divine Life Society*. May 2013. Web. 16 May 2013.

Morrison, Toni. *Sula*. New York: Alfred A. Knopf, 1973. Print.

Pater, Walter. "Winckelmann." *The Renaissance: Studies in Art and Poetry*. London: MacMillan, 1900. Print.

Samat, Talib. *The 99 Most Eminent Names of Allah*. Kuala Lumpur: Utusan, 2001. Print.

Woolf, Virginia. *Mrs. Dalloway*. London: Penguin, 1925. Print.

Φ (Flux)

WELLS LUCAS SANTO

If you open any work by Anne Carson, you will be greeted by a monolithic wall of ancient Greek or Latin. It's intimidating—scary, almost—how all these foreign words and symbols seem to just sit there, static on the page, and stare back at you with some great incomprehensible promise of meaning. But Carson is not afraid of these ancient languages. No, she revels in them—she loves them—and as *Eros: The Bittersweet* reveals, they are as important to her mind as the subject of love itself.

When you read a work by Carson such as *Eros*, you are not just reading the work of a translator who mechanically converts words from language to language; rather, you are witnessing a chase for new meaning in artifacts of the past. In the very first essay of her collection, Carson introduces a Greek passage from Sapphic poetry, where the word *glukupikron* appears. While the literal translation of this term would be "sweetbitter," Carson notes that "'Sweetbitter' sounds wrong, and yet our standard English rendering 'bittersweet' inverts the actual terms . . . Should that concern us?" ("Bittersweet" 3). From here, she begins to worry about meanings that may be lost in translation. When Carson uses the word *glukupikron* to describe this seemingly foreign notion of *eros*, or desire, she points back to the Greek and notices that the combined feelings of sweetness and bitterness invoke both the emotions of love and hate, and it is this duplicity of emotion that lies at the heart of desire.

But why, and how, exactly does this duality exist? Later in her work, Carson admits that "*eros* is a lack," which means that we desire what we do not have—in wanting it, we love it, but in not having it, we hate it ("Ruse" 12). For Carson, the existence of paradox is absolutely essential to the idea of *eros*, and this can be seen even in the growth of her short, simple, declarative sentences into complex, compound ones over the course of her writing. Over time, the use of more elongated structures that seem to pivot at the center reflects the growing presence of dualities in her mind and in the very subject of desire itself. As blocks of texts go by, Carson is unable to revert back to her terse and very pinpoint style of syntax because her very understanding of desire has also expanded from something that involves two entities to one that involves three. Meghan O'Rourke notes in *The New Yorker* that "the geometry of desire, which we usually take to be a two-way street . . . is actually a triangular circuitry of lover, beloved, and that which comes between them" (2). It's an apt summary of Carson's dynamic translation of Sappho's fragment 31 ("Ruse" 12-13). And it is this unique translation of the classic Greek poem from which Carson builds the rest of her argument.

At first glance, any reader might be tempted to interpret "that which comes between them" as a second lover who acts to complete the stereotypical shape of the love triangle, but Carson complicates the issue by admitting that the third component in desire is not someone or something. In fact, this third component is opposite of any *thing*: it is the space that lies between lover and beloved. Perhaps, then, the property of *eros* is not found in the simple hate and love of an object, or even in the unobtainability of that which is desired: it exists in the hate and love of this third component, of the very "space [that] must be maintained, or desire ends" ("The Beach" 26). We desire only because we wish to fill up the space of what we lack. It is paradoxical because we need the feeling of lacking in order to contend with the lack itself. In fact, in a characteristic move, Carson returns to the very etymological roots of desire and wonders "who ever desires what is not gone? No one," she replies, explaining that the Greeks "invented *eros* to express it," a line of reasoning which captures the paradox embedded in the Greek word itself, which, like the word *glukupikron*, is a meaning lost to translation ("Gone"11). This space, or lacking, characterizes the internally conflicting, paradoxical nature of *eros*.

Interestingly enough, near the end of *Eros: The Bittersweet*, Carson includes an essay titled, "What Is This Dialogue About?" which begins with a short haiku by Japanese poet Basho:

> old pond
> frog jumps in
> plop (165)

This poem is a translation from a foreign language as well, but beyond that, it seems wholly unrelated to the rest of Carson's work. How does Basho's haiku relate to the need for space, or to the concept of love at all? To contend with this question, the context in which this poem is written must be understood—that is, it must be read through the lens of Zen Buddhism. In this philosophy, it is believed that the moment of Zen, or enlightenment, is constantly in flux: enlightenment can only be obtained through the acknowledgment that each moment in life is ephemeral, fleeting, and impermanent (Suzuki 6). The old pond and the frog represent temporary silence, and the sudden "plop" at the end of the haiku is the breaking of that silence. For Carson, the fleeting moment of Zen is the same as the fleeting entity of love itself. Both must constantly be sought after. When one reaches for love, one can only grasp it for a moment before it crumples and changes and flees from one's grip, only to leave behind the space of lacking once more. In Carson's words, "Eros moves. You reach. Eros is gone" ("Dialogue" 166). The elusive explains much about why Carson's terse style and declarative syntax emphasize the abruptness of love. Her sentences are short. Quick. Momentary. Just as love can be.

All of this explains what Carson means when she states that "*eros* is a verb," for desire is a game of temporal, not just physical, chase ("Ruse" 17). As William Smoot explains in his review of *Eros*, "the lover wants to freeze the beloved in time" so that the lover may skip to the moment when the object of his desire is obtained and possess it forever (202). But this is a problem. As Carson rebuts, "a real love affair . . . must be lived out in time . . . it cannot be entered . . . or frozen," and for her, the "most erotic thing about eros" is the fact that it's not solid or static; it's elusive—evasive, even ("Dialogue" 165, 167). Perhaps, then, it can be said that Carson's true obsession is not about love or *eros* itself, but about the thing that makes *eros* so interesting: its impermanence. In *Nox*, a more recent work of Carson's, the poet Basho appears once more in section 8.2, followed by a very odd, abstract painting of the Biblical figure Lazarus, to whom she compares her recently deceased brother. What is immensely fascinating about this painting is that it is comprised of three images of *Enso*, a sacred symbol in Japanese calligraphy that represents enlightenment, space, and the fleeting moment. It is no coincidence that Carson places this painting after a Basho haiku, and it is definitely no coincidence that these symbols for impermanence rest at the heart of a work dealing with death.

Perhaps Carson puts together *Nox* because she has to deal with the absolute entity of death, which opposes the ephemeral and temporary entity of love. She mourns for her brother when she explains that "he's dead. *Love* cannot alter it. . . . No matter how I try to evoke the starry lad he was, it remains a plain, odd history. So I began to think about history" (*Nox* 1.0). What makes Carson so unique as a writer curious about the topic of love is her level of scholarship in classical texts and her ability to breathe new life into poems of the past through careful translation. But she cannot bring her brother back as she would the dead languages of Latin and Greek. No, she must do something different. For Carson, *Nox* is a collection of items from her and her brother's past that she desires to piece together and make sense of. Meghan O'Rourke explains this mindset in her review of *Nox*: "Because the dead person is absent and voiceless (the word *nox* both rhymes with the Latin word *vox*, or voice, and contains the English word 'no'), the bereaved is always experiencing the lost through other things: books, ideas, language, memory" (3). By making sense of these "historical" objects or memorabilia, Carson is essentially translating them into something comprehensible. Through translation, she is then able to *re*-visit and *re*-vision the past, and for a fleeting moment, to reconnect with what once existed—the love she felt for her brother. It seems, then, that translation is her *modus operandi* in continuing the eternal chase for what or whom she loves.

If the act of translation is what allows Carson to chase the memory of her brother by revisiting the past, perhaps the translation of ancient Greek poetry helps Carson to chase the fleeting entity of love in *Eros: The Bittersweet*, as well. By including blocks of ancient Greek or Latin text, Carson is not merely performing some etymological exercise to seize love from its historical roots. Rather, the act of translating these ancient languages is a necessity for Carson to keep the past—something that she loves fiercely—alive. Re-visiting and re-encountering the past is the only way she can keep reaching at the ungraspable entity of love. In this sense, the gap or space that exists for Carson in the "three-part structure" of *eros* is the space of time itself, and her act of translation is an attempt to transcend time and close the gap in order to reach for what she desires ("Ruse" 16). Indeed, what makes Carson's translation of ancient texts indispensable is that she does not simply convert words from one language to the other; rather, she breathes new life into the ancient and static by comparing them with things that exist later in time. In the essay "Gone," for example, Carson distills the messages of "various voices" throughout different ages of writing into a sort of "common perception" that acts to advance the meaning of ancient Sapphic poetry (11).

Instead of viewing objects of the past, such as ancient Greek poetry about love, as static and unchanging, Carson dares to see them in a constant state of flux. Just as she gives *eros* motion by describing it as the *action of lacking* rather than the object of lack itself, she gives motion to ancient Greek and Latin by showing that history isn't something that has already happened but something that is constantly happening and *re*-happening. What makes Anne Carson so important to us in the modern world is that she translates and transforms what we see as static and unchanging into things that continue to move, grow, and evolve. As Guy Davenport points out about *Eros: The Bittersweet*, "this book is about kinesis and balance . . . spinning, moving, fluttering," which Carson alludes to in the preface to her collection of essays (Davenport 185). There, she explains the mindset of the fictional philosopher from Kafka's story, "The Top," and how "catch[ing] a top still spinning makes him happy for a moment . . . [but] Disgust follows" (xi). Love is supposed to be active, not frozen in time, and for Carson, because the "suppression of impertinence is not the lover's aim," the viewing of history and Greek poetry as something frozen in time is not her aim either (xi).

What Carson sees that is of so much value is that "a meaning spins" and is not merely concrete or static (xi). The definition of love is not something that can be pinpointed and captured, and there is never a point in her essays when her chase for the meaning of love seems to stop or stall. But the meaning of love does not merely spin. In the field of physics, there are two types of motion: rotational and translational. Rotation describes things that pivot in place. Translation allows for such movement; it creates space through displacement, and this is what Anne Carson does with her own act of linguistic translation (Giancoli 249). She reminds us that the ephemeral moment of the chase is what matters, and that we must be forever concerned with the impertinence of existence and the transient nature of all things, especially history, life, and love. At the end of *Nox*, Carson includes the words of her brother's wife at his funeral service: "Yesterday you cannot change / Today you might alter. Tomorrow does not give any promise" (10.2). Carson writes to inspire us to see the world in terms of constant change and flux, so that we may continue to re-translate the past as we move into the future. So that we do not become complacent with that which is static. So that we may continue to love.

WORKS CITED

Carson, Anne. *Eros: The Bittersweet*. Champaign, IL: Dalkey, 2009. Print.
    "Preface." xi-xii.
    "Bittersweet." 3-9.
    "Gone." 10-11.
    "Ruse." 12-17.
    "Tactics." 18-25.
    "The Reach." 26-29.
    "What Is This Dialogue About?" 165-67.
—. *Nox*. New York: New Directions, 2010. Print.

Davenport, Guy. "Eros the Bittersweet." Rev. of *Eros: the Bittersweet* by Anne Carson. *Grand Street*, Vol. 6.3 (1987): 184-191. *JSTOR*. Web. 6 Dec. 2012.

Giancoli, Douglas C. *Physics for Scientists and Engineers with Modern Physics*. 4th ed. Vol. 1. Upper Saddle River: Addison-Wesley, 2008. Print.

O'Rourke, Meghan. "The Unfolding." Rev. of *Nox* by Anne Carson. *The New Yorker* 12 July 2010. Web. 6 Dec. 2012.

Smoot, William. Rev. of *Eros: the Bittersweet* by Anne Carson. *The Georgia Review*, 42.1 (1988): 201-203. *JSTOR*. Web. 6 Dec. 2012.

Suzuki, Daisetz T. *Zen and Japanese Culture*. Princeton: Princeton UP, 2010. Print.

Lost Girls

MEGAN STEINER

> "*Life* here is magic. Even *you* knew that, you girls / who seemed deprived of it, who were trapped in the city's / vilest streets [. . .] For each of you there was an hour, perhaps / not even a full hour, but between two intervals / a space not marked by the measures of time—, / when you had an *existence*."
>
> —Rainer Maria Rilke

> "I sit and dwell on faces past / Like memories seem to fade [. . .] / may these shadows rise to walk again."
>
> —Flogging Molly

It is the end of February, and it has been a cold winter. Then again, any winter feels cold when one is living on the street. I took up residency in Tompkins Square Park—I call it "my park"—nearly two months ago. Upon my arrival, I staked my claim on a particular bench. I guard it fiercely, for though it does not provide me with shelter, I cannot bear the idea of losing it. This bench is prime real estate. It sits beneath boughs of trees which, though bare, provide the illusion of a makeshift roof, of a makeshift home. It is located near the chessboards, where wizened old men with calculating gleams in their eyes sit bundled against the cold and play for hours.

I love to watch them play. Gloved hands move pieces back and forth across the board, locked in a mesmerizing dance: a piece is lost, then another, yet the game goes on. Watching the casualties of the game pile up—valiant little black and white monuments of expendability—makes me sad. While I love to watch them play, hearing that triumphant crow of "Checkmate!" sends a chill up my spine, for I've come to identify with those conquered pieces, defeated lives in miniature.

You see, stationed at my bench, watching the comings and goings of people who participate in the act of living, I experience the strangest feeling: I call it a voyeur's invisibility. I am isolated from everything that I see—from the chess players, from the men and women who walk by, from my fellow park tenants, from the squirrels who dart past my feet. My bench is tucked away in a quiet nook of the park (for not many people seem as intrigued as I by the pastime of old men). I am far away from the verdant hill upon which college kids congregate, coffees securely in hand. I am a world away from the jungle gym and the dog run, hidden from the respectable people, the proud parents and giggling children and tentative lovers who exude a sense of ease. I am, however, relatively close to "junkie row." Its occupants are my friends, my peers, but I am far too proud to claim my place among them, to share their benches. Instead, I cling to *my* bench, for when I sit here I can pretend at least to belong among the chess-players, if not among the respectable people. I can forget that I am fading into the colorless background of the winter landscape, blending in with the dead trees. I can forget how trapped and helpless I feel; how afraid I am of disappearing entirely. I only truly live through the chess players. I can imagine my hands directing the intricate dance; I can deny my kinship with those faceless, fallen pawns.

Curled up in my sleeping bag on the bench, I see a neon flash of vitality against the barren, faded landscape of winter. It is a little girl wearing a puffy pink jacket and matching sneakers, with two short blonde pigtails poking from the top of her head. She is smiling and skipping—she is bouncing. Her little pigtails bounce with her. It is as though the buoyancy of her happiness frees her from the pull of gravity for a moment or two. She is holding the hand of her mother, who is also smiling. Yet her mother's smile is different; she does not seem to evade gravity. There are cracks in the facade of her happiness—a corner of her upturned mouth twitches, the muscles pulling relentlessly downward, revolting against an expression rarely worn. Her pupils are dilated, and beneath them lie two dark circles, their darkness a stark contrast to the brightness radiating from her child. She glances over at me. I suppose I've been staring. Now the facade is smashed: when I look her in the eyes, I see despondence, apprehension, absence. I see a fallen pawn, a defeated life. Just as I cannot bear to look at the defeated chess pieces, I cannot bear to look at her. It's a cold day, I tell myself, and I burrow deeper into my sleeping bag. I pull it up over my head and tug it closed. It's just cold out there.

Though I wish I could, I cannot remain in my cocoon forever. I live in this park for a reason, aside from my fascination with chess. It is dusk; the families are long gone, and with them the laughter. The chess players have called it a day and gone home, taking their little black and white armies with them. The college students have scattered, leaving the hill naked. Only the junkies and I remain, and there remains nothing and nobody to separate us.

By day, the park is cacophonous: shrieks of amusement, strains of buskers' tunes, the hurried staccato of well-heeled footsteps and snippets of the too-loud musings of junkies intermingle. In the daytime, all I hear is white noise; like the many faces passing by, the sounds become a blur. But by dusk, I fall victim to dope-sickness, as all addicts do. I shake, and I cannot pretend that this chill is from the cold. My ears are suddenly attuned to the siren call of junkie row. The time for invisibility and voyeurism is over. It is time to join the dance.

I can no longer see clearly—sickness blurs the park I know so well—but, like a rat in a maze, I am on the scent of my reward. Burning need drives me towards the choreographer of the twilight dancers. I have come to purchase my medicine—that which will stave off the shakes, stave off the world, return me to blissful blurriness for a while longer. Oblivion is the sustenance—the lifeblood—of this netherworld. Though I may deny it, my separate bench does not negate my status as one of them, as one who comes to life only in the dusky world of shadows. Now shaking with anticipation, I snatch the poisonous treasure from his hands and shuffle away to attempt to lose my senses once more, to once more become invisible.

I do not return to my bench. I am ashamed of what comes next—I refuse to defile my sanctuary with my sins. A shadow takes my arm—it's strange, but I cannot make out its face or form. The shadow has a firm grip, and guides me to the bathroom. Blood is rushing to my head—I am hallucinating—and as I prepare my fix, I hear the sound of falling chess pieces, one after another, each landing a thunderclap echoing with finality. It will be over soon, and I can return to my bench. I shake my head to silence the hellish crashes. Then, the inevitable.

My veins ignite; the chill that has permeated my bones is replaced with reassuring warmth; the horrible din subsides, giving way to the usual white noise; I am safely absent once more. At some point, I fall to the floor. After a moment, perhaps an eternity, I open my eyes. I am lying on the black and white checkered floor like a fallen pawn, just as I lie here every night, my cheek against the cold tile. I catch a glimpse of a face in the grimy metal of a stall partition. Her skin is gray and smudged with dirt; she has sunken cheeks, matted hair, cracked lips, hollow eyes . . . *oh—her eyes!* In those eyes, I see despondence, apprehension, and absence. I see weariness, sorrow, and uncertainty. I see the falsely happy mother; I see another conquered chess piece; I see *me*. This ghostly thing—this zombie of a woman, this shadow on the floor—is what I have become. And I am terrified by this shock of reality. I claw at the sink to pull myself up from the ground and stumble away to flee my own image. I return to my bench. The chess players will be back soon.

Two years have passed since I struggled to rise from that freezing floor for the last time. It's strange how memory works. Sometimes, I feel as far removed from that version of myself as I once did from everyone who passed me in the park. Yet at others, that wraithlike, lifeless being that I once was feels inescapably close. She is haunting me; she appears everywhere.

Sometimes, when I catch a glimpse of my reflection in a shop window, for an instant I see *her*—the specter of my past—glaring at me judgmentally with cold dead eyes. Sometimes, I walk through Tompkins Square Park—these days my well-heeled footsteps add to the cacophony—and look at my old bench. It is often occupied; it is mine no longer. But often, when I allow my gaze to linger long enough, the oddest thing happens: the bench's current occupant looks up at me, and though I know it is an illusion, I see *my face*— as it was that February—instead of his or hers. I hate these moments most of all—when I subconsciously superimpose my own face upon that of another person. It happens so often. Each time it does, I am erasing the face my own replaces. I am turning a person into a faceless pawn. It happens so naturally, so easily. It's startling how easy it is to not see another human being.

Yet there are also some faces that refuse to be ignored. That effervescent bouncing little girl, for example—she was brimming with vitality, so alive in that particular moment that I can still see her skipping through my memory. But perhaps this is not quite correct: I can still see her bouncing pigtails, her pink jacket. Her face escapes me. And yet I do remember vividly the face of her mother; I remember vividly my own face reflected in the bathroom stall door. I cannot escape them. But these are my memories, my haunts. If you had seen these faces, perhaps they would escape you, or rather, perhaps you would escape them. We'll never know—you will never see these faces, at least not in the moments in which I saw them. I am sorry to say that I cannot truly share my memories with you, not completely. But I can share a photograph, and what is a photograph if not a captured moment?

At first glance, one is struck by the beauty of Lee Jeffries's photograph *Michelle* and by that of his model. She is young, perhaps in her early twenties, with long brown hair, high cheekbones, large, light eyes, and a delicate mouth. She stares up at us through her arms, her hands clasped behind her neck. The beauty of the photograph, however, does not come from the radiance of the model. It does not come from the sultry pout she wears. It comes from the flaws and the unmistakable sadness that are present in the face of a woman so young and so beautiful. Her hair is frazzled and unwashed, and premature strands of silver frame her face. Her skin is rough, every pore and freckle and line cast in relief by the harsh contrast of the image. There are even smudges of dirt visible on her wrists and forehead. The traces of a hard life are unmistakable, impermeably stamped upon her countenance.

Yet all these details fade into the background when one locks eyes with Michelle. Her gaze is riveting. Her eyes are wreathed in shadow, out of which they positively glow. One can stare into them for hours and still be struck by some new depth, some new emotion that reveals itself. Her soul is within her eyes, and it seems to be begging to be seen. Michelle's eyes tell of weariness, of sorrow, of uncertainty. The portrait is almost painfully intimate; it hurts to be allowed into her internal world. She looks so *lost*, and one can't help but ache for her. Yet from this woman who sits wreathed in shadow—from behind the veneer of dirt—emanates, more than anything, honesty. Yes, it is the honesty of the portrait that makes it gripping and unforgettable. Michelle bares her soul before the camera, stares directly into the lens, and in turn it feels as though one is bare before her. As we search her face, she searches ours in turn, and we are disallowed any pretense. Hers is a face that refuses to be ignored, or erased.

As I stare into her eyes, the old familiar ghost of Megan past rears her haggard head; she tries to subsume Michelle. But then the incredible happens: Michelle *banishes* her. This is not my portrait; this is not my moment; this is *not* me. However much kinship I may feel with her, this is Michelle. And while I allowed a zombie to replace me, erase me, make me a faceless chess piece, the incredible thing is that Michelle will not be replaced. There is something undeniably strong in her: she seems quietly yet adamantly to declare, "I am here." While I, beneath the crushing weight of a hard life, chose to slink into invisibility, Michelle remains visible. There is no danger of her disappearing into the background. And that is the most beautiful aspect of her portrait: the fact that she is wholly, self-affirmatively *present*, present in her filthy skin, present as the gray hairs grow in and as her skin grows weathered, and *unbroken* by it all. As someone who has been incapable of such presence, I stand in awe of Michelle.

But this is simply my impression of her portrait, of Michelle as she was in this particular moment. And in giving you my impression, I am imposing upon you—and upon Michelle—all of my biases. I am coloring her story with my own, but perhaps it is not my place to do so. In an interview recorded by the same man who photographed her, Michelle tells her own story. Her voice is melodic, lilting, a thick Scottish accent revealing her land of origin. At the time the photograph was taken, she is 22 years old. She lives in the doorways and sheltered alleys of London, and has for some months. She tells us that life on the streets is both scary and fun; there is danger from roaming drunks, but she feels uninhibited and freer than she could ever have imagined. Only when Jeffries asks her of her plans for the future—for getting off the streets—does uncertainty creep into her confident speech. She "emm"s and "ahh"s a bit, but in the end concludes with "looking at getting a flat" (Michelle). Jeffries himself comments on what we can only assume, what he's seen firsthand: "addictions keep her where she is; it's a vicious circle" (Bignell 1).

If her portrait is powerful due to its honesty and lack of pretense, I cannot keep up an idealized pretense on her behalf. She, as I once was, is a denizen of the netherworld. She, too, is a twilight dancer. I wonder how she copes; whether, when out of the camera's sights, she allows herself to disappear. I wonder if she too has found herself curled on a cold, unforgiving bathroom floor. I wonder if she has caught a glimpse of her own reflection and been shaken to her very core. I wonder if her own face has ever escaped her, if she has seen in a mirror that same deathly terror that I have.

When I look into her eyes, despite the honesty, the beauty, the trust that they contain, more than anything I see a look all too familiar—the look of the lost girl. Once you have worn it, you will always recognize it. Lost girls are characterized not merely by homelessness, nor by sadness, nor by addiction, but by the constant, looming threat of facelessness that you can practically see. It is woven around them like a net, and at any given moment the trap can be triggered and the girl ensnared, consumed by nothingness, rendered invisible. But perhaps it is the presence of this very real danger that made Rilke write that such girls know that "*Life* here is magic" (Rilke 43). Yes, I believe that Michelle and I—along with all the world's lost girls and faceless pawns—know this well. For when we begin to feel ourselves slipping away, being consumed by an unrecognizable other, everything around us seems sharper, more valuable, more *magical*, more *full of life*.

A game of chess becomes a life-affirming ritual. A child skipping becomes an expression of life itself. A reflection in a grimy door becomes a malicious specter. Jungle gyms, dog runs, and grassy hills become the landscape of a higher, heavenly realm. Indeed, when life escapes you, the world in which life goes on comes aglow. Even inanimate objects take on a glimmer of life's magic; you might find yourself believing that maybe—just maybe—when nobody is looking, those fallen chess pieces might right themselves—stand up off checkered floors and become their own choreographers—no players needed. You might find yourself able to see your face in the faces of others. I see now that when I do this, perhaps I am not erasing the faces upon which I superimpose my own. Perhaps, in some strange way, I am assimilating them. Maybe we engage in some magical exchange from which we both walk away transformed: maybe they impose some part of themselves upon me, just as I impose myself upon them, without either of us realizing it. I wonder if we all carry each face, each person in whom we see ourselves, within us—if others are living *through* us, through our memories, just as I lived through the chess players. And I wonder if we are all, by way of this exchange, living through others as well. I like to think so. Maybe this exchange is Rilke's *"existence"*— perhaps it is a sharing of lives, a sharing of life itself (Rilke 43). If this is true, then the cages of our current situations may always be transcended: though our bodies may rest upon benches, floors, or in alleyways, our souls and our faces go on living in that "space not marked by the measures of time," that eternal space of magic (Rilke 43).

WORKS CITED

Bignell, Paul. "What made an accountant dedicate his life to documenting the plight of the homeless?" *The Independent*. N.p., 9 Oct. 2011. Web. 22 Feb. 2013.

Flogging Molly. "Drunken Lullabies." Rec. 2001. *Drunken Lullabies*. SideOneDummy, 2002. CD.

Jeffries, Lee. *Michelle*. 2011. Photograph. *Flickr*. 28 July 2011. Web. 19 Feb. 2013.

Michelle. "Homeless, London." *Interview by Lee Jeffries*. Goear. N.p., 31 July 2011. Web. 22 Feb. 2013.

Rilke, Rainer Maria. "The Seventh Elegy." *Duino Elegies: A Bilingual Edition*. Trans. Edward A. Snow. New York: North Point, 2001. 41-45. Print.

On Constricted and Dimly Lit Spaces

MARIA STOJANOVIC

In a museum, you often see a person standing in front of a painting, completely still for minutes that seem like hours, trapped within the experience as though he or she is unable to crawl over and out of the experiential frame. Or it is as if a singularity has been created, a point in time and space that admits life's many trajectories so that they coalesce to erase boundaries such as outside and inside, past and present.

In his fifth postulate, Euclid says that if there is a line A and an independent point B, there will exist a line going through point B that will never cross line A. These two lines will be parallel. Also, if line A and line C are both parallel to line D, then line A and C will be parallel to each other. If we are blessed with more dedicated teachers, we may hear a thing or two about Lobachevski and his work on parallel lines in the field of hyperbolic geometry. There, in the world of convex and concave planes and more reflective of our own world than the planar world of Euclid, any two parallel lines can intersect at some single point before continuing on their journey into infinity. Two corollaries of Lobachevski's work are: if a space is curved enough, any seemingly unrelated set of three or more points can appear on the same line, and at each point in space, an endless number of different seemingly parallel trajectories intersect. It seems to me that it is just a matter of time until we find a point where everything—the lives of our friends, the lives of all people who lived before us and who will live after us—will come together as these hyperbolic parallel lines come together. On a smaller scale, such a realization of the convergence of many past moments, moments one person has lived through as well as those he knows others have experienced, is what happens to anyone trapped in front of a painting.

Connections with past experiences will differentiate the way one person sees a painting from the way another person sees it. One Thursday, I visited the Frick Collection and felt the need to stop in front of George de la Tour's *The Education of the Virgin*. Other more elaborate and colorful paintings outshone it; in fact, the *Virgin* had been slightly damaged in a restoration attempt. The painting shows a space very dark and closed yet partially illuminated. The main source of light comes not from the candle in the young girl's hand, but from the pages of a book that her disinterested teacher is holding. Light and knowledge radiate straight into the girl's intelligent and absorbing face, relegating her teacher and the rest of her surroundings to the realm of irrelevance and darkness. Interestingly enough, the girl's face is in the damaged portion of the painting: it was whitened too much during the restoration, only adding to the light's glowing effect. It might seem to a third party that I was attracted to this painting simply because, as someone of college age, I would enjoy the idea of being bathed in the scholarly light emitted by my textbooks. But this notion was only partially the case. After all, it is almost impossible not to see the association between the girl's calm smile and the comfort that such knowledge—one accumulated by, and passed down from past generations—brings. Yet, I felt moved by something deeper than the straightforward connection with education. After all, the education that the subject of de la Tour's painting is receiving is most likely a religious one, so, this would be an education perhaps not always well suited for the challenges I would face in the real world. It was something else in the painting that caught my attention and drew me in.

When I walked into the next room, I understood that this magnetic something was the way light interacted with the subjects of the painting. There hung Jan Vermeer's *Officer and Laughing Girl*, which depicts the next stage of a girl's education, beyond the ideal love that Christ has for humanity radiating from de la Tour's book. A man and a woman are sitting across from each other. They are in a room with a map on the wall, a table, and two chairs. The girl, wearing a black and gold dress that matches the upholstery of the chair and a white scarf enhanced by the light coming in through the window, is holding a glass and smiling nervously. The officer's face is not visible. His back is to the viewer and even the girl within the frame cannot see him well because he is in shadow. All light herein enters through the window, from the outside, from the real world. It casts brightness on the face of the woman, separating her from the man in shadow, implying a depth that transcends such simple concepts as foreground and background.

The room the officer and girl are seated in is small; they are brought together into a closed space with two possible exits. The first is the window, leading to a more open space, lit with the full magnitude of the sun, unlike the room into which only a few sunrays can enter. The other exit is the map hanging behind the girl, showing all of Holland with its seemingly endless combinations of places. But the map is closed off by a frame, a memento of a boxed-off finiteness that we are all trapped in.

You also feel that you know all you need to know about the young woman at that particular instant. She is politely, perhaps excitedly, enjoying the moment, the attention, the nice words, and if there were to be in their conversation a conflict, you would side with her because she seems so sweet. But there is no sign of a conflict, just a shadow. The brim of the officer's hat creates, in contrast with the woman's white, glowing scarf, a dark halo around him, making him seem both suspicious and mysterious. Who is he? What are his intentions? The young woman is being entertained by him. She laughs, she is happy; but one cannot tell how all this will end. Light, though, is usually a source of comforting reassurance. Whether it is the light of God's book educating the girl in de la Tour's painting or the light of exposure to the outer world, we associate it with "shedding light," overcoming the unknown. We are drawn to it because of these revealing powers. If the officer were to turn around, he would be caught in the light and would no longer remain a mystery. But, of course, he will not turn around, so this particular light is limited to a brief moment and cannot reveal the future. The viewer is left wondering whether this encounter will end well or whether the officer, to paraphrase Emily Dickinson's famous words, will "kindly stop for her."

People say that during near death experiences (or at the moment of death), a person's life reappears as a sort of instantaneous movie, a single scene with all other scenes within it and no logical boundaries of time, the sort of worldview Saint Augustine's three-and-four dimensional God would have. A walk in the Frick Collection is far from traumatic. Yet moving between *The Education of the Virgin* and *Officer and Laughing Girl* and seeing similarities in composition and meaning caused this very movement of moments for me, seemingly parallel lines from my past intersecting with that immediate moment. It reminded me of a third picture, albeit one not created by an artist's moment of inspiration and framed by mortals, but by natural forces instead.

My grandparents' village is a tiny point on the east Adriatic coast where everybody knows everybody else. The only stranger is a Russian tycoon who bought a summer house there a few years ago. He, his wife forty years his junior, and his bodyguard soon became accustomed to the rhythms and rituals of life in the Balkans. Every summer they would arrive followed by a truck full of furniture to replace everything that was stolen during the off-season when the house was empty. The village had given up whatever opportunities it may have had to develop as the center of the universe, to preserve its ancient, natural beauty. Unlike the more famous Duino Castle on the same sea, the village is tucked deep in a bay, and so the angry voice of the sea cannot be a source of inspiration. Instead, the water slowly overwhelms the shore that crawls upwards to become the surrounding frame of mountains that seem to touch the sky all around. In reality these walls are not that tall; they only appear so because the village and everyone in it are so small. Around noon, when the sun falls perpendicular to the sunbathers, leaving no dark place to hide, and when the heat becomes unbearable, I want to melt into the environment, relieved of any direct connection to the sun. Through this transformation of light and humidity, I become less aware of the enclosing magnitude of my surroundings.

On a summer day, with my mother and my aunt, I walk across the road around noon to get from our house to the other side of town where the graveyard is. A car approaches, and so accustomed are we to angry driving in the region, we hasten to get out of the way. Surprisingly, though, the young man stops and lets us pass while smiling, and I let his gaze follow me. My aunt teases me about it while I pretend not to care, putting on my somber face. We are going to put flowers on my great-grandmother's grave, and it is not the time to "stir dull roots with spring rain."

We arrive at the graveyard soon after. It is more of a cute little garden behind a church than the densely populated rows of single-filed headstones I had pictured. We reach the headstone engraved in Cyrillic with my great-grandmother's name. We set the flowers down. My mom asks me if I remember her at all. No, I say, but I do remember the photograph in which she is holding me as a baby. My mother then mentions that her uncle is planning to be buried in this plot, to which my aunt adds, "Mihajlo is too fat, he'd need to be cut up into three pieces in order to fit. Even then, it would be uncomfortably snug."

"I think that even if we cremated him, his ashes wouldn't fit properly," my mom continues. We stifle our laughter, as though the tombstones can hear—my great-grandmother's hand might rise out of the dirt and slap us on the wrist for making such cruel jokes! It is the type of gallows humor that can only exist at noon, when there are no shadows, when we are certain that the spirits of the dead are asleep, when we seem to be free from strange conjunctions.

It is the type of humor that keeps me up that night, when the postcard landscape gives way to never-ending black and navy. When the stars are visible, you can see the jagged outline where the mountains stop and the sky starts, and you are humbled by the greater force that surrounds you. When there are no stars, there is so much darkness around that you are blindfolded. There is no beginning, and there is no end, and you are trapped in a single dark spot. This is when you are alone with yourself and the tide brings the smell of rotting mussels and, with it, *thoughts* of rotting muscles. Jokes about the impossibility of properly burying a fat man turn into meditations on sickness, on aging, decaying, and dying, on cartilage, tendons, and flesh. During the day, cutting someone up into three pieces is a Tom and Jerry cartoon, but at night it becomes someone attacking with a meat cleaver. I try to think of the home where I spend the other ten months of the year, my quiet suburb in New Jersey that is in a time zone six hours behind that of this mountainous frame, where it is evening and there is still some light. I try to think of nice things, not of the mysterious splashing in the water or the graveyard down the road, which is no longer a garden resting place but a series of pits where we dump our dead.

A few months earlier, a young woman in my town in New Jersey had been killed by her jealous ex-boyfriend. She had been out for a jog, and as she crossed the street, he ran her over repeatedly with his car. Another man who was present rushed over and banged on the car window in a futile attempt to stop the crazed driver. I hadn't thought about the incident since it happened, but at that moment, looking at an infinite sky, I conjured up memories I had never had. I heard the crunching of bones and the screeching of tires, sounds that I'd never heard in real life. I smelled something awful and indescribable, and I saw the dark stains on the concrete. I thought of the gaze of the smiling boy who stopped for me and let me cross the street earlier that day and whether or not he had the capacity to do the same thing to me. I suppressed a scream and fell into a fitful sleep that later disappeared with the delayed arrival of sunlight, delayed because the sun's rays had to push themselves through the mountainous frame.

I do not know whether Vermeer intended for viewers to look at his painting and connect his ideas and use of shadows and highlights to the chiaroscuro of their own daily lives, or whether any artist plans to create an effect like this. But, in one way or other, perhaps each and every moment of a life can be painted in chiaroscuro. Every moment is a point and we, in a very closed and framed space, see only that particular moment as illuminated, like the light shining only on Vermeer's girl or sunlight peeking over dark mountains. While some trajectories from the immediate past are like beams of light, most lead to a moment that is obscure to us and out of our control. The future remains dark, no matter how we might pretend otherwise.

Combinations of darkness and light, the closed spaces with hints of ways out into openness, burrow themselves deep within us and affect our subconscious. Rather than individual moments not connected to one another—the skeletal combination of lines and points in a sketch—our most moving thoughts are those that result from combinations of meaningful memories triggered by the way our surroundings are molded, impressions of color made clearer by the filling in of depth and shadow. All of our memories—those that have actually happened, those that we have imagined happening, and those that we are still waiting for—attach themselves to the light and the dark, the open and the constricted. This is why I am uncomfortable when I am in a small room, or when I look at a painting of two people in a small room. I am taken back to that sleepless night framed by mountains where, in turn, I was taken back to a different moment in New Jersey, at the intersection of sidewalk and street, of running sneakers and rubber tires. *This* is why different people are moved by different paintings. In each mind, memories are evoked by different associations, and the parallel lines drawn from a moment in the past to the present intersect. They converge upon and diverge from me as they cannot for others. The associations I make come from the arrangement of light and spatial orientation. Someone else may react to a specific cascade of notes. Another may find that a certain smell causes a rush of moments. The associations we make with our surroundings, whether they are about constricted and dimly lit spaces or not, begin to form patterns in our lives, patterns that eventually settle down and become a part of the consciousness we don't normally access. When I turn the lights off to go to sleep, I don't usually panic and think of death and the unknown, and I can safely assume that most other people are not paralyzed on a daily basis by the sudden onslaught of thoughts when a small association is made. It is only when the right combination of lines, of moments, unites perfectly at a specific point in space and time that we are overwhelmed with memory and freeze into statues before a work of art in a museum, realizing how intertwined our lives really are.

WORKS CITED

Blackburn, Paul. "The Once Over." *Break, Burn, Blow: Camille Paglia Reads Forty-three of the World's Best Poems*. Ed. Camille Paglia. New York: Vintage, 2006. 185. Print.

Dickinson, Emily. "Because I Could Not Stop for Death." *Break, Burn, Blow: Camille Paglia Reads Forty-three of the World's Best Poems*. Ed. Camille Paglia. New York: Vintage, 2005. 95. Print.

de la Tour, Georges. *The Education of the Virgin*. 1650. Oil on canvas. The Frick Collection, New York.

Vermeer, Johannes. *Officer and Laughing Girl*. 1657. Oil on canvas. The Frick Collection, New York.

Finding My Role in Visual Art

MADDIE HILL

Lights up on Mark Rothko, the famous abstract expressionist painter of the 1960s. He stands stoically, examining one of his Seagram Murals. But to the audience, the painting itself is invisible. They see him looking directly at them. He contemplates them in a prolonged silence as he enters a mysterious yet intimate exchange with them—a communion. When Ken, his new assistant, walks in, Rothko immediately hushes him.

"What do you see?" Rothko asks (Logan 9).

After a moment Ken simply replies, "Red" (10). And we sense the passion suggested by the color, sense the life that will fuel *Red*'s inquiry into the profound interaction among the characters: the art, the audience, and the artist.

Playwright John Logan gives the actor playing Ken little direction about the moment in which he contemplates Rothko's painting. When I first read the scene, I was at a loss. I could not imagine what was going through Ken's head until I went to see a Rothko painting myself. On a rainy Sunday in early October, I spent an afternoon at New York's Museum of Modern Art. I had heard that the MoMA did not have a Rothko painting, so I went without an agenda. And while other pieces sparked in me a range of emotions, I wanted to see a Rothko. So I asked the security guard if there were any.

"Nope," she curtly replied, "We don't have any."

As I thanked her and walked away, she began to chase after me calling, "Wait! I think we do. I just remembered."

She directed me to the very last piece I saw that day: *No. 16 (Red, Brown, and Black)*—the piece that still affects me.

Many in the crowded room walked straight past the enormous painting without a second thought, while others posed in front of it for a photo. But I decided to spend some time with *No. 16* because I wanted to experience what the real Mark Rothko intended for me as a member of the audience. Yet as I stood before *No. 16*, the first thought that popped into my head was, "So?" For the first few moments, I felt stale. It was not stirring me. I felt as if I had no relationship with it. We existed separately—almost as if I weren't there.

In *Red*, we meet Rothko doing something that makes us uncomfortable. He stands in prolonged stillness giving his total attention to a painting, allowing it to "pulsate" and "work on [him]" and "wrap its arms around [him]" as he "engage[s] with it" (9). When I sat frustrated before *No. 16* that day at the Museum of Modern Art, I wondered how I might be able to find a similar connection, how I might "engage" with paint on a canvas. I did not know if I was supposed to act or if I would be acted upon. I just wanted to let the painting do its work. I, like Ken, had to learn to let Rothko's work "pulsate" for me.

In her essay "Art Objects," Jeanette Winterson grapples with learning to understand and interact with art, explaining that for her, at that moment of first encounter, art demands a new and unfamiliar language. She tells the story of being struck by a painting that "had more power to stop [her] than [she] had to walk on"; she found herself uncomfortable with the painting because it, like "all art . . . is a foreign city" with a different language and way of thought (89). She wants us to know that to understand art, we must adapt and learn about the world of the piece, separate from the world in which we live.

After sitting before *No. 16* for a few moments, I realized that I was unable to look away. Something foreign had happened to me and in me that I could not name. I had been affected by visual art before, but never so intensely. This piece was different from the others I had seen that day. Perhaps it was the genius of Rothko's deceptive simplicity. Perhaps it was because I had gained some insight into the mind of Rothko through *Red*. There is no way to know. The only thing that mattered in that elongated moment was the painting's powerful hold on me—an almost otherworldly hold. I was beginning to exist in the foreign city of *No. 16*. It felt as if another being were acting upon a part of me that I had not known existed. In a way, it was magical.

In her interview with *Time* about her career and craft, Tony-nominated actress Michelle Williams explains that some of what she experiences as she acts comes from an "unknown" place, and that it has an "element of magic." As an actor, I long for the moments in which I am acted upon by a force outside myself that comes from that "unknown" place. This is, perhaps, why I found my moment with Rothko's work so powerful and so cathartic. I was taken into the imaginary world of the painting where I experienced something that cannot be wholly nailed down. I cannot say what powerful force brought me there. There is no way to know.

My acting teacher tells us to "take each other in" so that we will not think about our actions but will allow them to flow freely. As I take in a scene partner, I want nothing. I expect nothing. I simply wait for something to strike me. While I need simply to be present to have a genuine interaction with my scene partner, I must usually be active when I look at a painting. I must fuel an interaction. And yet both kinds of "taking in" bring me out of this world into another. I am pulled into something so vivid and truthful that words fail me when I try to describe the sensation. The interaction is not of the mind but of the gut.

Sometimes, that gut reaction is not pretty or comfortable. In an early exercise, my partner and I were going back and forth until out of nowhere I shouted to her, "Shut up!" I did not realize what I had said until seconds after the sound left my mouth. The "Shut up!" had come from that same foreign place within myself that *No. 16* had somehow reached, a place that sometimes brings out ugly, disturbing experiences. In *Red*, Rothko calls for a painting (like his own) that "[lets] out a silent howl of something feral and foul and primal and REAL. Not nice. Not fine. Real. A moan of rapture" (51-52).

Immersed in *No. 16*, I felt in the middle of my chest the beginnings of grief as if I had just lost a loved one. As the grief began to overtake me, sadness surfaced as well. I was unsure if these feelings were merely brought to the surface by the painting, or if they had been created by the art. My face began to feel red and hot as these emotions took hold of me. Tears welled in my eyes. Looking back, I still cannot pinpoint why I was moved so greatly. What I do know, however, is that this painting made me feel something truthful. Although the experience was not pleasant, it was satisfying. Cathartic. Beautiful. The art "worked on" me and I on it. This was also an experience I wanted. I was open to it. And although in the moment, the intense sadness was frightening, I was proud to have taken a step in my understanding of the work of art.

Logan's Rothko calls the people who do this active work with art real "human being[s]" because they are in touch with the part of their humanity from which the artist created the art (10). They are fully alive because they are not shutting off pieces of themselves to hide from pain, discomfort, and anguish. Winterson explores what the audience must give to a painting and concludes that art demands "increasing discomfort," "increasing distraction," "increasing invention," and "increasing irritation" for the sake of full comprehension and experience (91, 92). And if art is truly born of the human experience, it must demand from us things that we might not enjoy giving. In my acting training, we struggle to allow the unpleasant moments to affect us. When our partner screams, "Go to Hell!" it causes us pain. But we must learn to take it in, if we are to create our art. For me to have that very personal moment with *No. 16*, I had to give myself over to the painting so that it could do its "work" on me, even if the process yielded pain. In the molding of *No. 16*, Rothko also shaped me. But he was only able to do this work on me because I gave myself permission to surrender, something I had not done before.

Rothko's goal is to bring us together with the art, to create "[a] place of communion," as he explains to Ken (17). Christians recognize the doctrine of communion as a coming together, a spiritual exchange. But for this exchange to happen, the supplicant must have faith. Growing up in the Christian church, I heard time and time again that all I had to do was believe to feel a connection with God. I know now that submitting to any great unknown can reap its own rewards even as our submission puts us at risk. Because I went into my exchange with *No. 16* with faith that I could gain from it something new, I was more susceptible to its power. It did not necessarily mean that I would experience something profound, but faith created the possibility. I had to have faith in the art, faith that I was not being ridiculous as I stared at a painting alone for a prolonged period. Giving oneself over into another world is in and of itself an act of acknowledgement about the power of art.

When I stood to leave *No. 16* I found it very difficult. I had to pull my eyes away. Even leaving MoMA, I could not shake the image or its effect. Through some kind of "magic," we created a symbiotic need for one another.

John Berger speaks of symbiosis in his essay "Steps Toward a Small Theory of the Visible," explaining that we look at paintings because they offer "us company . . . when the painted image is not a copy but the result of a dialogue, the painted thing speaks if we listen" (39). I craved that dialogue, faithful that it could occur even in a world that Berger notes is full of solitude. The comfort and hope that company can give fuels a great desire in us to commune with art. He compares this relationship between audience and art to the relationship between Heaven, a place whose existence is contingent upon faith, and earth. He notes that "the difference is infinite between heaven and earth, yet the distance is minimal" and so it is with art and the viewer (35). The viewer stands but a few feet from the painting; if she does not give herself over to the painting, the space between them is unbridgeable. Without the communion between Heaven and earth, art and audience, the "dialogue" is lost; symbiosis ceases.

In *Red* we learn that Rothko paints for the people. He does not paint for himself, just as the actor does not lose herself in a character for self-pleasure. Rothko paints so that he might affect his world, the world from which he is physically separated, but with which he is in constant communion. He hopes that his Seagram Murals will be "inescapable and inexorable, like doom" so that those who come into communion with them will be forced to recognize their own place in the world (16). Ultimately, art—visual and performance—aims to affect its audience by showing them something about themselves they may not have known. Rothko stares out at us, at the painting that occupies the same place as our bodies, "invisible, unenterable but infinitely close" and he invites us in, asks for our faith and our participation so that we might be transformed (Berger 35).

WORKS CITED

Berger, John. "Steps Towards a Small Theory of the Visible." *Writing the Essay: Art in the World, The World Through Art*. Ed. Darlene A. Forrest, Benjamin W. Stewart, Randy Martin, and Pat C. Hoy II. New York: McGraw, 2012. 35-40. Print.

Logan, John. *Red*. London: Oberon, 2010. Print.

Rothko, Mark. *No. 16 (Red, Brown, and Black)*. 1958. Oil on canvas. Museum of Modern Art, New York.

Williams, Michelle. "10 Questions for Michelle Williams." Online interview by Natasha Deltoro. *YouTube*. 27 Jan. 2011. Web. 21 Sept. 2012.

Winterson, Jeanette. "Art Objects." *Writing the Essay: Art in the World, The World Through Art*. Ed. Darlene A. Forrest, Benjamin W. Stewart, Randy Martin, and Pat C. Hoy II. New York: McGraw, 2012. 89-96. Print.

The Human Narrative

ALEX LINZMEIER

Before *Homo sapiens* walked, he crawled; before he hunted, he gathered; before he killed, he crafted tools from sticks and stones. But once man developed more weapons and began to focus less on other tools, the evolution of the human narrative took a troubling turn. Humans began devoting more effort to domination, to war, than to their original need to thrive in nature, and, paradoxically, the system of evolution that helped to preserve and expand the human race began to destroy it. In the aftermath of the relatively recent conflicts of World War I, World War II, and the Vietnam War, civilians and soldiers alike have shared their stories in an effort to expose the animalistic atrocities committed in war, humanize the victims, combat evil with factual truth, and reach a common understanding of morality for the purpose of promoting peace.

Author John Berger initiates the monumental task of understanding the progression of human history by first exploring the hardships of a few of its characters. In his essay "Hiroshima," he examines those affected by the Allies' dropping of the atomic bomb; he quotes six survivor accounts from the book *Unforgettable Fire* in an effort to "re-insert that [event] into living consciousness today." He argues that the use of nuclear bombs "can never be justified" (Berger 106-7). Berger classifies the dropping of the bomb as an act of terror and evil because it was done with the intent of killing innocent civilians and producing a "shock effect on political decision-making by their government," but he acknowledges that these abstract appeals or "epithet[s]" do not enrage us as much as the words of the "*hibakuska*—'those who have seen hell'" (106, 104). In survivor accounts of Hiroshima, Berger discovers the idea that a weapon's victims provide a more authentic representation of a weapon's destruction than statistics provided by the attackers, and he hints at a much larger realization: truth, a nonfiction retelling of events, implicitly opposes evil weapons without invoking abstractions such as morality. The *hibakuska* don't generalize; they don't pass judgment. They have no need to. They describe hair standing straight up, skin peeling off, and parents dying before their children's eyes. Our resulting outrage and instinctive inclination declares that *"this should not happen again (here)"* (106). And so we, as the audience to these horrific stories, reach a level of consciousness in regards to our own powerlessness, an awareness of truth, but we lack the tools necessary to "release an energy for opposing evil and for the life-long struggle of that opposition" (106). As observers in a state of paralysis, we respond to our neutralized desire by listening to more stories in an effort to experience truth and evil in different forms, to understand the inner workings of the human narrative, the result *and* the outrage.

In his essay "How to Tell a True War Story," Vietnam veteran Tim O'Brien portrays truth as a malleable entity that changes and evolves with every telling of a given tale. The storyteller, as a function of his telling, adds and subtracts details, "making up a few things to get at the real truth" (81). O'Brien writes, "In any war story, but especially a true one, it's difficult to separate what happened from what seemed to happen" (67). The holistic, emotional impact of the story supersedes the boundaries of the actual occurrence, and, therefore, truth depends more upon the authenticity of a story's fiction than it does upon the facts themselves. According to O'Brien, "You can tell a true war story by its absolute and uncompromising allegiance to obscenity and evil" (65-6). O'Brien works effectively by crafting and reshaping the classic core elements of "story": exposition, plot, and conflict. Ultimately, he creates a lasting and deep impression.

Such tales live beyond the death of their authors because they not only capture the author's mind but also manage to speak directly to us as if we were listeners. Storytellers like O'Brien also help preserve and expand the human race not by producing literal offspring, but rather by giving birth to stories that have the strength to survive on their own; they compel us to pay attention. Ernest Hemingway, a WWI veteran, often encapsulates truth through the exploits of his fictional character Nick Adams, who only loosely reflects Hemingway's own war experiences as an ambulance driver but who nonetheless remains true to the human narrative. In his novel *Death in the Afternoon*, Hemingway states, "If a writer of prose knows enough about what he is writing about he may omit things that he knows and the reader, if the writer is writing truly enough, will have a feeling of those things as strongly as though the writer had stated them" (192). Hemingway and O'Brien's war stories resonate because they draw the foundations of their fiction from within their own real-life, nonfictional narratives; the derivative story upholds the authenticity of the original. Each truthfully effective story inherits the characteristics of its author and adapts to the reader's worldly context to become slightly different, slightly more evolved. Indeed, even non-autobiographical fiction maintains both the writer's authentic voice and fruits of experience.

Regardless of the subtleties among Berger's, O'Brien's, and Hemingway's three different shades of truth, all agree that the truth depends on details. O'Brien writes, "True war stories do not generalize. They do not indulge in abstraction or analysis" (74); Berger writes, "I refrain from giving the statistics. . . . Such statistics tend to distract. We calculate instead of judging. We relativize instead of refusing" (105-6); and Hemingway writes in *A Farewell to Arms*, "Abstract words such as glory, honor, courage, or hallow were obscene beside the concrete names of villages, the numbers of roads, the names of rivers, the numbers of regiments and the dates" (161). Ultimately, the abstract words that Berger and O'Brien allude to and that Hemingway lists dehumanize conflict and fail to account for the people ravaged by war's weapons, the people blistered, blinded, and burned by the mustard gas of WWI, the people charred, radiated, and evaporated by the nuclear bombs of WWII, the people roasted by the napalm of the Vietnam War.

Thus far, we have examined narrative methods for raising consciousness of evil, but before we can equip ourselves with the necessary tools to oppose evil and promote peace, we must weigh the narratives of civilians and soldiers against the arguments of those who propagate war so that we can see if the human side of the story actually withstands the destructive paradox of man's evolution towards conflict.

Robert McNamara, the Secretary of Defense from 1961 to 1968, embodies the ideal opposition to Berger, O'Brien, and Hemingway. To justify the escalation of the Vietnam War, he relied solely on number crunching, aggregate statistics, and mass-generalizations. In the documentary *The Fog of War*, directed by Errol Morris, McNamara explains the "false interpretation" of "political and military arguments" that Berger references but does not fully contextualize (Berger 105). McNamara says, "Killing 50% to 90% of the people of sixty-seven Japanese cities and then bombing them with two nuclear bombs is not proportional," but he doesn't criticize the bomb itself: "What one can criticize is that the human race prior to that time and today has not really grappled with what are, I'll call it, 'the rules of war'" (Morris). McNamara proposes that we reach a common understanding of morality by externalizing ethical right and wrong into a set list of do's and don'ts. This yes/no mentality for combatting evil, however, vastly oversimplifies its complexity and our willingness to be influenced by it.

Evil, like the human narrative told to subdue it, has evolved and adapted to withstand opposition. Berger writes, "The concept of evil implies a force or forces which have to be continually struggled against so that they do not triumph over life and destroy it" (106). Evil embeds itself in the same arena as truth; it attempts to hide behind a "mask of innocence" (107). Evildoers tell the same types of narratives as Berger, O'Brien, and Hemingway, but do so using lies to pass off evil acts as if they were justifiable. Berger suggests, "Nobody can confront the reality of 6th August 1945 without being forced to acknowledge that what happened was evil. It is not a question of opinion or interpretation, but of events" (106). Only by telling the stories of the truth and reality that contain implicit evil, evil in its purest form, can we expose indifference. Once we clearly identify and deconstruct "evil's principal modes of being," people may call themselves to action (107).

Our initial urge, however, to simply ban weapons has repeatedly failed. Bombs, grenades, landmines, chemical agents: they all kill people in horrific ways, and always will. Every now and then, though, I'll turn on the History Channel and watch *Vietnam in HD*. I'll hear stories of the Vietcong capturing American soldiers, chopping their penises off, and stitching them inside the 18-year-olds' mouths. This can be done with nothing but a butter knife and floss. We don't criticize butter knives and floss; we criticize torture, the intent behind violence. But even rules of war such as the Geneva Convention do not prevent terrorists and large nations alike from committing atrocities such as 9/11 or the torture of prisoners at Guantanamo. Evil lives within our ignorance of its origins, within the very fabric of what came before the weapons and the intent to harm.

Without acknowledging this record, we are doomed to make the same mistakes over and over again. We cry evil without examining the words that *are* evil: "*He looked miserable—burned and sore, and naked with only pieces of his gaiters trailing behind as he walked. . . . Skin of a girl's hip was hanging down . . . a girl of about three years of age brought some water in an empty can she had found. She was trying to let her [dead] mother drink from it*" (Berger 104-05). We return in a loop to McNamara's original flawed logic of oversimplification. Without an exploration of the human side of things to further our understanding of truth, evil, and morality, we return to where John Berger says he started at the beginning of his essay "Hiroshima." After receiving a copy of the book *Unforgettable Fire*, Berger did not open it for three months. He writes, "I didn't consider the book urgent; I believed that I already knew what I would find within it," but we cannot know anything until we read the stories themselves, until we retrace our reasoning back to the human level (103). To wit:

August 9th: On the west embankment of a military training field was a young boy four or five years old. He was burned black, lying on his back, with his arms pointing toward heaven. (Berger 107)

Four guys go down a trail. A grenade sails out. One guy jumps on it and takes the blast, but it's a killer grenade and everybody dies anyway. Before they die though, one of the dead guys says, "The fuck you do that for?" and the jumper says, "Story of my life, man," and the other guy starts to smile but he's dead. (O'Brien 80)

Norman Morrison was a Quaker. He was opposed to war, the violence of war, the killing. He came to the Pentagon, doused himself with gasoline. Burned himself to death below my office. He held a child in his arms, his daughter. Passersby shouted, "Save the child!" He threw the child out of his arms, and the child lived and is alive today. (Morris)

In all of these stories I see redemption: an appeal to a higher power, an attempt to save comrades, the sparing of a child. I see a desire to alert others to the destructiveness of war. I see an emerging movement to salvage humanity. I see storytellers using the effects of war's worst weapons as tools to promote peace. For us to do the same, we must become consciously competent, not only aware of truth, evil, morality, and evolution, but also capable of telling and being aware of the human narrative. For us to begin the lifelong struggle against evil that Berger outlines, we need storytellers, perhaps storytellers like Berger who spread the word of others, perhaps storytellers like O'Brien who blend fact and fiction, or perhaps storytellers like Hemingway who apply real life inspiration to the realm of fiction. Or, better yet, we might imagine a new species of storyteller evolved from those who came before us, seeking to capture both truth and evil so that we might live in peace.

WORKS CITED

Berger, John. "Hiroshima." *Writing the Essay: Art in the World, The World Through Art*. 11th ed. Ed. Darlene A. Forrest, Benjamin W. Stewart, Randy Martin, and Pat C. Hoy II. Boston: McGraw, 2012. 103-07. Print.

Hemingway, Ernest. *A Farewell to Arms: The Hemingway Library Edition*. Ed. Sean Hemingway. New York: Scribner, 2012. Print.

McNamara, Robert. Interview. *The Fog of War*. Dir. Errol Morris. Sony, 2003. Film.

O'Brien, Tim. "How to Tell a True War Story." *The Things They Carried.* Boston: Mariner, 2009. 64-81. Print.

The Passion: A Celebration of Suffering

DREW STEINER

This time, the guards reach for the flagellum, a wooden handle dangling strips of leather: attached to it are blades, razor sharp blades. They show it to Jesus, taunting him, before they begin. And then, with a wave of the overseer's hand, the torture starts all over again. The guard reaches back, flagellum in hand, and swings; the blades rip across Jesus' side, and blood sprays from five gashes. The count has begun. "Two!" He gasps, his breath taken away by the horrific pain. "Seven!" He cannot stand anymore, but they do not stop. His skin is torn to ribbons, but still they do not stop. "Ten!" The blades stay lodged in his side this time, and as the guard pulls away, flesh and blood fly from his body. They laugh. The count continues. "Sixteen!" There's hardly any skin left on his back. "Twenty-Two!" More. "Twenty-Seven!" More. "Thirty Five!" Finally, the overseer stops them. Jesus lies on the ground, his body torn apart, but at last there is this moment of respite. A guard comes over and undoes one shackle but leaves the other locked; he flips Christ over. The next strike slashes his stomach, and blood sprays over the guards. The count begins anew.

It is this terrible violence that preoccupies much of Harvey Blume's essay "Hammer," in which he discusses the similarity between Mark Burnett's reality television programming and Mel Gibson's *The Passion of the Christ*; he believes each to have an "aesthetic or narrative fundamentalism" (109). Blume writes that, for all their differences of subject matter, the two men compose their stories in a similar fashion. Commenting on the "fundamentalism" that runs through both media, Blume writes: "Burnett and Gibson aim to cut through complications . . . to give the sensation of raw truth . . . and they place enormous emphasis on the power of ordeal to seal their pact with reality" (109). Both employ a fundamentalist story-telling style wherein depicting visceral reality is of paramount importance. They seek to portray "raw truth" and "reality," and do so through "the power of ordeal." Ordeals, depictions of horrible experiences meant to convince viewers of the image's truth, are the main device both men employ to show the brutal "reality" of their characters (109, 110).

Blume, though, takes issue with this supposed "reality." While Gibson conceives his film as if it were history played out upon the screen, Blume accuses Gibson of being disingenuous about his source material, Sister Anne Catherine Emmerich's *The Dolorous Passion of Our Lord Jesus Christ*. Sister Emmerich, an 18th century German nun, describes her visions of the Passion in the first person, as if she were truly there. It is this sentiment that Gibson is attracted to: a personal attendance to Christ's Passion. It seems that Gibson achieves his goal, at least in the view of Pope John Paul II whose supposed review of the film was "it is as it was" (109). Yet Blume objects, offering the controversy around Sister Emmerich as proof that Gibson has a flawed sense of canonical "reality": "Doubts and complexities may gather around Sister Emmerich's tales, but Gibson will not so much as acknowledge them" (110). Taking for the moment a religious perspective and assuming a Biblical interpretation to be "real," Blume still finds that the use of this non-canonical text in a film that supposedly depicts reality dupes the audience. He also finds reality television guilty of the same tricks, seeing it as a doubtful depiction of reality taken from a source of shaky integrity, a manufactured scenario in which producers push their contestants toward outrageous behavior. Ultimately, he connects the two through their tones, suggesting that the programs "share one thing, at least, with *The Passion of the Christ*—its pessimism" (110). Blume believes Gibson's film highlights the depravity and sinfulness of man in order to invoke guilt, while reality television merely garners laughs at the expense of its ridiculous contestants. With regard to Burnett and Gibson's "narrative fundamentalism," he writes: "they are storytelling revivalists, demanding narrative return to its roots. And they place enormous emphasis on the power of ordeal to seal their pact with reality" (109). Gibson especially comes off as a "revivalist" zealot, depicting a violent religious event and portraying it as brutal reality. Burnett and Gibson each aim to take something contrived and deliver it to their audiences as a realistic, visceral experience.

In *Regarding the Pain of Others*, Susan Sontag discusses art's tendency to depict suffering, violence, and war in graphic, realistic detail. Analyzing Francisco de Goya's etching *The Disasters of War*, which depicts the atrocities committed by Napoleon's army against Spanish rebels in 1808, she writes, "The ghoulish cruelties in *The Disasters of War* are meant to awaken, shock, wound the viewer" (44). Goya's depiction of the violence puts the viewer through an intense ordeal; we are shocked into recognizing the pain of others. Sontag also emphasizes the value of art's authenticity. It is easier to look at a violent image if we can dismiss it as fake or fictionalized, yet when an artist depicts an event "as it was," the image and its assumed reality gain the power to shock the viewer into attention.

Blume's purported connection between reality television and *The Passion* holds true only so long as the audience's acceptance of the "reality" of the work in question is not shaken. If the viewers think the show is scripted, then ratings will drop; the show will have lost its spontaneity in the eyes of the viewer and thus cease to be compelling. If audience members do not believe in Gibson's portrayal of the Passion, or in the truth of the Passion itself, the film inarguably loses some (if not all) of its power: it becomes torture porn instead of a spiritual meditation. Yet here the functions of the two works seem to diverge, "one heading toward church, the other towards celebrity" (Blume 112). Still, though, Blume asserts the similarity between the two, writing, "But bringing religion into it at this point only clouds the issue. It's when you put aside the religious content of *The Passion of the Christ* for a moment that Burnett and Gibson have a lot in common" (109). At this point, Blume's argument loses force, as he has committed the same sin he accuses Gibson of: "cut[ting] through complications, irony, self-reflection" (109). How can one discuss a movie about the Passion of Christ without discussing the religious motivations involved, as well as previous representations of the Passion in art?

Sontag helps again in this regard, as she also examines the history of torture and pain in art in *Regarding the Pain of Others*, highlighting works from ancient Greece (*Laocoon and his Sons*) to 19th-century Spain (Goya's *The Disasters of War*). Discussing a photograph of the blown-apart face of a World War I soldier, she writes, "Perhaps the only people who have the right to look at such images of suffering of this extreme order are those who could do something to alleviate it . . . or those who could learn from it" (42). The horror of the photograph is almost impossible to behold, and Gibson's film certainly belongs in this same category. It is one of the most violent films ever to be shown so widely, to be granted mainstream success despite its depiction of horrific, stomach-turning gore. Blume, as previously stated, believes the film to be nothing more than an "ordeal" designed to shame and shock the viewer, and perhaps that is partly true, but Blume's criticism does not represent the whole. The film is as shocking as Sontag's WWI photo, but that also means that we can "learn from it" and help "alleviate" the suffering depicted therein. First, it gives a visual representation of the Passion, the Stations of the Cross come alive, and the lessons in that Biblical section have much to teach. Second, it depicts a distinctly Catholic perspective of the "alleviation" of

Christ's suffering. By viewing the film, one stands in solidarity, like Simon of Cyrene, with Christ. Other saints like St. Francis of Assisi took part, very literally, in the Passion through the suffering of stigmata and were the better for it. Perhaps modern man does not need to make such a literal sacrifice to understand Jesus' suffering; instead, recognition of the pain he suffered and compassion for Christ may be enough. Yet there is something even more elemental at work here: suffering itself, the ritual absorption of pain, a constant theme in much religious art, is on display.

Blume ignores the possibility that we might learn from the *Passion*. He blasts Gibson for not contemplating the theological consequences of portraying Jesus' death. Yet in his film, Gibson only continues an age-old tradition of depicting violence in order to shock the audience into recognizing Jesus' suffering. For centuries the Church has promoted solidarity with Christ's suffering so that followers may participate in the Resurrection through countless pieces of art, especially during the Italian Renaissance, depicting the violence of Christ's sacrifice. Coincidentally or not, a panel of the Maesta of Duccio in Siena depicts the same scene Gibson illustrates in his film in the graphically violent *Flagellum* (1308-1311). Blood runs down Christ's body as a crowd of Pharisees, Romans, and perhaps some disciples whose look of horrible pity and intense emotion we share, look on. Ludovico's *Lamentation* (1582) displays Christ's body laid upon his fainting mother, surrounded by weeping women and St. John. The depiction of Christ's body is extremely realistic; his hand is broken and his left arm seems dislocated (Sorabella). *The Passion* visits this same scene with a backwards tracking shot, starting close in on Mary's tearful, bloodstained face, then slowly pulling further to reveal a tableau of mourners: the Virgin holds her bloody, dead son as St. John and Mary Magdalene mourn next to her. It seems almost to be a painting rather than film; Gibson pays his dues to tradition.

The Renaissance painters used the tools they had to depict the Passion as realistically as possible in order to create a meditation on Christ's suffering. Gibson achieves the same goal through a different art form: film, perhaps the most powerful medium available today. With its immediate presence, film attacks our senses: the most poignant images are burned into our minds, and, by accessing our memories and imaginations, we can sense everything. Above sight and sound, we can also imagine or recall the textures, smells, and even tastes of the depiction on screen. Gibson's film exemplifies and implements the sensory power of film. Through its brutal reality, we can feel much that Christ felt: the blurred vision, the sound of his heavy breathing, the rusty metal of the nails piercing his hands, the smell of blood and sweat, the taste of vinegar. *The Passion* is based in realism, and yet it is a stylized realism designed to optimize our empathy; slow motion emphasizes Christ's pain, while point of view shots and an access to his visions place us directly in his mind. Through skillful implementation of markedly cinematic techniques, Gibson creates a realistic depiction of Christ's torture and brings the pain of the ordeal to the fore. Because of film's arguable power to make us *feel* more than any other medium, it is perfectly suited for Gibson's violent, graphic depiction of the *Passion*.

In fact, Gibson's is just the latest in a genre of Passion films propagated by great, often controversial directors. Martin Scorsese, raised Catholic, succeeded in his version of *The Last Temptation of Christ* (1988), connecting the viewer to Christ by stressing his humanity. Italian filmmaker Pier Paolo Pasolini, an atheist, made the classic *The Gospel According to Matthew* (1964), which depicted the latter half of the gospel, including the Passion. In fact, cinema has produced Passion plays dating as far back as 1897 (Grierson 35).

While rooted firmly in the cinematic Passion genre, Gibson's film is distinct in its depiction. Yes, he provides a greater context to Christ's suffering and creates a realistic depiction of the Passion in order to give the audience a devotional image for meditation; there is that noble goal, but there is something else present as well, another driving force. Blume describes an Abu Ghraib photograph in which a "hooded man, recently identified as Abdou Hussain Saad Faleh, [stands] on a box, wires fastened to his outstretched arms and genitals, terrified that if he falls off he'll be electrocuted" (114). This is just one example of the depravity committed in the American prison camp in which guards tortured men suspected of terrorism. Yet what may be the most disturbing part of the photograph is the guard visible in the right of the frame, taking his own picture. The photographers are almost gleeful in their commemoration: "Look what we've done!" they seem to say. There is an uneasy similarity in Gibson's film. He depicts the Passion not as an onlooker but as a participant. His brutal cinematography becomes self-indictment as Christ dies for man's sins. He, like the guards, participates in a ritual torture, filming it in order keep the memory alive.

The Passion, Sontag's numerous examples of graphic art, the Renaissance paintings, and the Abu Ghraib photographs all immortalize suffering. Yet there is another question that these works are pondering, one that Blume and Sontag fail to explore. They ask as we would: "What is the meaning of all this suffering?" The Abu Ghraib guards might have felt torture to be a form of pay-back for previous sins committed against their country. Gibson might say Christ's Passion is redemption for man's sins. There is an uneasy similarity between the two. For both, inflicted suffering is too easily attributed to unexamined notions of justice and reward.

Pope John Paul II explores a similar dilemma in his Apostolic Letter "Salvifici Doloris." Citing Job as a man of suffering, he writes, "*It is not true that all suffering is a consequence of a fault and has the nature of a punishment.*" He suggests something contrary to the motivation of the guards and perhaps even of Gibson: that suffering is not always part of justice. This limited notion of the nature of suffering may be a post-modern idea, rather than a theological one. Suffering does not necessarily result in a meaningless world, however; it can present opportunities for purification. Gibson shows how Christ's suffering allows for such purification, but what we glimpse seems insufficient. Because we all suffer, we all can enact purification for ourselves. Christ is not the only one who can suffer viably. Perhaps the question should not be the impossible "*why* is there suffering?" but the more tangible "*how* should we suffer?"

In such light, *The Passion* becomes not only a devotional film but a documentation of perseverance in the face of suffering, the glorification of a universal theme. Gibson's Jesus is not so much a teacher or religious leader as he is a soldier who marches on in the face of death and pain. He provides a model of fortitude, of faith in the future. The risen Christ's appearance in *The Passion* lasts only a few moments, yet the inclusion is key, completing the arc of suffering that leads to transformation. This model challenges us all: religious, atheist, anything in between. We must ask how we can use our own, non-fictive ordeals to save ourselves, instead of relying on a divine sacrificial lamb.

WORKS CITED

Blume, Harvey. "Hammer." *Writing the Essay: Art in the World, The World Through Art*. Ed. Darlene A. Forrest, Benjamin W. Stewart, Randy Martin, and Pat C. Hoy II. Boston: McGraw, 2012. 109-14. Print.

Carracci, Ludovico. *The Lamentation*. 1582. Oil on Canvas. Metropolitan Museum of Art, New York. *Metmuseum.org*. Web. 11 Nov. 2012.

Di Buoninsegna, Duccio. *Maesta: The Flagellation*. 1308-11. Tempera on Wood Panel. Museo Dell'Opera Del Duomo, Siena. *Abcgallery.com*. Web. 11 Nov. 2012.

Grieveson, Lee, and Peter Krämer. "Film projection and variety shows: Introduction." *The Silent Cinema Reader*. Ed. Lee Grieveson and Peter Kramer. New York: Routledge, 2004. 31-40. Print.

John Paul II. *An Apostolic Letter Issued "Salvifici Doloris."* Washington D.C.:
    Office of Publishing and Promotion Services, United States Catholic
    Conference. 1984. Print.

Sontag, Susan. *Regarding the Pain of Others*. New York: Farrar, 2003. Print.

Sorabella, Jean. "The Crucifixion and Passion of Christ in Italian
    Painting." *Heilbrunn Timeline of Art History*. The Metropolitan Museum
    of Art, New York. Web. 11 Nov. 2012.

The Gospel According to Matthew. Dir. Pier Paolo Pasolini. Perf. Enrique
    Irazoqui, Margherita Caruso, and Susanna Pasolini. Arco Film, 1964.
    DVD.

The Last Temptation of Christ. Dir. Martin Scorsese. Perf. Willem Dafoe and
    Harvey Keitel. Universal, 1988. DVD.

The Passion of the Christ. Dir. Mel Gibson. Perf. Jim Caviezel, Monica
    Bellucci, and Maïa Morgenstern. Newmarket Films, 2004. DVD.

Broken Bridge II

HANNAH BEVILACQUA

At the Paris Triennial in 2012, Nigeria-based artist El Anatsui covered an entire outside wall of the fun-to-say Musée de la Mode de la Ville de Paris with mirrors and rusted tin. He named it *Broken Bridge*. An employee of the High Line Art group saw it and thought it would make a perfect addition to the collection of art they've amassed and scattered along the High Line, a mile-long converted freight train track in Manhattan. Anatsui chose a site, reconfigured the piece for a larger area, and a few months later—slipped in between two tall buildings on 21st Street—there was *Broken Bridge II*. It is 37 feet tall, 157 feet wide, and so far as public art goes, it's massive. It isn't, however, intrusive, obnoxious, or even, in fact, immediately noticeable, especially to anyone not 30 feet above ground on the High Line's path. Most of the surface of the flat sculpture consists of patches of recycled, pressed tin folded, bent, and interwoven. Breaking up the rusty, metallic tapestry are immaculate mirrored squares that appear in three formless swirls out of the middle of the rust and run up to the top of the sculpture until they meet the sky they reflect.

From a distance, I imagine the pressed tin would look similar to the walls of the hundred other old buildings in the neighborhood, while the mirrors would be indistinguishable from the sky. If you were on street level, and you didn't know that *Broken Bridge II* was there, it wouldn't exactly catch your eye; walking along the High Line, though, it's impossible to miss, despite the fact that it looks as if it's doing its best to blend in. At the bottom of the rectangular structure the tin creeps out in jagged patches onto the bricks of the building behind it, making the building appear as if it has been eroded to reveal these rusted folds lying underneath. It's as if the art is encroaching on space it wasn't meant to, as if it's slowly enveloping a piece of the urban environment.

We, as viewers, are not accustomed to such aesthetic transgression; the effect it can have on a person is the subject of Mark Doty's essay "The *Panorama Mesdag*," wherein he recounts his visit to another piece of large-scale art. The *Panorama Mesdag* is a 120 meter long painting that encircles viewers so that they can vicariously experience the late-19th-century Dutch seaside that's painted on the inside. Adding to the illusion, the bottom of the painting has been buried in sand and driftwood to obscure the bottom and dissolve boundaries. As you stand under a thatched roof, which itself is under an oculus in the ceiling, natural light floods the round room and illuminates this edgeless rendering of reality. Doty, although not impressed with the painting itself, is quite struck with the hubris behind its creation. "A great ambition," he reckons, "to take us inside, for art to subsume reality" (228). He is fascinated with the idea of art that refuses to be held in one place, confined to an area we can easily grasp, and he asks, "What if art refused to stop there, on the museum wall? Wouldn't the result be revolution?" (228). *Broken Bridge II* performs an impressive feat, simultaneously grabbing the attention of pedestrians with its technical intricacy and camouflaging itself into the wall and the sky, making it difficult at first glance to determine where it ends and where the world begins. It is edgeless and encompassing in the same way as the *Panorama Mesdag*; it feels like the kind of art Doty said "refused to stop," and yet the High Line doesn't really feel like a hub of impassioned emotional reactions, let alone the site of a revolution (228).

Emotions of revolutionary caliber are more likely to be experienced in galleries or museums, places people visit with the explicit intention of experiencing art. Visitors are more likely in such places to read the work closely, and to expect themselves to react to it. The heart of a gallery is the art inside it, but outside, in the public arena, our buildings, roads, and parks define the landscape against which everything else comes second, including public art. When it's up against the structures we need for living and working, public art can feel like decoration. *Broken Bridge II* serves no function other than being an object to look at. If it were in a gallery its appearance would automatically be studied for meaning and no one would ask twice why it was there, but outside the first thing people notice is that it's not a building, and so its first duty as a piece of art has been to interrupt the urban environment. When art is placed in a public space and so not afforded the reverence and attention gallery pieces receive, it is, in a way, stripped of some of its power to affect people. It's not giving itself to those who seek it; it's something to pass by on the way to the places we need to go. *Broken Bridge II*'s position amongst apartments and offices potentially overshadows its artistic merit.

This is not to say that the High Line is simply a scenic tour of office blocks. Climbing the stairs from 10th Avenue onto the High Line is like walking into rarefied air, and the first thing you notice is how much cleaner and quieter it is 30 feet off the ground, especially if you've just spent hours walking around in the Meatpacking District on streets that always seem to be wet no matter the weather. Before the High Line became the park it is today it was a long disused rail track that sat untouched for decades until 1999 when, just as its rusted, weed-covered remains were threatened with demolition, a group of citizens lobbied the city to transform it into a public park. They won, and in addition to the installation of footpaths and benches, in came the art, "site-specific commissions, exhibitions, performances, video programs and a series of billboard interventions" chosen by the park's full-time curator Cecilia Alemani (High Line Art). Its design boasts a very trendy mix of minimalism and eco-friendly ambience which is visible in the unfinished wood benches, the small cafés that break up the mile long walk, and the original railway sleepers that were taken out, tagged, restored and put back where they had been. The High Line itself feels as if it's under the same kind of tight control as the journey along its narrow unbending path. It seems designed to ensure that all visitors would share an analogous experience by walking the same way, being shown the same art objects in the same order, taking photos, pausing at the café, and then exiting back onto the New York street. *Broken Bridge II* is a piece of this experience, an element of the High Line's "art safari." Aside from a ceiling, there's not a whole lot separating the High Line from the Guggenheim, which on the one hand, could lend *Broken Bridge II* the weight and attention of a gallery piece but, on the other, could potentially undermine its unique status. When your experience in a place such as the High Line is very much controlled by the people responsible for it, after all, every part and every choice they've made feels deliberate, including the introduction of art work, and when art is introduced simply for its own sake and not necessarily as an expression of the artist's emotion and intention, it runs the risk of feeling merely decorative.

How art appears is, of course, subject to the judgement of the individual observing it, but there have been trends when it comes to how the public views public art, and what exactly its objectives are. Such notions have been constantly evolving since the first NEA-commissioned piece appeared in

1967. In her essay "Sitings of Public Art: Integration versus Intervention," Miwon Kwon details the evolution of the public's perception of what public art should accomplish in an examination that spans early pieces, "often enlarged replicas of works," early pieces normally found in museums and galleries, to where we are now at the "art in-the-public interest model" (5, 4). People expect their public art to make "genuine gestures towards public engagement," and to offer "aesthetic edification or urban beautification" (8). Altering the aesthetics of a site is one of the easier tasks a work of art has to accomplish, since it only has to be visible and in that space to achieve it. The task of public engagement, however, requires effort on the part of the public; specifically, it requires some form of response, because without a response there can be no interaction. Art that doesn't engage the public is often criticised as being "at worst . . . an empty trophy commemorating the powers and riches of the dominant class" (8). In other words, art for the sake of art. This is one of the critiques Doty levels against the *Panorama Mesdag*, when he calls it "an immense, flashy commission" (227), aware that the painting's integrity is compromised by its association with "bourgeois boosterism" (229). Similarly, *Broken Bridge II* is a flashy commission, as well as an enlarged replica of a work, and so it could certainly be interpreted as the kind of art Kwon says we are trying to move away from, the kind that only serves to decorate rather than provoke.

The people *Broken Bridge II* is designed to interest and engage are a mix of tourists wishing to see the city, locals wishing to see the top of their city, and pedestrians looking for a faster way to walk up 10th Avenue. All must squeeze by each other along the concrete path. That such an intermingling of tourists and locals might cause some friction seems a certainty; these tensions are explored in Dean MacCannell's essay, "Staged Authenticity: Arrangements of Social Space in Tourist Settings." MacCannell references the work of Erving Goffman and elaborates Goffman's theories concerning division of space in a given urban area and his approach of dividing areas into "front" and "back." "The front," MacCannell reiterates, "is the meeting place of hosts and guests," while conversely "the back is the place where members of the home team retire between performances" (590). Because these "front" spaces are constructed to give visitors a positive impression of the community, there is always a certain amount of what MacCannell considers "mystification" at work in them; that is, the intention is "to create a sense of 'real' reality" in a place where reality is not the desired outcome (591). If the High Line is considered a "front" space, then *Broken Bridge II* could be considered a component of its mystification; it could be interpreted less as a work of art and more as a functional symbol meant to represent culture at large and help establish the High Line as an "arty" destination.

It wouldn't be the first "arty" destination in New York, and it won't be the last. Another group that works to bring art to the public is called First Street Green, a collective that successfully turned a vacant lot famous for its unholy number of residential rats into a park complete with its own art collection on East 1st Street. One of the two parks on 1st Street is empty, open and centered on a tall, rusted iron sculpture by Robert Sestok. The other is cluttered and full of plants and trees. They aren't the kinds of places high on the tourist to-do lists. Instead, they seem as if they were purposefully built for residents of the area who want to look at art in nature instead of a colony of rats. Goffman's theory of the division of space, when applied to these two parks, helps one imagine what the initial response may have been to First Street Park, small and tucked between two apartment buildings, and a representative of the "back" region, as opposed to the High Line's trendy "front." A few visits to the renovated rail line, though, provide evidence that complicates Goffman's idea. During some of my trips I watched constant streams of tourists move in crowds so thick everyone had to travel at a constant, shuffling pace. On another trip, the path was freed up, as the few people there were families sticking to the edges while building snow sculptures for a High Line-organized competition. In the mornings there are joggers braving Hudson River winds. In the afternoons people with briefcases take the scenic route home. Weekends are packed and weekdays are more peaceful. Those enjoying the High Line at any point in time are in a constant state of flux, and although this is particularly true of this park, it is also true of many other outdoor settings. *Broken Bridge II* might feel more like a gift bestowed upon New York City's visitors and art buffs alike than a token "front" space monstrosity if you take into account the complexities of the site: Goffman's division of space, it turns out, is more problematic to put into practice than to theorize with. In the case of New York City, packed as it is with tourists and inhabitants, there simply isn't enough room to indulge in wholly divided spaces.

About 100 yards down the road from *Broken Bridge II* stands Allen Ruppersberg's striking *You & Me*, another High Line Art commission. It is a billboard covered in blown up versions of Ruppersberg's rainbow-bright posters that say to the viewer in huge black font phrases like "Me and me and you and you." It's aggressively eye-catching, and as it sits, billboard-sized and angled towards motorists and pedestrians, it certainly receives more attention than *Broken Bridge II*. *You & Me*'s bright colors explode out from amongst Chelsea's subdued industrial facades, but it's hard to imagine High Line Art expected a similar visual punch in *Broken Bridge II* when it flew El Anatsui all the way from Nigeria. Did someone really stand in Chelsea, the world's largest concentration of art galleries, and say, "What this community needs is more art to look at"? Probably not. Do we expect public art merely to sit while we observe? Do we require it to surrender its fascinating, dazzling essence to as large an audience as possible with the least amount of effort asked of us lest we brand it an overly-academic waste of time and money? Public art is capable of achieving more than art in a gallery can achieve, because it has more materials at its disposal than just those that comprise its form; it has the entire outside world to draw from. *This* is where *Broken Bridge II* succeeds as public art, and where other kinds fail. *You & Me* is designed to be seen, confined to its frame while the bright colors mingle with each other, trapped, as they are, in a grey landscape; you can look in, then look away. *Broken Bridge II* is more complicated than that.

At the very top of the sculpture it's tricky to see exactly where the mirrors of the sculpture end and the sky begins. You can discern where it ends, because your eyes can follow the line of the roof, but staring at those identical hues of blue you might as well be staring at an unbroken plane. Anatsui wanted his sculpture to give New York City something its own design and density rarely permits: open sky. Also reflected in the mirrors is a wobbly replica of the Manhattan skyline, including the tip of the Empire State Building, so that from certain vantage points we may peer into an alternate reality in which New York is more open and breezy, and New Jersey has its own Empire State Building. Gazing at *Broken Bridge II* reveals the intricacies of the sculpture and its evocations of traditional tapestry techniques. Looking at the plaque next to it reveals its statement about consumerism and Anatsui's predilection for using recycled materials sourced from his town. Standing in its presence, however, reveals a space full of tensions you wouldn't have seen had you looked at it too closely and not acknowledged the surroundings of the sliver of space it occupies. Only when you take it all in can you see how its ability to blend seamlessly into the Chelsea environment is at odds with its enormous size, how its glistening mirrors look identical to the silvery, futuristic buildings dotted around the High Line while its rust and decay recall the age and history slowly being erased from the area. The way there's sky where there shouldn't be, and buildings where they shouldn't be, and despite how you might think you had become desensitized to the look and feel of this city, this building, which appears to be fading in and out of existence, throws time and space askew. *Broken Bridge II* represents the kind of public art that doesn't just give to the public a simple message, a cultural reference, or even an uncomplicated aesthetic beauty worthy of only marginal attention. There is a constant flow of give and take and distortion between art and space as the pressed tin continues to rust alongside old Chelsea fences and the mirrors throw the image of a city at that particular point in time back at itself. Half of *Broken Bridge II* is falling back into the past while the other half is moving forward in real time with the rest of us, and it's this disruption of time and space that makes it such a captivating piece.

Doty saw something similar at work in Mesdag's *Panorama*: "It wishes to place you in the center of a moment, wishes to colonize your attention for a while, while time seems held in suspension" (229). For him, it was a difficult painting to pin down, evoking comparison with other illusion-based Dutch art, such as *anamorphosis*, one of "those peculiar paintings that are unreadable till reflected in a curving mirror" (230). *Broken Bridge II* is unreadable until it is given a city to subsume. The sculpture would be entirely different if it were placed inside the Guggenheim's white walls with no old buildings to grow against and no skyline to remake. The best kind of public art doesn't make itself the best by simply being outdoors, nor does it achieve anything through being seen by the most people. Public art should move time and space the way something in a gallery, confined to itself by the sterility of its surroundings, never could. "Walls are meant to block views," remarked Anatsui, "but they only block the view of the eye—the ocular view—not the imaginative view" (Brooklyn Museum). Anatsui created a wall that opens up more space than it could ever close off. It forces you to engage with your environment and use your imagination, skills easily forgotten when living in a visually repetitive urban space. All public art should strive to reengage the public, not just in regard to their city, but also in regard to their own ability to think creatively. Every piece of public art runs the risk of becoming just an attractive spanner in the inner-city works, but if it can achieve the level of engagement with its environment that *Broken Bridge II* has achieved, then it has justified its placement away from the galleries in the outside world, and no one can say, regardless of the connotations of the space it inhabits, that it's just decoration.

Now that I've revisited this space so many times, *Broken Bridge II* doesn't look like an art installation anymore. It looks as if it grew out of the High Line over the span of a few decades, like a virus that eats away at buildings, causing them to decompose until they disappear. In a few months, when summer ends, *Broken Bridge II* will end its residency and disappear, and I only hope that it gets to live somewhere else, so its beauty can eat away at, while transforming, someone else's city.

WORKS CITED

Anatsui, El. *Broken Bridge II*. 2012. Pressed tin and mirrors. High Line, New York.

Doty, Mark. "The *Panorama Mesdag*." *Writing the Essay: Art in the World, The World Through Art*. Ed. Darlene A. Forrest, Benjamin W. Stewart, Randy Martin, and Pat C. Hoy II. Boston: McGraw, 2011. 225-30. Print.

Brooklyn Museum. "Gravity and Grace: Monumental Works by El Anatsui." *Brooklyn Museum*. Brooklyn Museum, Jan. 2013. Web. 5 Mar. 2013.

High Line Art. "High Line Art." *The High Line*. 2000. Web. 8 Feb. 2013.

Kwon, Miwon. "Sitings of Public Art: Integration versus Intervention." *Massachusetts Institute of Technology*. The MIT Press, 2002. Web. 2 Feb. 2013.

MacCannell, Dean. "Staged Authenticity: Arrangements of Social Space in Tourist Settings." *American Journal of Sociology* 79.3 (1973): 589-603. Web. 2 Feb. 2013.

Ruppersberg, Allen. *You & Me*. 2012. Poster. High Line Art, New York.

Amor Fati

MAXIMILIAN CHIS

On the shore of Coney Island, white foam forms and merges, twisting in the surf, yielding shapes. Each shape is unique, not only in its momentary appearance but also in its transfiguration over time. Eventually, each returns to the waters that made them like continents crumbling to the ocean floor.

And yet we don't like to think of our own continents as being as precarious and fragile as those white shapes on the waves. We prefer to think that the land beneath our feet and the civilizations we build upon it will last forever. I need only look in front of me at Coney Island proper, at the bright red Parachute Drop rising out of the horizon, to see this line of thought in effect. A great blaring mass of steel, the Parachute Drop has been defunct for over 40 years, but that does not keep it from standing tall and pretending it is everlasting. I wonder how many people, so familiar with the island, look at the tower and think it will be there forever. It's just too large, too iconic, too proud to fall.

Coney Island has always had a relationship with the proud and ostentatious. It began its vibrant and at times lurid history with the establishment of the Coney Island House in 1829, one of many retreats for the wealthy, accessed by a carriage road laid with seashells. Over the years, Coney Island was lavished with ever more hotels, eye-catching amenities, and a bevy of roller coasters and theme parks. Perhaps the most recognizable representation of Coney Island is the famous Elephant Hotel, its facade shaped like its pachyderm namesake. The "island" was a place of money and vanity, and by the late 1800's it was known as "Sodom by the Sea," and with good reason (Meier).

Yet I need only look to my left to see a broken pier, torn apart by Hurricane Sandy and closed for repairs. One can only wonder what happened to all those other bright and seductive attractions Coney Island is so famous for. The antique roller coasters were condemned as death traps and closed (most notably the "Roosevelt's Rough Riders'" coaster, which threw sixteen people off "from a height of 30 feet, killing three") (Meier). The Elephant

Hotel burned down, as did many other relics of earlier decadence. Indeed, it was the tendency for the fires, along with the economic tumult of the Depression, that led to many of Coney Island's attractions being closed. One of the most famous attractions, Luna Park, was shut down after an economic decline (Meier).

And what has become of Coney Island today? Crime abounds. The local news recently reported the killing of a homeless man, Julian Salley, with no arrests made as of this writing (Fractenberg). The legendary theme park itself fares no better. On the official Coney Island website, the iconic mad grin of the Island's mascot leers from the top of an atrociously-designed page adorned with manifold pleas for financial aid and support. An aged man in an antiquated top hat and white button-down shirt with chest hair poking out from the top crosses his arms and gazes, self-satisfied, at the camera: he is the Coney Island artistic director. Beneath his picture is an announcement that the opening of the park will be delayed because of the damage from Hurricane Sandy.

One might say Coney Island is dead, has been for many years, but I would argue that's not the case. Coney Island is now what it has always been, a contorted Frankensteinian combination of mad hubris and pitiless reality, a desperate attempt to cling to a fantastical representation of a life that never really existed. But to consider Coney Island a unique phenomenon in this respect is disingenuous. Coney Island is nothing more than another piece of collateral damage in mankind's losing war against nature and its overwhelming force.

The attempt to deny the ebb and flow of life is a trend mirrored in all of art, which so often attempts to replace the force of nature with pleasant, monotonous fakeries. In his essay "The *Panorama Mesdag*," writer Mark Doty finds himself impressed by the ostentatious hubris of the titular panorama, which attempts to imitate a beach pavilion, yet is static and unchanging. It seeks to pass itself off as a replacement for nature, with artificial sand and beach debris, a panorama painting that attempts to imply that it is more than just a canvas. The *Panorama* was painted in an era in which works of art and literature attempted to encapsulate the entire world within their frames or pages, betraying both a certain arrogance and ambition we have since lost (226). What impresses Doty about the *Panorama* is its attempt to create a virtual world that is somehow superior to the original. What impresses him even more is how it has failed; the forces of nature still press upon it, and the owners must constantly renovate the *Panorama* to keep it in its seemingly eternal state (228). In response to the renovation, Doty says:

I confess: I would have loved the *Panorama* more in disarray; I'd have loved to have seen it with stains of mildew creeping through its skies, or a worry of unraveling the mice had done down in the sands beneath the high dunes of Scheveningen. Then, in the face of time's delicate ruination of human ambition, I would have been moved. (228)

There is something truthful about such decay. In contrast to many paintings kept flawless under layers of shellac, the *Panorama* lies naked and crumbling, revealing the impermanence of our art, our creations, and ourselves. But the *Panorama* constantly attempts to keep that decay at bay, which is, perhaps, exactly what is missing from much artwork—an acknowledgment of decay, of change, and perhaps ultimately of rebirth.

Not all modern art is like the *Panorama*, of course. There are some works that distinctly acknowledge the ravages of time, as Doty would prefer. Upon visiting the Carnegie Museum of Art in Pittsburgh last year, I beheld one of Alberto Giacometti's *Walking Man* sculptures, a bronze piece depicting a tall, emaciated, and fragile humanoid who presses onwards despite the forces working against him. The sculpture endures as a powerful symbol of human fragility and perseverance. Whether or not one agrees with the implications of Giacometti's rather dreary style, there is something unique about art that does not deny the complexities of nature but rather embraces them, that acknowledges the cycle of birth, death, and rebirth.

Some may think such art tragic in its acknowledgment of death and decay, but I do not. There could be no rebirth, no regeneration, if there were no decay. Renovations such as those made to the *Panorama* maintain a comfortable illusion. But like the *Panorama* itself, all things will fall apart in time. Facing such truth, we see more clearly that our art, the trappings of our civilizations, cannot protect us from the ever-encroaching primal void. In time we all will come into contact with nature and its inevitable decay, as Coney Island reminds us. What purpose does it serve us to believe we won't all ultimately fall?

The concept of *amor fati*, Latin for "love of fate," suggests that all things in life, joys and tragedies alike, while perhaps not comforting, are necessary to the achievement of our greatest fulfillment in life. Perhaps we should cease trying to fortify our manmade constructs against the ravages of nature. Perhaps it might be best to give into *amor fati* and acknowledge that we cannot resist the ravages of fate and time, that our constructs will fall, and that we must find purpose within the context of such knowledge.

And I wonder, is that acquiescence enough for us? The Parachute Drop demonstrates the human impulse to try to overcome fate, to stand tall and proud against the forces of wind, rain, and gravity. And I wonder too if we can ever really accept our own powerlessness and own up to our inability to change fate.

An answer of sorts can be found in the most un-Lynchian of David Lynch films, *The Straight Story*. It is the tale of Alvin Straight, an elderly man who seeks to make amends with this brother Lyle who has recently suffered a stroke; neither man has much longer to live. Unfortunately, Alvin's legs and eyes are too worn down by the years for him to get a driver's license. This handicap, however, does not stop him; instead, he drives his lawnmower across Iowa and Wisconsin, a 240 mile trip of meditative interludes and quiet conversations with strangers on his path to make amends with his brother. At the end, the two reunite and share a moment of quiet emotion.

It is not a typical happy ending. The two brothers are frail and will die soon. Indeed, in the grand scheme of things, neither has altered his fate in any significant way. Yet at the same time, there is a change which gives the end of this journey meaning. One brother has gone to great lengths to make amends, and both of them are the better for it. Perhaps that human need for reconciliation distinguishes us from all the other complex natural rhythms that govern our lives. We need not avoid our ultimate fates, but we might dare to make the journey with a bit more awareness of what makes ours distinctly human.

Suppose Straight's brother had never answered the door. Suppose, as is sometimes the case in life, his brother had died before they could make amends. Does that mean that Straight's journey was all for naught? I do not think so. Even if his brother was not there, there still remains the memory of those long meditative drives, those deep and at times not-so-deep conversations with the people he met. There still remains the fact of what he did, the accomplishment itself. Can the winds blow apart an accomplishment? Can the waves wash away the conversations? Or do our risks and our efforts linger, not simply in the physical world but in the land of memories, deeds, and meaning? The things we build, like Coney Island or the *Panorama*, may not last, but their destruction does not diminish their significance. They give testimony not only to human vanity, but also to human stubbornness and determination in the face of seemingly insurmountable opposition. Our creations may fail and crumble, but the record of their existence matters. As inevitable as the crashing white-capped waves might be, they do not defeat our human passion for creating and restoring. In these stories of decay and re-creation, we find the essence of our human will to survive, and our art should serve as a continual reminder of our changing, but ever persistent, struggle against the fate that enlightens us.

I think back to a trip I made to Coney Island several weeks ago. There, I saw many seagulls: they lay in the water not far from me, wings tucked, rocking in the surf. They had such looks of concentration and calm, like little avian Buddhas on the waves. At times, they would rendezvous on the beach, their stick feet awkwardly padding along the sand, ill-at-ease. Soon enough, they would flap their wings and take to the sky, where the winds would blow them in ways they did not anticipate, sometimes back to the water where the waves pushed them in whatever direction the ocean chose. I could not help but admire them.

WORKS CITED

ConeyIsland USA. *ConeyIsland.com*. The Not for Profit Arts Center at
    Brooklyn's Beach. n.d. Web. 29 Apr. 2013.
Doty, Mark. "The *Panoroma Mesdag*." *Writing the Essay: Art in the World, The
    World Through Art*. Ed. Darlene A. Forrest, Benjamin W. Stewart,
    Randy Martin, and Pat C. Hoy II. Boston: McGraw, 2012. 225-30.
    Print.
Fracetenberg, Ben. "Homeless Man Shot Dead in Coney Island, Police
    Say." *DNAinfo New York*. 24 Apr. 2013. Web. 29 Apr. 2013.
Giacometti, Alberto. Walking Man I. 1960. Bronze. Carnegie Museum of
    Art, Pittsburgh.
Meier, Allison C. "Brooklyn History: Coney Island." *Brooklyn Based*. 5 June
    2012. N. pag. Web. 29 Apr. 2013.
The Straight Story. Dir. David Lynch. Perf. Richard Farmsworth. Walt
    Disney, 1999. Film.

In the Land of Gods and Monsters

RILEY FOLSOM

> I feel spontaneously attracted by everything that is beautiful.
> —Leni Riefenstahl (qtd. in Sontag "Fascinating Fascism")

How do you talk about Leni Riefenstahl without discussing Hitler?

It actually is quite simple. You start at the beginning. You start with the image of a young woman.

As the fog clears, her figure appears sitting barefoot on a rock on the top of a ragged mountain peak. Snow that looks like glitter begins to fall from the heavens as she bends down and picks up a glowing blue crystal. Behind her, an enormous waterfall plunges into the depths below. Mist wets her tattered clothes.

The first time we are shown Junta in Leni Riefenstahl's 1932 film, *The Blue Light*, we see her as a goddess. She is literally radiant; light flows from her body. Making her way down the mountain, she finds other crystals and places them in her small straw basket, collecting them the way a child might collect flowers for her mother. She is sweet and powerful, humble and strong, framed by Riefenstahl in such a way that the audience is expected to fall in love with her. We expect the townspeople at the base of the mountain to praise her as we do. When they don't, when they see her as a witch and blame her when several young boys climb the mountain and fall to their deaths, we still take Junta's side because she has already captured our hearts.

But in the end, it is Junta's very beauty that leads to her downfall. An attractive scholar travels to the mountain town, falls in love with her, and, thinking that the villagers will accept Junta if they understand that she is the source of light, leads them to the crystals. But the townspeople are greedy and take all the gems for themselves, leaving none for Junta. Her mountain path grows dark, and she falls, plunging from the peak into a flowerbed on the mountainside.

A beautiful woman killed by others' greed. A beautiful woman killed by love. A beautiful woman killed by nature. A beautiful woman slips and falls.

When she is twenty-two years old, Riefenstahl sees an image that drastically changes her life. She stands on the subway platform, favoring the foot she hurt dancing, waiting for a train to take her to a doctor who is going to treat her injury.

A poster catches her eye, an advertisement for a film. A man is climbing over a towering mountain chimney. Minutes later, Riefenstahl is in the theater watching *Mountain of Destiny*. Clouds, rocks, alpine slopes, and mountains flash before her eyes. She is captivated by their force and power. Sitting in the darkness, she commits those vivid black-and-white images to memory. "I had made up my mind to get to know those mountains," she writes in her memoir (42). She decides to become an actress.

Riefenstahl spends the next eight years visiting various mountains all over Germany: acting, skiing, climbing, laughing, crying. She learns to climb, to push her body to its limits, to sit in the snow for hours. She comes to the Brenta Dolomites, the mountain range that she uses for her first film, *The Blue Light*. She searches for the best way to amplify nature's natural beauty. She is both Romantic and romantic; she knows the terror of these peaks, their sense of the sublime, but she also feels a kind of nostalgic sentimentality. The forests, the lakes, the animals all remind her of the fairy tales of her childhood, so she tugs on her memories for the images that will haunt her and us. As a child she sleepwalked when there was a full moon, so she uses the moon as the leading part in *The Blue Light*. She also invents a special filter that creates a moonlit effect by shooting on infrared film negative. It is organic, pure, striking. Like Junta, whom she plays in her own film, she is bringing light to the world, harvesting crystals of natural desire.

Enter the attractive scholar—or at least, the failed art student. Hitler. He sees *The Blue Light* and approaches Riefenstahl. He wants her. It is debatable whether this desire is sexual, or professional, or both. He has the ability to change everything about her situation, and her reaction upon meeting him is powerful: "I had an almost apocalyptic vision that I was never able to forget. It seemed as if the earth's surface were spreading out in front of me, like a hemisphere that suddenly splits apart in the middle, spewing out an enormous jet of water, so powerful that it touched the sky and shook the earth. I felt quite paralysed" (Riefenstahl 101). It is worth noting the violent naturalism of her vision. Water does the impossible—cracks the earth, rises up, overcomes gravity. Riefenstahl believes she is doing the opposite of falling.

It is the fact that Hitler intimidates Riefenstahl that draws her to him.

Riefenstahl decides to join Hitler and his retinue, becoming a lone female in an all-male pack of wolves. She travels in an exclusive circle, positioning herself always in relation to the alpha male, the Führer. She decides to prove the ones who distrust her wrong. She will make a film worthy of his greatness, as good as any demagogue could desire. Employing a crew of one hundred and seventy men, she films the 1934 Reich Party Congress in Nuremberg. The film of this event, *Triumph of the Will*, becomes her magnum opus. She invents new techniques, builds cranes and tracking rails. Thirty cameras are used to capture a rally that will change history forever.

If you have ever seen a documentary about Germany, or any from the 1930s, it is almost certain that you have seen a few moments from *Triumph of the Will*. Young boys, all between the ages of ten and twenty, pound fiery cadences on drums. They are preparing for a daytime rally in the vast Nuremberg Youth Stadium. Their fresh, well-scrubbed faces match their neat attire. They are Hitler Youth. They know nothing of the gas, fires, or purges that will come. They look innocent. Trumpets and flutes join the drums for a fanfare. The boys crane their necks, sit on each other's shoulders, jump as high as they can, desperate to get a peek of their Führer. Hands turn almost simultaneously across the stadium as Hitler makes his way through the excited throng. He is handed flowers plucked from fields all over the Reich. At the podium, he stands with his hands interlaced, eyeing the massive crowd. He seems pleased with himself. He has persuaded these people of something that is never quite said. Perhaps he has persuaded them to accept *her*. Close-ups of smiling boys' faces appear on the center of the screen. They clap, drum, and stomp in unison. Hitler steps into his car, driving through their salutes. The camera pulls back from the crowd. There are miles and miles of Hitler Youth; the mass is never-ending.

Triumph of the Will dramatically elevates Reifenstahl's status. She wins multiple cinematic awards, and personal accolades from Hitler. She has given him an image to reflect and consolidate his ambition. She has given him his light.

A beautiful woman slips and falls.

In 1933, Joseph Goebbels is appointed Propaganda Minister for the Third Reich. His preference for propaganda tends towards the subtle and artsy. Hitler, on the other hand, wants a more direct approach: blunt, explicit expressions of desire. What makes him "sick," he reportedly says, is "political propaganda hiding under the guise of art. Let it be either art or politics" (qtd. in Welch 37). Goebbels takes issue with this rejection of artfulness. He thinks that "the moment a person is conscious of propaganda, propaganda becomes ineffective" (qtd. in Welch 38).

In his book, *Propaganda and the German Cinema: 1933-1945*, David Welch characterizes these different approaches as "lie direct" and "lie indirect" (37, 38). We are perhaps used to thinking of *Triumph of the Will* as a clear instance of "lie direct," as an expression of the National Socialist point of view. In the film itself, Goebbels says, "May the bright flame of our enthusiasm never be extinguished. It alone gives light and warmth to the creative art of modern political propaganda." For a man interested in subtlety, it's a pretty direct sentiment.

In 1965, Riefenstahl is interviewed by Charles Wasserman for the Canadian Broadcasting Corporation, who asks if she knew of Hitler's plans. She stiffens, her eyes widen, and she jolts in her chair. Her voice peaks like her faithful mountains, then drops below the surface. She protests. She says she was unaware. Then she is suddenly calm and ladylike again. When she talks craft, she is a new woman, recalling exactly how each shot was achieved, the color of the filter, the brand name of the camera, and how many rolls of footage were used. She is wholly different from the defensive, self-justifying woman who first argued that *Triumph of the Will* was a documentary, and then said "Reality doesn't interest me." Wasserman asks her if she believes *Triumph of the Will* is a propaganda film. She stiffens again and responds in choppy English: "If I would see this film today, after we know everything what happened, I would say yes. In this time, '34, natural no, because a propaganda film must have a commentator . . . I only made what I have seen, and I have spoken nothing, only the natural things" (CBC).

If Riefenstahl can't classify *Triumph of the Will*, how can we be expected to? It is a shocking comment in a number of ways. What was Goebbels in her film if not a commentator? What is a director—if not an arranging, composing, commenting hand? Yet what seems even more shocking is the afterthought of her answer, that almost offhand characterization—"only the natural things." The rally, then, was natural. She says it so coolly, as if she had stepped outside to film a mountain. And how does one film only the natural but not care for the political reality?

In *Triumph of the Will*, it is the filming itself that transforms reality into fantasy. Her craft makes it so. The way the crowd falls at Hitler's knees, the way he is flown in from the clouds on a plane, the salutes, the chants, the drumming, the coordination of the marching—it is all a form of beauty. In the world of Riefenstahl's film, everything becomes rhythmic and harmonious, takes on the easy symmetry of a natural world. She cannot admit that this rhythm, and that the film's transformation of the "natural," comes from her technical skill.

To admit that *Triumph of the Will* is beautiful is a difficult thing to do now. We can't look at Riefenstahl's film without the hindsight history provides, without the knowledge of all the horror and pain these young boys would go on to inflict on others. Yet is it fair—to her, to our understanding of art—to see so much beauty in *The Blue Light*, and ignore it in her next film? It's true that on the surface of it, *The Blue Light* and *Triumph of the Will* seem like very different films. One is set in nature, the other in a city. One captures solitude, the other seeks the collective. One follows a woman, the other a crowd of young men. One is about being undone. The other is about being overcome, transfigured, made whole. We could say that Hitler ruined Riefenstahl with her second film, set her off on a course from which she never recovered. She slipped, thinking all the while that she was rising upward. But *The Blue Light* and *Triumph of the Will* are twins, in a way, even if they are fraternal, not identical. In each, the light is a source of obsession. In each, Riefenstahl focuses on the purity of desire. Men lust after something greater, something that is exciting, captivating, and deadly for all parties involved. They see the crystals and Hitler as heavenly gifts, given to them in a time of need. Perhaps we overlook the similarities between the films because her love of nature, which is so present in *The Blue Light*, veils a number of problematic "truths," including the notion that man can be so easily persuaded to destroy the thing he loves. We could say that *The Blue Light* is Lie Indirect, and *The Triumph of the Will* is Lie Direct. But to make this kind of distinction seems spurious. We—or rather, I—don't want to. I want to assume instead that there is a clear distinction between the beauty in one film and the beauty in the other. Junta seems so far away from Nuremberg. How can this goddess be the same as the boys in the stadium? I do not want to believe that both are natural in the same way.

We might think Riefenstahl has solved the problem herself with her next film, *Olympia*, a four-hour black and white movie comprised of two parts, *Fest der Völker* (Festival of the People) and *Fest der Schönheit* (Festival of Beauty), which documents the 1936 Olympics in Berlin. The Prologue sets the scene of the games' origin, the camera tracking through temple ruins and classical statues: we are in ancient Greece. The camera settles on a statue of a discus thrower. In slow dissolve, the statue comes to life in the form of a German decathlon champion. The camera moves to show other classical sports, each dissolving from marble and stillness into flesh and movement. The shot-put thrower tosses the ball in a rhythmic, dance-like motion. His hands dissolve and are replaced by the feminine hands of a dancer. Nude women circle around each other, throwing their hands in the air (though the camera angle hides her face, Riefenstahl is one of these women). They line up; only their hands extend out. From the ground, a flame rises. It encloses the women, yet they are untouched. The flame becomes the Olympic torch. These are women come down from the mountaintop, transfigured, immortal. History comes alive through the lens of Riefenstahl's camera and with one, simple technique. It takes one cut in an editing room to bleed the past into the present, to connect the Greek gods with the German athletes of 1936. The statues themselves are also lies—"direct" or "indirect," it doesn't matter. Riefenstahl is able to reach backwards in time and reconstitute, reread history, cinematically exemplifying the long-standing superiority of the Aryan body. The Olympic Games provided the perfect opportunity for the Nazis to display their supposed dominance over all races, and they won more medals than any other country that year. We see Hitler in the crowd, watching the events, his presence somehow overshadowing the athletes. Even when he is not there, he is. She barely lingers on his face, but one shot is enough. In the film, the athletes' natural beauty is accentuated, almost sharpened, by the dominant political atmosphere. The body is, indisputably, a "natural thing," but the sources of its power, here, are dangerously unclear.

Riefenstahl spends eighteen months in the cutting room, stitching together thousands of black and white negatives to make *Olympia*. She forgoes meals and sleep. She is so focused that she says she misses the political change that is occurring outside her office (Riefenstahl 213).

World War II begins. Riefenstahl attempts to make another film as the battles rage on. Her brother dies fighting. It takes her years to make another film, and when it is finally completed, the French confiscate it. She is labeled a Nazi sympathizer and held for four years by the Americans and French for de-Nazification. She protests, says she is innocent, but no one believes her.

Six thousand miles away in the United States, another artist, Ansel Adams, spends these years looking over his own photographs in his lab. He is also interested in capturing the natural. His Sierra Mountains are Riefenstahl's Dolomites. He is another technical obsessive. In the 1930s, Adams masters the manipulation of darkness and sunlight, using it to elevate the natural wildness through seasons and spaces. Using a large depth of field, his black-and-white photographs capture oak trees in snowstorms, branches above clouds, lakes and trees in front of endless mountains. And like

Riefenstahl, Adams had a similar epochal awakening, a realization akin to the one she had standing on that subway platform in 1924.

It is interesting to note that both Riefenstahl and Adams had other life plans. Riefenstahl wanted to pursue dancing further, and Adams wanted to be a pianist. But Riefenstahl injured her foot, and Adams' family could not pay for the expensive lessons. The tiniest twist of fate intervened: Riefenstahl saw a poster and Adams was given a book about Yosemite. "From that day," Adams writes in 1916, "my life has been colored and modulated by the great earth gesture of the Sierra (qtd. in Turnage "Adams"). Both Adams and Riefenstahl found a new source of beauty and never looked back, and if you look closely, you begin to see patterns between Adams's photographs and Riefenstahl's films; they are attracted to the sublime sense of power in nature. Waterfalls, clouds, and mountains take on a greater meaning, become driving forces in their work.

If Adams and Riefenstahl are comparable, then there is recognizable evidence that Riefenstahl is not the only person to create a world where politics lurks beneath the natural world. Adams's majestic pictures now represent the cause of wilderness protection in the popular imagination. The Sierra Club uses his photographs to advertise. But Adams would only be considered a propagandist by the most churlish. If he is known as one thing other than an artist, it is simply an environmentalist. It makes sense that the Nazis were environmentalists. They advocated vegetarianism, organic agriculture, and forest preservation. During their rule, the Nazis maintained the idea of "Blood and Soil": a nationalist ideology, popularized by race theorist Richard Walther Darré, that advocated rural living and valued the German Aryan peasantry above urban dwellers and immigrants. The Nazis were desperate to regain the sacred land that their predecessors had held. They saw the forest in relation to themselves: strong, healthy, and far-reaching. Yet if Riefenstahl is known as one thing other than as a female artist, it is as a Nazi. Had she chosen to continue with the fantasy stories of her childhood, her life, her legacy would have ended with her art. The irony is that her lack of awareness destroyed her career—but now, she will never be forgotten. For Riefenstahl, her art has been "saved" because it is the "lie direct." *The Blue Light* is only watched because of *Triumph of the Will*.

Riefenstahl is only in the news again these days because of the supposed directness of that lie. When Kathryn Bigelow released *Zero Dark Thirty* in 2012, the noted feminist polemicist Naomi Woolf accused Bigelow of being the American Riefenstahl of her time because of her supportive—or at least neutral—portrayal of torture and the CIA's tactics in the hunt for Osama Bin

Laden. Wolf argued that Bigelow made "heroes and heroines out of people who committed violent crimes against other people based on their race." And, perhaps because there are so few well-known female film directors, Wolf found it easy to draw a distinct line from Bigelow to Riefenstahl. In a letter to the *Los Angeles Times*, Bigelow addressed Wolf's criticism: "Those of us who work in the arts know that depiction is not endorsement. If it was, no artist would be able to paint inhumane practices, no author could write about them, and no filmmaker could delve into the thorny subjects of our time." By her logic, Bigelow needed to show the interrogator—capable of stringing a man up for days—striding through very ordinary corridors in Washington, casually sitting with departmental heads in the CIA. She needed to make this man's passage between our world and another shadow world so natural that we would in turn reject it as unbelievable—and reflect, in turn, on our own shock (in a way, this sense of moral "dissolve" is very similar to *Olympia*). It's the last part of Bigelow's justification that seems debatable—can she really rely so faithfully on an audience's capacity for self-reflection? She seems to want to think that *Zero Dark Thirty* will influence our thinking without its making a direct statement or endorsement, that we will be fascinated enough with her craft to offer our own interpretation.

What the comparison between Bigelow and Riefenstahl does reveal is that these women will be remembered, not because they are women, but because as women they are able to take on such grandiose subjects and master their art so well that it tugs at our heartstrings. These heartstrings are not the lovely, gushy ones that are manipulated by many female directors like Nancy Meyers and Nora Ephron, but the deeper emotions of pain, horror, regret, and those that are tied up in much bigger events that we carry with us, that are released in the darkness of the cinema. These women might say that they filmed whatever their talent found available, but it appears their talent is (their) tragedy. They bring out the upper case in us—the defensive desire to think of Lies and Women and Propaganda. Even if they don't want to, they make us aware that what we are watching might be dangerous, might be insidious, might be a lie that brings out an even more uncomfortable truth.

In 1962, at age sixty, Riefenstahl travels to the Sudan in search of new beauty, this time in the form of a Sudanese tribe, the Nuba. She makes short films and takes thousands of photographs of these natural, dark, nearly naked humans. The Nuba are physically flawless. The oil on their large muscular bodies glistens in the sunlight. The way they dance is slow, rhythmic. They bring Riefenstahl some renewed prominence. Critics say she is exploiting the

Nuba, using their beauty to absolve her previous transgressions. Yet Riefenstahl never saw her earlier work as a transgression; she was invited to film an event and used the talent she had. It seems, rather, that it was mutually beneficial. She used Hitler for his status, and he used her for her sheer talent. They both benefited and they both suffered.

Adams has been criticized for the lack of human presence in his pictures, but this absence has also ultimately saved him. We think the human form—however natural—has not "corrupted" his art. We are, supposedly, not able to see ourselves in his pictures. But humans are in the forefront of Riefenstahl's films and photos. We can see, in Riefenstahl's decision to photograph the Nuba, her desire to become Junta again. Critics and historians label her as immoral, as failing to adhere to accepted moral standards. But it is only after studying this woman, watching her films, listening to interviews that I realize something so minute that it is easily overlooked. She is not immoral, but amoral. Or rather, she thinks herself amoral. Riefenstahl saw her subjects only through her camera lens. Beauty blinded her judgment. She never took a moment to step back, to step aside. She was not aware another eye would ever evaluate her because she controlled every part of the process so intently. She saw the human body as natural, but then she went and filmed thousands of bodies doing very unnatural things. Maybe this is why we punished her. We can't face the fact that the Hitler Youth believed that what they would go on to do was, in their minds, natural. We see them as barbaric, as creatures who are not humans. We, "the good ones," could never do that. And yet Riefenstahl provides clear proof that humans can. It is a haunting thought. Riefenstahl does not show any of the cruelty. How could she? At the time, she didn't know what was to come. But her art will be forever wrapped up in a historical event that cannot be forgotten. She was on the wrong side of history, and for that her art will both perish and be saved.

It is almost funny to think that all of this might never have happened. To think that so much was set in motion by a twist of an ankle is haunting. In many ways it's easy to believe that this was her twist of fate, that she was destined to play a part in history. But what does that say about the nature of creativity? That art will always be overshadowed by history? Should creativity be sequestered from history? Yet art is self-expression, and so separation between artists, history, and their art is really impossible. When it comes time to critique such connections, one also comes up against the complexity of the individual; Riefenstahl, in particular, contained so many lives. We need to know who she was before *Triumph of the Will*, because it is only then that we can sense her multiple transformations. Beyond the murky ethics that overtake our discussions of her work, Riefenstahl's art reveals more about the world than we want to know. It is almost too unbearable to admit that both the Nuba and the Nazis can exist simultaneously in the same filmmaker's world.

At age seventy-two, Riefenstahl takes up underwater photography and learns to scuba dive in Africa. In the Indian Ocean, she finds a different world. The creatures below only see her as a human. They can't understand her past. They don't know who she is. She is alone. Again, she has returned to water. The power of this image brings me back to the image she created when she first saw Hitler: *a hemisphere that suddenly splits apart in the middle, spewing out an enormous jet of water*. Now there is no violence, no spewing forth, not even the crashing of the waterfall that first began her career. This new picture is silent, calm, a fluid movement. She has survived the dive, almost in spite of herself. She spends the rest of her life paddling, trying only to support herself so she can get enough air to breathe.

In her debut as an actress, in *The Holy Mountain* in 1926, Riefenstahl plays Diotima, a dancer, who begins an affair with a skier. Before venturing on a ski trip that will ultimately end in his death, Karl is warned: "You seek Gods – but it's people you must find." It seems, knowing what choices she was to make, that these words were better suited for Riefenstahl, who sought out the Gods, who believed she had found one in Hitler. I don't think she even realized how symbolic her life was, how that line of dialogue and how her first film had mapped out her history. She saw a poster for the *Mountain of Destiny*. She stood no chance against kismet.

I think if she had waited, if she had taken a step back, if she hadn't been so "spontaneous," so blinded by beauty, she would never have stepped inside that theater. But I don't think she would have had it any other way.

WORKS CITED:

Bigelow, Kathryn. "Kathryn Bigelow Addresses '*Zero Dark Thirty*' Torture Criticism." *Los Angeles Times* 15 Jan. 2013. Web. 20 Apr. 2013

The Blue Light [*Das blaue Licht*]. Dir. Leni Riefenstahl. Perf. Leni Riefenstahl, Max Wieman. DuWorld Pictures (USA), 1932. Film.

Canadian Broadcasting Corporation. "Leni Riefenstahl in her Own Words." CBC Digital Archives, 11 May 1965. Web. 23 Apr. 2013.

The Holy Mountain [*Der heilige Berg*]. Dir. Arnold Fanck. Perf. Leni Riefenstahl, Luis Trenker, Frida Richard. Universum Film UFA, 1926. Film.

The Mountain of Destiny [*Der Berg des Schicksals*]. Dir. Arnold Fanck. Perf. Hannes Schneider, Frida Richard, Erna Morena. Berg-und Sportfilm, 1924. Film.

Olympia. Dir. Leni Riefenstahl. Tobis Filmkunst, 1938. Film.

Riefenstahl, Leni. *A Memoir*. New York: Picador, 1995. Print.

Sontag, Susan. "Fascinating Fascism." *Under the Sign of Saturn*. New York: Picador, 2002. Print.

Triumph of the Will [*Triumph des Willens*]. Dir. Leni Riefenstahl. Universum Film AG, 1935. Film.

Turnage, Robert. "Ansel Adams: The Role of the Artist in the Environmentalist Movement." *The Ansel Adams Gallery*. Web. 14 June 2013.

Welch, David. *Propaganda and the German Cinema: 1933-1945*. London: I.B Tauris, 2001. Print.

Wolf, Naomi. "A Letter to Kathryn Bigelow on Zero Dark Thirty's Apology for Torture." *The Guardian* Apr. 2013. Web. 19 Apr. 2013.

Zero Dark Thirty. Dir. Kathryn Bigelow. Perf. Jessica Chastain. Columbia Pictures, 2012. Film.

Opening the Door

HOPE WHITE

Sunlight falls upon an orange tabby cat stretched out on a table. Surrounded by several cube-like structures made of slender bamboo sticks, he playfully bats at them while lying on his back. Behind the cat are three men. One of them is renowned Chinese artist Ai Weiwei.

"Let's start," Ai softly suggests. "We have a lot of dogs and cats," he tells his interviewer. "Out of the forty cats, one knows how to open doors." He continues, "If I'd never met this cat that can open doors, I wouldn't know cats could open doors."

The camera shifts from Ai to a stark white door. Beneath it is an orange cat, perhaps the same cat as before. The cat looks up at the handle, prepares himself, and leaps up to pull down on the lever. The door pops open, and the cat slips outside.

All of this takes only two and a half minutes, but the sequence feels much longer as a result of the camera's slow, deliberate movements. We are already mesmerized by Ai's world before any of the action begins. Alternating between scenes of gallery installations and Ai's playful rebellion against China's harsh government, American filmmaker Alison Klayman's documentary *Ai Weiwei: Never Sorry* follows Ai over the course of three years as he rises from a member of China's cultural elite to an international superstar of art and activism. Under China's repressive regime, with its strict censorship policies, Ai was forced to turn to the international stage and gain his popularity primarily through his blog and Twitter account. With the help of these social media utilities, Ai conducted a massive investigation into the government cover-up of thousands of children's deaths in the 2008 Sichuan earthquake, petitioned his Internet followers to record themselves reciting the names of the victims, and created several art installations inspired by the events, spreading awareness to millions (Ai and Klayman). The Chinese government began to watch Ai with ever-increasing scrutiny as Klayman filmed the documentary.

Never Sorry treats Ai as an artistic genius. If his work had not first been encountered with prior awareness of the current sociopolitical issues in China, one might easily have written him off as not much of an artist at all. Consider Ai's exhibit *Sunflower Seeds* at London's Tate Modern from 2010 to 2011: to the uninformed visitor it looks as if the artist took a trip to Costco, purchased a bunch of sunflower seeds in bulk, and poured them onto the gallery floor. The one hundred million black-and-white striped husks look real, but they are in fact made of porcelain and hand-painted by 1,600 Chinese workers hired by Ai ("Sunflower Seeds"). While virtually any "Made in China" product could have been used to represent China's mass production of goods, Ai deliberately chose sunflower seeds for both personal and political reasons. He grew up in a rural area during Mao Zedong's Cultural Revolution of the 1960s and 70s, where ubiquitous "propaganda images depicted Chairman Mao as the sun and the mass of people of China as sunflowers" beneath him ("Unilever"). But despite the oppression and restriction associated with Mao's reign, "Ai remembers the sharing of sunflower seeds as a gesture of human compassion" ("Interpretation"). When viewed through the layers of cultural context and personal associations that define it, *Sunflower Seeds* morphs from intellectual garbage to evocative sculpture. Ai's predominant goal throughout his entire body of work is to encourage free speech and the sharing of ideas in China, instead of dogmatic belief in one particular ideology. The seeds encourage us to celebrate our individuality and in doing so condemn mass production—not of goods, necessarily—but of the identities of individual citizens.

But what makes this work so compèlling (and it is) as evidenced by the multitude of visitors pouring into the museum from all over the world, is that an extensive knowledge of Chinese history is not necessary to appreciate the installation. Klayman demonstrates the approachability and joy of Ai's artwork when considered apart from its inspiration by first introducing us to *Sunflower Seeds* in the Tate with little contextual information, the same way many museum visitors would encounter it in real life. There is no barrier between the museum-goers and the work. *Sunflower Seeds* invites its viewers to interact with it by walking on or lying in the seeds. For these visitors, Ai's exhibition is more reminiscent of a picnic in Central Park than a trip to the museum. By capturing the variegated nature of the viewing experience, the film shows us how Ai's installation alters our preconceived notions about how art can be experienced.

Klayman reminds us that despite the sensationalism that surrounds him, Ai is not only China's top maverick but also China's most popular artist.

Though Klayman states in an interview with *PBS NewsHour*'s Jeffrey Brown that she sees Ai as an artist "first and foremost," Ai responds that he cannot define himself only as an "artist or as a so-called activist," because he does not know "what [he] will be next." "But to him," Klayman later asks Brown, "what is the definition of an artist? It's someone who is interested in communication, who is interested in engagement, who has to be talking about things that are relevant to the world around him or her." By this definition, Ai is surely an artist, but this definition of the word "artist" is nearly indistinguishable from that of "activist," one who "advocates or engages in action" (*OED*). Ai's seemingly dual identity makes it difficult to analyze his work as either a product of protest or as a work of art.

But it is important to realize that Klayman and Ai are not in personal conflict. In fact, their disagreement stems from an ideological debate about art that dates as far back as the Renaissance. Various fine arts academies established during that time sought to define art, once and for all: they established "ideologies, rules, [and] procedures" to help pin down the concept (Boime 203). Esteemed art theorist Albert Boime, however, asserts in his essay "The Cultural Politics of the Art Academy" that such institutions aimed to resolve more than traditional "stylistic or practical issues" and "function[ed] as part of a distinct social and political agenda" (203). In the contemporary art world (outside China), the Academy's definition of art is no longer enforced and has become increasingly malleable. According to artist Marcel Duchamp, whom Ai claims to be his biggest influence, "anything can be turned into an object of art if the artist decides it to be" (qtd. in Dercon and Lorz 7). Duchamp and Ai's take on art contrasts starkly with the traditional beliefs set forth by the academies of Europe (which regarded painting as the highest medium), as well as the Fine Arts Academy of the People's Republic of China, which exists, in part, to prevent the vocalization of dissent through art (Boime 211). In *Never Sorry*, Beijing-based artist Chen Danqing tells Klayman that Ai is "not the kind of person we are familiar with in China. He doesn't work within the system. He's just himself." It is clear from Danqing's usage of "we" and "he" that Ai is in a category all by himself in the context of Chinese contemporary art—or, perhaps, he is undefinable because he is not simply "just an artist."

The beauty of *Never Sorry* is that it presents the information necessary to make an informed decision on where to draw the line between art and activism. The Academy, rather, forces the viewer to believe one view over the other. Many of Ai's installations selected for the film, like *Sunflower Seeds*, can be interpreted as either as activist *or* artistic. Another such example is *He Xie*, a pile of 3,200 porcelain crabs on display in the Hirshhorn Museum and

Sculpture Garden in Washington, D.C. (Ai and Klayman). The inspiration for the piece clearly comes from a moment in *Never Sorry* when Ai invites his Twitter followers to a feast of 10,000 river crabs following the government's unexplained announcement that it would demolish Ai's newly-built studio in Beijing that the authorities had in fact invited him to build there. Why crabs? They are "laced with political satire," we are told in the interview with Brown. In Mandarin, the word river crab sounds the same as the ubiquitous government slogan "harmonious society." Ai's sarcastic pun points out the government's hypocrisy in calling their highly restricted society "harmonious," highlighting the fact that this perceived harmony is actually a result of governmental force rather than of free will. With the government's impending demolition of Ai's property, the river crab becomes the perfect entree to protest the restriction of individual rights.

He Xie also demonstrates Ai's obsession with using massive quantities of a given material in his artwork: both *He Xie* and *Sunflower Seeds* use a vast number of small symbolic items to create a single installation. In the work of a social and political activist, it seems apt to consider this habit as representative of Ai's interest in the concept of individual citizens who come together to form a cohesive society. In an interview about *Sunflower Seeds*, Ai says he feels that the seeds reflect what he is doing on Twitter in that they represent the sharing of information among individuals. Though Ai's statement is more of a contemplation of the piece itself than a description of his underlying intention, it nevertheless implies that he recognizes the value of social media's power to disseminate information to people around the world easily and quickly. In fact, the truest expression of Ai's artistic goals occurs via Twitter because through this medium his clever messages and offbeat images force his followers to pause and reflect not only in a museum or gallery but out in the world where politics and policy truly matter.

And yet Ai's Tweets, though there are many in the film, are not highlighted as works of art in Klayman's account. They function only as transitions during moments of conflict and high intensity in the film's narrative. The structure of *Never Sorry* has a distinct pattern that repeats itself throughout the film's length: first, we see Ai in his studio or installing a work in a gallery, then an incident in which he acts out against the Chinese government (often supplemented by footage from his own documentaries), and then the Tweets that Ai posted during or after the event. This habitual sequence unfortunately makes his online statements seem more like afterthoughts or commentaries than integral components of his artistic process. But Klayman does not completely ignore the power of online media: in the director's commentary of

Never Sorry's DVD, she describes Twitter as a "tool" for change in China and encourages us to think about the possibilities of Twitter in the U.S. (*Never Sorry*). The power of Twitter, she adds, depends on the context in which it is used and how you "curate" your Tweets. What makes Ai's Tweets so powerful is the large number of supporters they have earned him. His online communication encourages participation in the process of making change and, of most importance, teaches Chinese citizens about "using resources," as Ai calls it, in order to do so (*Never Sorry*). Klayman does use an artistic vocabulary to explain Ai's use of Twitter, but the fact that her acknowledgement of the power of Ai's Tweets is buried in the director's commentary rather than being highlighted in the movie points to a need for a greater analysis of social media's role in activism in order to fully understand Ai as an artist.

Popular writer and journalist Malcolm Gladwell examines the effects of social media on activism in his *New Yorker* article "Small Change: Why the Revolution Will Not Be Tweeted." Gladwell seeks to prepare us for the imminent failures of this social media revolution and to make us critical of activists' use of Twitter as a tool for change. Gladwell does not outright dismiss the benevolent intentions of today's activists but rather points out a difference in the amount of change contemporary activism elicits compared to activism of the past. According to Gladwell, radical change has not been produced by Twitter activism because social media activists ask very little of us (3). Mareike Schomerus of the London School of Economics and Political Science agrees with this analysis and deems the social media method of change "slacktivism" because it "implies that by clicking on a link and forwarding something you have done your share" (qtd. in "Kony2012"). The guilt we create through documentaries and other modes of persuasion is relieved too easily through sharing, and the desire to go out in the world and act is thereby eliminated.

Invisible Children, Inc.'s *Kony2012* campaign, which set out to make Ugandan war criminal Joseph Kony infamous for his crimes, exemplifies Gladwell's claim that large numbers of online supporters do not necessarily produce big change. Jason Russell's documentary prompted the world to spread awareness on Facebook and Twitter. His message went viral within 24 hours, receiving just shy of one billion views as of this writing (Russell). Though Russell portrays himself as leading a massive movement for change and actually achieving something of merit, he is in reality decidedly not. Despite all the followers, likes, and shares, there has been almost no change on the ground in Uganda, and "Kony is still at large" and active; the viral sensation that was *Kony2012* is now largely forgotten (Barcia).

The big difference between Ai and Russell is that Ai's use of social media extends well beyond "slacktivism." Instead of making us feel as if we are making a difference simply by donating or sharing a link as Russell does, Ai makes us critically aware that we are not doing anything to produce change by consuming his Tweets. Rather than trying to get each and every one of his followers to feel as if they are producing change, Ai only seeks to point out that change is necessary; by giving us less, Ai tells us we need to do more. His ability to awaken a deathless desire for revolution in his followers, something Russell's fading movement has not done, frightens the Chinese government immensely, as is evident in their attempts to silence and censor him. "What can they do to me? None other than deportation, kidnapping, and imprisonment . . . or make me completely vanish," Ai tweeted in November 2009 ("Top Ten"). In early 2011, Ai did in fact disappear. We later discovered that he had been detained by the government for "tax evasion." He was released eighty-one days later, and his return home is somberly depicted at the end of *Never Sorry*. The prescient Tweet served to turn his eventual political oppression into a kind of artistic performance, one that prompted his followers and others to think more carefully about the Chinese government's censorship.

Until his goals for China are achieved, Ai will not stop. Rather than proposing a simple solution, and telling us how to solve our problems as other activists do, Ai works to *show* us what needs to be changed. While activism endeavors to persuade us that something needs to be changed, social media only allows these ideas to permeate our personal networks. However, such ideas are not close enough to our hearts for them to incite effective action. This is why art, in any form—whether it is sculpture or Tweets—is necessary. It asks us first to feel, and only after, to think. Ai Weiwei's art wins our hearts with its wit and its solicitations to contemplate the state of things. For now, we spread ideas through social media; Ai shows us through his artful approaches that we must act on them.

Never Sorry doesn't have a happy ending, and it doesn't offer us an opportunity to turn things around as Russell does. When Ai returns from his imprisonment, reporters follow him down the road, their cameras illuminating a remarkably skinnier and wearier Ai than the one we have known throughout the film. He is under strict orders not to speak with them and closes the door in their faces as well as ours; we learn in the next moment, though, that Ai is not defeated even in his temporary silence. Within months he is Tweeting and speaking to the press again.

Like the cat in the opening scene of the film, Ai uses social media as a lever to open the door to China. Just as Ai says he would not have known cats could open doors until he saw one cat do it, much of the world did not know that it is possible to spread the seeds of change within China until Ai made himself a household name through his pioneering art and social media presence.

Klayman's ending offers us a frustratingly perfect image; there is still more to be accomplished in China. We must see that important doors are still closed and important statements still go unsaid. Ai appears to be a tragic figure in our final glimpse of him. But if *Never Sorry* offered a happy ending, we as viewers would not be inspired to do the hard work of opening our own doors to change.

WORKS CITED

"Activist." Def. 2b. *OED Online*. Oxford UP, 2013. Web. 30 Mar 2013.

Ai Weiwei: Never Sorry. Dir. Alison Klayman. Perf. Ai Weiwei. MPI, 2012. DVD.

Ai Weiwei. "Ai Weiwei: Sunflower Seeds" Embedded video. *The Unilever Series: Ai Weiwei: Sunflower Seeds*. Tate Modern, 22 Oct. 2010. Web. 14 June 2013.

"Ai Weiwei's Top 10 Tweets." *The Telegraph* 5 May 2011. Web. 5 Apr. 2013.

Ai, Weiwei, and Alison Klayman. Interview by Jeffrey Brown. "Art, China, and Censorship According to Ai Weiwei." *PBS NewsHour*. PBS, 11 Dec. 2012. Web. 27 Mar. 2012.

Barcia, Manuel. "Whatever Happened to Kony 2102?" *Al Jazeera*. Al Jazeera America, 18 Jan. 2013. Web. 4 Apr. 2013.

Boime, Albert. "The Cultural Politics of the Art Academy." *The Eighteenth Century* 35.3 (1994): 203-22. *JSTOR*. Web. 6 Apr. 2013.

Dercon, Chris and Julienne Lorz. "So Sorry." *Ai Weiwei: So Sorry*. Munich: Prestel, 2009. 7. Print.

Gladwell, Malcolm. "Small Change: Why the Revolution Will Not Be Tweeted." *The New Yorker* 4 Oct. 2012: 42-49. Web. 1 Apr. 2013.

"'Kony 2012' and the future of activism." *Al Jazeera*. Al Jazeera America, 11 Mar. 2012. Web. 4 Apr. 2013.

Russell, Jason. "KONY2012." Online video clip. *YouTube*. Invisible Children, Inc., 2012. Web.

"The Unilever Series: Ai Weiwei: Sunflower Seeds: Interpretation Text." *Tate Modern*. Web. 1 Apr. 2013.

Medicating the Cultural Subconscious

JACQUELINE YI

Johnny was a difficult child, always screaming, running, and rough-housing, much to his parents' dismay. He could not sit still to watch a single television show or focus on playing with his action figures for more than a few minutes at a time before he was up and about again, being disruptive and, on rare occasions, destroying his toys and other items around the house. When his mother told him to hold her hand while walking across a busy street or to stay close to her cart at the grocery store, Johnny disobeyed. His mother would think to herself, "I guess he's just a runaround, rowdy kid." But as he grew into an adolescent, Johnny increasingly found himself in "time outs" or scolded by his parents and teachers. He felt terrible about being a disappointment, and despite his efforts to be good, he continued to misbehave. Eventually the doctors became involved, and Johnny was diagnosed with attention deficit hyperactivity disorder (ADHD). The doctors assured Johnny and his parents that ADHD was not a rare condition: 11% of school aged children—roughly 5 million American children—are diagnosed with ADHD, and about two-thirds receive psychoactive medical treatments such as Ritalin and Adderall stimulants, which alter a child's brain chemistry in such a way that he becomes more docile and focused (Schwartz 1). This number seems so alarmingly high that many people have begun to question what drives this prevalance of ADHD in our culture. Are there just more Johnnys out there today, or could this incredible rise in diagnoses be the result of something more troubling?

Recently, numerous documentaries and talk shows have raised public awareness of the disorder, and now that ADHD has become more familiar, some might not be alarmed about the high percentage of children diagnosed with ADHD. What, really, is the worst that could happen if a lot of children are "hyperactive"? The title seems harmless, but a medical diagnosis of ADHD becomes a lifelong label. Most children with ADHD continue to take Ritalin or Adderall into adulthood, creating a huge dilemma: if the child were to stop showing hyperactive symptoms, would doctors be able to know decisively whether the drugs had cured him or if he had simply aged out of his hyperactivity? Our current solutions to ADHD seem quite straightforward: if you have symptoms A, B, and C, take pill X to get better. It is a tangible, logical solution—one that is simple and reasonable considering our limited resources, However, these pills, although shown to make dramatic differences in children's behavior, are not entirely safe and come with a multitude of known side-effects and many unanswered questions. What are the long term effects on a child's developing brain? Could we be altering children's personalities just to make them more manageable?

According to psychiatrist Sami Timimi's thoughtful but adamant argument in "ADHD is Best Understood as a Social Construct," the rapid increase in ADHD diagnoses can be partly attributed to the current state of the medical field, with its unreliable "profit-dependent pharmaceutical industry" (8). Marcia Angell digs deeper into the pharmaceutical industry's ties to mental health care in her essay "The Epidemic of Mental Illness, Why?" Angell assesses arguments offered by three critics—ranging from concerned to outraged—of the pharmaceutical indsutry, and she sides with their critiques. There is immense bias in the accessible research on mental disorder treatments because "drug companies make very sure that their positive studies are published in medical journals and doctors know about them, while the negative ones often languish unseen within the FDA" (Angell). As a result of flawed studies and misleading or incomplete medical literature, there are many ineffective and possibly dangerous antipsychotic drugs on the market today, some of which have been shown to create long-lasting differences in brain function—such as a compromise of neuronal pathways and shrinkage in the cerebral cortex. With this kind of evidence available, you would think that the rate of medical ADHD interventions would decrease in an effort to protect our children.

With such high stakes, we need a deeper, more sustained investigation of mental disorders and the way we treat them. Timimi advocates for a "cultural perspective" to "explain the recent rise, to epidemic proportions, of rates of diagnosis of ADHD" (8). He theorizes that rather than being an objective mental illness, ADHD is a social construct—a permanent label that we put on individuals who do not meet the societal standards of how a "normal" person thinks and behaves. We give the ADHD label to a "runaround kid" like Johnny, who becomes restless and reckless after sitting in class all day. But what causes Johnny to behave this way in the first place? We all agree that a child's mental health can be negatively affected by a "loss of extended family support," "pressure on schools, a breakdown in the moral authority of adults,"

and many more situational aspects of a child's life, but we do not usually recognize these social problems as legitimate triggers of psychiatric disorders
(8). Instead, we use the specific criteria printed in the current United States
version of the Diagnostic and Statistical Manual of Mental Disorders (DSM)
to establish who does or does not get labeled with ADHD. Also, the DSM's
wording is actually quite different from the guidelines printed in the world-
wide manual of disorders, the International Classification of Diseases (ICD).
This discrepancy shows that different cultures have different expectations of
behavior; so do the doctors—human beings with their own definitions and
opinions on how a "normal" child behaves. With all of these varying, circumstantial factors, we are forced to evaluate the validity of an "objective" ADHD
diagnosis, or any mental disorder diagnosis for that matter.

This is not to say that ADHD and other psychological disorders are not
"real," or that the suffering of those who are diagnosed is not legitimate.
ADHD is complex; the social construct theory may explain one child's diagnosis, while another's can be attributed to other factors. We cannot discount
the unlimited number of variables in ADHD diagnosis, and we cannot view
the increase in ADHD only through the lens of biology. Mental illnesses
"cannot be understood without understanding the ideas, habits and predispositions—the idiosyncratic cultural trappings—of the mind that is its host"
(Watters). We must not underestimate how much power the human mind has
over the human body, or how much culture and personal experiences affect
our conception of what is normal and healthy. Johnny's mental health is
affected by the town he grew up in, the parents who raised him, the teachers
who taught him, the siblings and peers who played with him, the television
shows he watched—the list of factors is nearly infinite.

The mental lens through which we view our world is not fixed: the mind
has an immense capacity to alter, complicate, and transform our understanding of the world. It is malleable and ever-changing because *we* are ever-changing. We are masters of adapting to our social environments, and these
changes often happen unconsciously. The subconscious is so strong, has so
much of a hold on our physical selves, that it may lead us into delusion and
can even begin epidemics. Susan Dominus in her essay "What Happened to
the Girls in Le Roy?" employs the term "mass psychogenic illness" to
describe the mental phenomenon found in eighteen schoolgirls from Le Roy,
New York (293, 291). The outbreak started with Katie Krautwurst, a high
school cheerleader and straight-A student who woke up from a nap to discover her chin had begun to twitch uncontrollably. A few weeks later, her best
friend and fellow cheerleader Thera Sanchez began to flail her arms and hit

herself so violently that she constantly had bruises all over her body. In the span of a few months, the tics started to spread throughout the high school social hierarchy, from the popular cheerleaders to the lower-status girls. A neurologist located in Buffalo proposed the diagnosis of "conversion disorder," suggesting that the girls were "subconsciously converting stress into physical symptoms" and spreading these symptoms to their fellow peers (293). This was extremely unsettling to the concerned parents and community of Le Roy; they could not grasp how this invisible, mental process was causing their girls to be so visibly, physically sick: "How could one person's illness be reflected in another person's neural pathways, playing a trick on consciousness, convincing the host that it originated in her own body?" (298). Dominus establishes the role of physiological processes in one of the most important capacities that humans have: "empathy" (298). Through a process called the "chameleon effect," we recognize the emotions and actions of others through the use of "mirror neurons," which fire both when we observe and when we imitate an action performed by another human (298). Our minds use mirror neurons so effectively that in some cases the behavior of others can unconsciously manifest itself in our own physical functions, as demonstrated by the Le Roy girls' mental distress and their resulting physical symptoms.

Even when we are presented with evidence, we are still very skeptical of the relationship between our peers and our physiology. As Derek Summerfield observes, the medical literature hardly ever mentions how "Western mental-health discourse" involves "a theory of human nature, a definition of personhood, a sense of time and memory and a source of moral authority"—none of which is "universal" (qtd. in Watters). Whether it is a conscious or unconscious decision, each individual uses his cultural beliefs and expectations to make sense of his situation and to respond with certain behaviors. In his essay "Drinking Games," Malcolm Gladwell explores different cultural perceptions of alcohol and how they affect people's physical behaviors. He contrasts the drinking patterns of the Bolivian Camba and the Italians of New Haven with those of the American population at large, stating that the effects of drunkenness, such as aggression and self-inflation, differ from culture to culture. Although the Camba people of Bolivia drink laboratory alcohol every night, there is, according to Dwight Heath, "no social pathology. . . . No arguments, no disputes, no sexual aggression, no verbal aggression"—behaviors that are typically associated with America's "picture of alcohol" (qtd. in Gladwell 73). Gladwell states that "culture is a more powerful tool in dealing with drinking than medicine, economics, or the law" (76).

Instead of a specific gene among the Camba and the Italians allowing them to drink heavily while still behaving non-violently, there are "ideas, habits and predispositions" that produce specific cultural conditions (Watters). These are what influence the Camba to "drink only within the structure of elaborate rituals," the "heart of Camba community life"; rituals influence the Italians to view alcohol as "food, consumed according to the same quotidian rhythms as pasta or cheese" (Gladwell 72, 74, 76). And American culture influences us to be "loud and rowdy" in a crowded, dim lit bar on a Friday night (74). The chemical effects of the alcohol seem to matter far less than the cultural conventions that surround it.

These social structures are most effective when influential people reinforce them. To explain the influence of the "popular" cheerleaders of the high school in Le Roy, Dominus asserts, "Cheerleaders frequently come up in case histories of mass psychogenic illnesses at schools, partly because psychogenic outbreaks often start with someone of high social status" (298). Katie Krautwurst and Thera Sanchez, two girls at the top of Le Roy High School's social ladder, first exhibited their symptoms, which then "seemed to flow . . . to those who looked up to them" (302). High school culture is defined by those of lower social status eagerly desiring to identify and belong with the "popular" group. But this social structure, seen and silently acknowledged by the school's population, lies just under the surface. Another significant and often deeply hidden part of these girls' environments lies within their family dynamics. Dominus discovered that of the girls with conversion disorder that she interviewed, "none had stable relationships with their biological fathers"; several had very low income levels; and one girl was juggling being a single mother at nineteen, going to school, and cheerleading (301). There was a "commonality of a certain kind of vulnerability," and these shared, circumstantial factors that combine to form the Le Roy girls' culture needed to be taken into account in diagnosing their mental disorder (302).

An assessment of social and familial conditions relies heavily on qualitative analysis and subjective interpretation. Afraid of appearing irrational or too abstract, we often neglect the significance of cultural and social contexts in investigating our physical responses to outside stimuli and turn to more concrete and measurable explanations. We search for reasons to be skeptical, and in qualitative analysis there is plenty to be skeptical of, as it offers possibility and probablity rather than the certainty of fixed numbers. Unwilling to accept the "psychogenic illness" diagnosis and all the social and familial introspection that such a diagnosis might have demanded, the Le Roy parents pointed fingers at contaminated water, soil, decades-old toxic waste spills—

they wanted test tubes and hard numbers (294). We measure our problems with biology and math, and then let pharmaceutical companies sell us a chemical cure. We may be uncomfortable with how much control our sub-conscious minds and our cultures have over our bodies, with the idea that pills cannot solve our problems nor ethanol explain our aggression. But denial produces a mindless and possibly dangerous understanding of the world.

As we continue to seek understanding in a complex world, we are most comforted by empirical, "logical," straightforward evidence because the alternative would be to face the nuanced and uncertain interactions between body, mind, and environment. Our unspoken cultural conventions convince us that it is ridiculous for the Le Roy girls' minds to have been converting conscious, stressful emotions into subconscious, involuntary, and severely dangerous motor movements. We are uncomfortable with this concept because we do not want to accept that the human subconscious has more power over us than our conscious minds do. In searching for a satisfying explanation of the girls' disorder, the town of Le Roy discounted its real roots, forfeiting an opportunity to solve some of the genuine problems that faced them. It is all too easy to discard the ideas that we find illogical and absurd, at the expense of the truth; it is all too easy to homogenize the girls in Le Roy and the hyperactive Johnnys of the world. Often we reject the fact that we are products of our environments, wanting to believe that we have total control over who we are and how we act. However, our surroundings, our personal backgrounds, our genetics, and moreover, our cultures define us along with any personal agency and autonomy we may have. Any singular diagnosis that a doctor might give us is but one component in a complex array of variables regarding our health or our identities. Any singular pill that solves the "problem" of a robust and rambunctious child should be considered an incomplete response to a complex problem.

WORKS CITED

Angell, Marcia. "The Epidemic of Mental Illness: Why?" *The New York Review of Books*. 23 June 2011: N.p. Web. 28 Apr. 2013.

Dominus, Susan. "What Happened to the Girls in Le Roy?" *Advanced College Essay*, 5th ed. Ed. Beth Boyle Machlan and William M. Morgan. Boston: Pearson, 2013. 291-305. Print.

Gladwell, Malcolm. "Drinking Games." *The New Yorker* 15 Feb. 2010: 70-76. *Gladwell.com*. Web. 30 Apr. 2013.

Schwartz, Alan and Sarah Cohen. "More Diagnoses of Hyperactivity in New C. D. C. Data." *New York Times* 01 Apr. 2013: 1-2. Web. 28 Apr. 2013.

Timimi, Sami and Eric Taylor. "ADHD is Best Understood as a Cultural Construct." *British Journal of Psychiatry*. 184 (2004): 8-9. *BJPsych*. Web. 28 Apr. 2013.

Watters, Ethan. "The Americanization of Mental Illness." *New York Times Magazine* 8 Jan. 2010: N.p. Web. 11 May 2013.

Buried in the Synapse

ALEX THOMSON

Even buried in our synapses, memories change, and the past that shapes us shifts. In his February 2012 article for *Wired* magazine, "The Forgetting Pill Erases Painful Memories Forever," scientific journalist Jonah Lehrer describes a neuroscientific model for memory that proposes "a molecular explanation of how and why memories change." According to this model, the "chemistry of the brain is in constant flux," and "the very act of remembering changes the memory itself." Lehrer describes how past memories are affected by present emotions—a process called "reconsolidation." Characterized by a constant process of revision, reconsolidation means that "every time we think about the past we are delicately transforming its cellular representation in the brain, changing its underlying neural circuitry."

Neuroscientists have discovered the crucial protein that would allow human beings to erase painful memories, everything from our earliest memories of pain—Lehrer calls them the "cliché cinematic scenes from childhood"—to "the persisting mental loops of illnesses like PTSD and addiction—and even pain disorders like neuropathy." Such conditions could conceivably be deleted through the administration of a protein-inhibiting drug. Here's how that deletion might look as a scientific procedure: to forget a traumatic experience, a subject would be asked to go through a series of steps, including writing down the memory and "retell[ing] it aloud several times." After this recounting, the subject would be administered "a drug that blocks PKMzeta," a protein that stabilizes neural circuits to create memories. The painful memory would disappear entirely, while leaving the other parts of recollection intact: "if the drug is selective enough and the memory precise enough, everything else in the brain should be unaffected and remain as correct—or incorrect—as ever."

While this part of Lehrer's article presents a rather breathless vision of a world without PTSD, childhood trauma, or addiction, messing with our memories may cause more problems than it solves. Though we might be tempted to turn away from them, painful memories *orient* us, shape our thoughts and habits. Reminding us of past mistakes, they allow us to change direction as we navigate the unpredictable pathways of our lives. Lehrer's article, though, seems to suggest that all memory, far from being the dutiful recording machine people imagine it to be, is fundamentally unreliable: "though every memory feels like an honest representation, that sense of authenticity is the biggest lie of all" because "the very act of remembering changes the memory itself" on a chemical level. This phenomenon of reconsolidation, Lehrer tells us, is nearly chemically identical to forming an initial memory. Memory is like wet clay—touch it and it's impossible not to leave a fingerprint, impossible not to alter its shape. Every moment, we're sculpting what we remember, remaking it as we put the parts back together, so lost in the process of remembering that we don't realize we're changing the form of the memory.

Perhaps because we've always known how selective and unreliable memory is, we've invented dutiful machines—such as cameras and other recording devices—to help us remember, to give ourselves a false sense of permanence. According to recent brain research, each of these machines is far more faithful and accurate than our own brains. During reconsolidation, Lehrer reminds us, "the structure of [memories] in the brain is altered in light of the present moment"—in other words, feelings distort one's view of the past. People warp the fabric of memory every time they recall something, though often the alteration is subtle. Think of an artisan making a mosaic, using a photograph as the template for the thing he's piecing together, tile by tile. Memory is a composite experience of many things—emotions, suggestions, narratives, sensory flashes—and the picture thus produced cannot be identical to the original experience. Each time it is reproduced, the original is in danger of being changed beyond recognition.

Other complex networks—cities, for instance—mirror the structure of the brain on a more massive scale. In her essayistic short story "Portrait of a Londoner," Virginia Woolf portrays her subject, Mrs. Crowe, as a vital synapse in the neural network of London. For six decades, Mrs. Crowe has been reconsolidating the memories of not just one life, but thousands of lives: taking stories from her guests, she assembles the parts into a "lively, comprehensible, amusing and agreeable whole" (119). Resting "in an armchair by the fire," always with "someone in the armchair opposite, paying a call" (117), Crowe is a like a pre-digital Wikipedia, endlessly gathering pieces of the city's information, preferring "conversation" to "intimacy" (118). Through her fireside chats with visitors and her "deftness in extracting" sharp particulars from them, she assembles a portrait of the vast, unknowable place that is London (119).

But in making that portrait, the parts change. Woolf tells us that to merely "record the fact" is not enough for Mrs. Crowe, who adds "a sprinkle of amusing gossip" to the recollection (119). Embellishing "bright and brilliant" pictures representing "the pages of London life for 50 years past," she cannot produce an exact replica of events as they occurred (119). Mrs. Crowe has a powerful memory, but even still, the sheer quantity of information proves too much for her. With the passage of years, "her knowledge became, not more profound . . . but more rounded," and if someone was too specific in their account, or said something "brilliant," it was considered a "breach of etiquette" (118-19). She's already consolidating so much information that one fact more would push another detail out.

Assembling the memory of such a large, multifaceted place is probably always a doomed project—destined to be forever incomplete—but Woolf insists that for certain inhabitants of London, Mrs. Crowe comes to embody their city to such an extent that "nobody can be said to know London who does not know" Mrs. Crowe (117). Using her powerful ability to understand and catalog such a vast amount of information, she is able to condense into a digestible form the essence of London, "making the vast metropolis seem as small as a village" (118). But this process is probably more dilution than "essence." Mrs. Crowe's history is actually a composite of many stories, stories that undoubtedly change as they get passed on. Yet Mrs. Crowe's sources, "her own cronies," are essential despite their fallibility (119). They allow her to round out the story of a place much larger than herself. Perhaps, then, we can say that such reconsolidation of memories comes not only from within ourselves, but from those we depend on to fill in the gaps in our shared experiences. Woolf's "Portrait" reminds us that memory is socially as well as neurologically constructed. Though we like to think of ourselves as the protagonists of our lives, our life stories have many authors. We depend on others not only to give us different perspectives on our shared experiences, but to fill in the gaps of what we haven't experienced or can't recall.

My first memory is not a comprehensive whole—it's a jagged piece of a much larger event, like a fossil I can dig up but not fully understand. When I was four years old, camping with my parents near Sacramento, I was stung by wasps—or so my parents tell me. All I remember is the buzzing and the removal of the stingers: the before and after parts of the experience. I don't remember the actual pain of being stung; having the stingers taken out seemed much more agonizing. As irrational as this seems to me fourteen years later, the synaptic pain of being stung persists. Even now, buzzing wasps seem to live in some part of my brain, and my body remembers in flashes: head ducking, arms flying up, torso hunched over, stomach churning. My parents, of course, remember the whole thing, and have given me a context for knowing why even hearing a buzzing sound can make me flinch.

Maybe what's more intriguing than memory itself is the way we *make* memories. Hearing this story recounted, attributing to it this set of bodily instincts, my brain sets to work filling in the holes, reconsolidating this information as if I recalled it myself. I cannot be sure if I am recalling the event itself, or if I am recalling a picture my mind created after hearing about the event. It is possible that the emotional memory is real and the visual, pictorial representation comes from my parents, but the two cannot be distinguished with any certainty. Once alerted to a gap in memory, reconsolidation attempts to rebuild the lost picture, taking fragments of its new mosaic from anywhere within reach, then solidifying the result as its own. In testing this phenomenon, the "psychologist Elizabeth Loftus has repeatedly demonstrated that nearly a third of subjects can be tricked into claiming a made-up memory as their own. It takes only a single exposure to a new fiction for it to be reconsolidated as fact" (Lehrer).

Bernard Cooper understands the unreliability of memory's structures all too well. In his essay "Labyrinthine," Cooper describes how aging corrodes his memory, making it malleable, adding bits that do not belong while pushing others into an indefinite fog. As a child, Cooper feels empowered by his love of mazes. "Even when trapped," he feels "an embracing safety" within the walls (345). His parents refuse to solve these mazes with him, especially his own sprawling creations which consume entire sheets of shelf paper to accommodate his "burgeoning ambition" (346). As he grows older, Cooper finds this dynamic inverted. Life itself becomes a maze filled with uncertainty and discomfort. He tells us that he feels "lost in the folds and bones of [his] body" and has trouble with memory (347). To his dismay, "remembered events merge together or fade away," leaving a "jumble of guesswork and speculation" (346). Due to his inability to stop this process, Cooper begins to feel helpless, his tone becomes resigned: he begins with phrases like "When you've lived as long as I have" and "I suppose it was inevitable" (346-47). Instead of wishing for his memories back, he shows his grudging acceptance of fate. Cooper feels too sharply the reasons why his parents were unwilling to "get mired" in his mazes; his "days encase [him], loopy and confusing" (346). He feels "tiny, pungent details poised on [his] tongue," but they never come fully to the front of his memory (346). This loss of control over the past is extremely disconcerting and "sometimes [Cooper is] not sure if [he has] overheard a story in conversation, read it in a book, or if [he is] the person to whom it happened" (346). Instead of filling in the gaps between buzzing and stingers to create wasps, instead of creating false memories, Cooper is losing true ones. Presented with such scattered fragments of the mosaic, memory's only option is to generalize. Thus, for Cooper, the past becomes a soup in which "uncertainty is virtually indistinguishable from the truth" (346-47). Reconsolidation doesn't help. It merely mixes fragments together, providing Cooper with a frustrating representation of the past. He often wonders "whose adventures, besides [his] own, are wedged in [his] memory" (346).

Like Cooper, Woolf's Mrs. Crowe has other people's memories wedged into her own. And like Cooper, like all of us, this prodigious matron's recollection is selective. Woolf reveals that Mrs. Crowe's fireside guests each have to be a member of the "club" (118). Like her avian namesake, Mrs. Crowe gathers scraps to make a kind of social nest until "the outer world [has] not a feather or twig to add" (119). Woolf's talk of "class" and "privilege" when describing Crowe's meetings reinforces this sense of exclusion (118).

I wonder what Mrs. Crowe would make of Cooper—Mrs. Crowe who is "merely a collector of relationships," who doesn't want her conversations to go too deep, and who doesn't want to look too sharply into the past (118). If Cooper were to be admitted to Mrs. Crowe's front-drawing room, would he, lost in his mazes, be able to command the old woman's attention? He might receive a stern rebuke about spending "too much time on the past" (Woolf 119). But Cooper might also approve of the "layers of complication" in Mrs. Crowe's knowledge of the convolutions of genealogy (Cooper 345). Both figures might find they have something to say to the other about the things buried in their synapses—perhaps their conversation about the world of memories might be worth remembering.

Even if we don't undergo the futuristic procedure described in Lehrer's *Wired* article, we are, like Cooper, destined to find ourselves lost one day—overwhelmed, "mired in a maze" (Cooper 346). We're destined to lose our memories, one way or another. Ultimately, like Mrs. Crowe, we'll die, and like Mrs. Crowe's London, our world will still exist after we die. In the meantime, we're left with those strange and sometimes unpredictable machines: our brains. If our memories are being constantly shifted, reworked from our initial picture into a series of mosaic images, then with each retelling we overwrite the remembered bits, intensifying or adding details. Knowing that the neurological process of reconsolidation exists cannot prevent it. Each time we recall our pasts, they will be a little different, and in the future we might have the option of intentionally editing our memories to remove the most painful, stinging bits.

Perhaps memories, even painful ones, *need* to be remade—after all, they're not recordings being repeated, but structures that we make over and over, altering them with our continuing scrutiny and our lived experiences. Recordings, after all, tend to capture only the most literal aspects of our experience, usually leaving out nuance and enigma. Without the remaking process that is memory, we might be left with only unconnected images: a little boy who can't remember being stung; a child absorbed in a maze the viewer can't see; a woman in a London drawing-room without company, the fire gone out. Perhaps only by remaking memories, by assembling bits from ourselves and others, can we discover their richness and the richness of the lives we are living.

WORKS CITED

Cooper, Bernard. "Labyrinthine." *Occasions for Writing: Evidence, Idea, Essay.* Ed. Robert DiYanni and Pat C. Hoy II. Boston: Wadsworth, 2008. 345-47. Print.

Lehrer, Jonah. "The Forgetting Pill Erases Painful Memories Forever." *Wired Magazine.* 17 Feb. 2012. Web. 8 Oct. 2012.

Woolf, Virginia. "Portrait of a Londoner." *Occasions for Writing: Evidence, Idea, Essay.* Ed. Robert DiYanni and Pat C. Hoy II. Boston: Wadsworth, 2008. 117-19. Print.

There Are Angels

EVAN BOBELLA

His heartbeat is a fluttering moth, a sputtering flame. I can feel it in my palm. The heat of it. There are several rapid beats per second, but they are irregular and faint. His beady black eyes shine hardly at all in the white fluorescent light of the waiting room, matte sheets of weary pain. Once, he stretches his forelimbs and curls those cloudy gray claws as a great yawn consumes his fragile and boney body, exposing with a shiver the pink of his small mouth and the perfect, miniscule fangs that reside therein.

I have him swaddled in the red blanket, fittingly, in which I first brought him home only a year before. It was clean, then, unsullied with the lost hairs, brown pellet food, and various bodily fluids that would eventually come to define it. It lacked too that special, sleepy smell that hundreds of hours of his little sleeping body would lend it and that no amount of washing could expunge—a comforting smell, musky and real, a primal and animal indicator of rest and warmth and happiness.

I have a diminutive silver chain around my neck. It is beautiful, but slippery and smooth, and so I hardly feel it as I anxiously run its length through my fingers.

Finally, after about a half hour, they call my name. I fill out a few forms about insurance and the status of the animal, writing "ferret" on the small blank next to the word "Other," and then I'm sitting in a happy yellow room with children's jungle wallpaper and green Formica countertops, the barking, whining dogs from the waiting room barely audible. Dante's breath, though, I can hear plainly, and his faint wheezes fill the room with melancholy, with ancient mortal grief, as we huddle and hunch together on a blue plastic stool and wait for the vet to arrive.

Dramatic, maybe, the way my memory handles these things. What's the life of a cheap, dumb animal when there is no dearth of real tragedy to attend to? Aren't our lives shaped by caskets and last conversations, by broken hearts and dreams deferred? There is no place in the cavalcade of entropic failure that is real life to mourn the passing and inconsequential; if you believe the epic poets and the body collective of human myth, we mark the passage of days by the broad and sweeping, the epic reckonings and calls to witness. After all, we have songs for Heracles and Perseus, dirges for Orpheus and Cassandra and Oedipus, but it is a rare moment when we glorify or savor the innocuous, incidental flickering of an artificial light in an oft-trafficked hallway or let our fingernails pause on the nearly imperceptible defects of silver chains. And yet, and yet.

The interior of the Cristal Hotel, Abu Dhabi, UAE. Polished black marble forms every fixture, and the heady smell of chlorine from the swimming pool permeates all thirty floors. Five times a day the state of the art sound system, an interconnected network of high-end white JBL speakers hidden cleverly throughout covert alcoves so as to be audible from even the most remote and recessed places in the whole of the building, plays the Muslim call to worship, a warbling, penetrating, decidedly foreign melody with ululated quarter tone ornamentation like fluttering, feathery wings and a breathy drone beneath. A good portion of the patrons here will each time remove their shoes and make their way to one of the many prayer rooms to supplicate themselves before Allah, to impose rigorous and regular transcendence onto the shape of their days.

There are sandstone-colored mosques, beautiful and often dead, on nearly every street corner—beautiful things with graceful minarets and fascinating Moorish arch work—that can be seen through the ceiling-length windows of the hotel. Even behind these tremendous panes of glass, the stifling heat of the Persian Gulf spring sun and the smell of stinging desert sand in a cool breeze make themselves apparent if only by some vague and vicarious process. Spend a moment wandering the plushly carpeted halls and you will hear the German and Russian of well-to-do businessmen and families on holiday intermingle with the Arabic and Urdu of the native Emiratis and expat Indian workers, an intoxicating mix of lilting and barking sounds that is nothing like the twang of American English. The boutique in the lobby, named in gaudy green neon letters "So-Pretty Clothing," features a comic distribution of *dishdasha*-ed men and *abayah*-ed women alongside more Western tourists buying brand names like Guess and Gucci, an amicable mixing of cultures that is all smiles and heartfelt greetings and conspires, in a decidedly unsubtle way, to remind you of the import of these moments, of the potential for depth and profundity that swirl in this alien and singular place.

And in a very real way, I am here. I am consumed. I am a devoted cultural voyeur, I am painfully and acutely aware that this is a formative experience, that *life* itself is in these halls in some immeasurable way, hiding in every facet of this lively and vivacious excursion, in the well-tended hotel rooms and sacred, sequestered ablution halls and empty burning deserts. Shivers dimple the skin on my arms every time the clock strikes a holy hour and groups of devotees bustle to commune with their God. And yet, for all the faith and godliness that suffuse this place, the dedication to deities and *dirham* alike, there are no angels I can find; I am sublimated by my own attentions and by the wealth of reality, and so my thoughts float over all these far-reaching differences like a flat stone skimming over the surface of a glassy lake, and I find that, no matter how I try, I cannot feel my necklace. Vast arrays of information will be taken in and internalized on this trip; a grand narrative will form in hindsight, I know; but it will be hazy and distorted like a distant mirage, an artifact encased deeply in gauzy and obscuring cloth, a travelogue as travelogues are. The whorls on my fingertips find no purchase as I wander, and divinity is absent from my heart.

I've grown pensive. A friend asks me how I like the trip thus far. I say, "I am surviving." I do not think she understands.

The veterinarian is a smallish woman, maybe five foot three, with black hair tied behind her head and kept in place with a pebbled brown many-limbed butterfly clip. Her sterile white lab coat and cork clipboard grant her a certain air of off-putting officiousness, but she plays it easily behind a well-polished smile. All business. She asks me, glancing at her charts, if this is Dante, and what can she help me with today; I tell her of his erratic eating habits and his over-sleeping, his general malaise, the extreme skinniness that pushes his brittle spine through his patchy fur.

A deep V is impressed upon her forehead as she listens attentively, making but a couple quick notes on her clipboard. The way she nods belies confidence, empathy, understanding. She speaks to me about the potentialities of this particular situation as she feels with steady hands along his frail body, checking his digestive tract for discernible lumps; in the middle of explaining to me the genetic predispositions for these animals to certain types of cancer, her cool look of medical beneficence fades for a brief moment into one of genuine weariness as her probing fingers catch, and her manual exploration comes to a resigned rest.

Life clips on around us. An orderly knocks on the door and leaves some paperwork. Somewhere behind the walls of the examination room a heavy piece of machinery hums serenely into life, only to fade quickly into ambient buzzing. We are surviving, and I cannot stop toying ineffectually with my chain.

Two X-rays and a brief, courteous discussion of financial considerations later, his tiny head is cupped in my hand as she presses a thick syringe into his abdomen. She is aiming for the liver, she says, which will help to disseminate the chemical quickly and efficiently, with little pain, to shut down all the biological systems as rapidly as we can manage. I can feel the taut muscles of his neck twitch slightly as the needle penetrates him, but his eyes don't seem to really change, nor does his rapid breath. The black eyes focus somewhere in the middle distance, and the ragged heaving comes shallowly, unperturbed, from his sable, furry face.

I cannot help but wonder if he has any concept of soul-baring vulnerability in this moment. Does he stare at death as it encroaches upon his fragile form? Does he exult in the unique confluences of his life, in the inexorable pull of past and future on his tiny constitution, does he sing to the high heavens his fear and his praises and his curses? Is there an angel in this moment or is it another plodding, coursing figment like so many mornings and nights before?

Rainer Maria Rilke tells us, "Every angel is terrifying" (11).

But then, my fingertips falter on a chain link upon which there's a small deposit of rust-red oxidation. I never noticed it before. There are hot salty tears on my nose—I am acutely aware of their slick lugubrious scent, their cloudy, heady sting. I can feel every detail of Dante's head in my fingers, the gorgeous slightness of his jawbone that protrudes through paper skin, the pulsing esophagus now going dry as the poison does its heavenly, dirty work, the bristly protuberances of his stiff whiskers. I can see the muscles in his eyes relax as the pain-knit fibers relinquish their hold on his beautiful, minute irises; I watch in admiration as the small spark of his mind is snuffed out into black smoke.

This is not nearly the greatest tragedy I have known, and yet for some reason its implications work their icy fingers through a wide, bright hole deep in my mind. It is easy to live dutifully and purposefully with a confidence in the depth of one's own experience, to think that by some force of will we can wring from the fabric of being purpose in abundance and justification in all moments, but we do not choose our visitations. All we can do is try not to deny them when they deign to arrive.

So, I go forth in that miraculous Middle Eastern jewel of a city, into the hot Arab night, restless and overwhelmed, playing with my chain once again.

I stray from the hotel in the sacred hours past midnight, down the broad avenues towards the city's waterfront corniche and towards the ocean, past the hordes of lean and mewling Arabic cats and the white Toyota taxi cabs and the crowds of impoverished Indian workers that huddle in alleyways beneath crumbling Soviet-bloc style facades. Strange smells of roasting meat and saltwater air and ethereal breezes tantalize my nose, bond themselves to my memory, burn themselves through layer upon layer of my waking faculties, and I just so happen to prod a kink with my cuticle.

Then, inexplicably, there are angels in the subtly shifted stars, the twinkling pinpricks of light that seem rotated on their axes and yet outline somehow the same shapes they did at home. They are in the familiar globules of artificial light that distort the night air into hazy coronas of blue like beaded pearls on an endless string, so ordinary and yet lighting up palm trees where I am used to seeing maples or pines. They leap from the license plates of parked cars, familiar Hondas and Subarus except that their identification codes are ten digits long, all numbers, the first five characters separated from the last by a small black silhouette of an eagle in flight.

The closeness of links on a masterfully crafted silver chain can at first blush make it seem one object; they fool the senses, these tiny, nearly imperceptible things, and it is so damnably easy to believe there is nothing between them, that this is a chain like every other chain you've felt, a familiar sensation, links affixed to links, a stock and rote part of life. It is not; they are not. It is the smooth and shifting skin of a desert snake, the nearly silent sussuration of lapping waves on an Arabic shore, the shuddering, dying breath of the smallest of creatures; they are halos and pure, cutting notes, reckonings and calls to witness, clarity and purpose incarnate, and they will show themselves to be distinct in the strangest of moments.

Cling to this truth. It is everything.

WORKS CITED

Rilke, Rainer Maria. *Duino Elegies and the Sonnets to Orpheus*. Trans. Stephen Mitchell. New York: Random, 2009. Print.

Moving Stillness

ERIC LENIER IVES

There are moments of my life that I remember as gerunds. I am *falling* from the tire swing into crisp, white snow. I am *lying* in chilled sand late at night as lightning rips through the clouds offshore. I am *hiding* my mother's whiskey. I am *kneeling* next to my grandmother for the last time, and she winks at me. These words extend beyond the moment they were lived, as if those moments were still alive, as if they never faded. These words assert, "*I am*," and flourish this claim with proof and inspire action. Something, someone, after all, must be behind the doing. Yet gerunds are at once malleable and non-specific. They allow moments to endure; they allow them to grow. The present progressive tense is just that: both present and progressive. For a memory to endure in this tense is for it to be molded by time and perspective, instance and progression. It is appropriate that a painting should immediately come to mind. The word "painting" is, by definition, a verbal noun, a thing in motion. Harmoniously both the action and the moment, a painting is a thing—but it is also so much more.

It is three o' clock in the morning, and there is a portrait before me. A figure reclines on a bed of pillows. The right hand lies over the belly; the legs are turned to the side, clasped together and drawn to the hip. They seem bound, forced into the frame, locked in place. Indeed, within the frame, the entire body is contained by a looming darkness overhead, but the figure asserts a faint glow. Warmth emanates from a delicate, white bosom that precedes a flushed neck and a rosy face. While the torso is soft—a gradient of gentle pinks and inviting flesh—the face grows harsher: lines of black from the cosmos above seep into the figure's eyes and lips, hardening them, closing them. Even in technique, this contrast persists: the carefully blended colors blossom this figure out of darkness, shield him within their glow, yet sharp strokes of a palette knife smear and cut the paints to harsh points. There is almost an androgyny about this figure, a confusion or, then, a fusion. A fusion of soft and hard, light and dark, mind and body. This last pair I must linger on: body lying limp and cuddled in warmth amid darkness, this figure could be sleeping, yet I know that he is not; eyes shut, the world invisible to him, this figure could be dreaming, yet I know that he is not. This figure could be many things, yet I know that he is, most obviously, me.

I know because I held myself on my childhood bed for hours to see him come to life. I know because I lived this. I felt sensation depart from each part of my corpse. First my legs, then my back, then my arms, each in its turn until it was only my face that was soft and not buffeted by rigidity. The blood left all non-essential appendages. In the end, it seemed no part was particularly essential: each cried out a final hum before fading into numbness. Viciously aware of what I could not sense, *feeling* the numbness, I found it strange that our word for "dulled feeling" warrants an entire sensation of its own. Feeling my entire body strained, focusing on nothing, and yet able to feel everything, a queer wholeness made itself known: though the parts of my body fell, each in its turn, to a deliberate stillness, each was now unified by this feeling. Just as a painting inhabits both an instance and an action, so, too, does a feeling, it seems. It is both an instantaneous impulse and a long, drawn-out echo, changing in time, progressing. Yet this figure in the painting now before me is, at once, not me. He is not the experience that I have just lived, the feeling I have endured and even now hear the echo of. He is something else entirely.

He is the skin that someone else wears; the entire work is this skin. There is another in this painting, though not represented obviously or outright. Rather, this shadow figure is in everything, lying beneath the obvious. The image of "me" is a boy as seen by someone else, a painter whose sight was morphed by love, morphed by fantasies of a boy purer than I am, purer than I was. The psychic forces that conspired with and against this painting are vast and varied, but understand that though colors and strokes have been arranged to bear a striking resemblance to my physical order—androgyny not excepted—I am not the only subject of this work. Rather, the one wearing my face, the one glowing back to me, is another: Brittany. After four years of notes, letters, sweet-nothings and ugly-somethings, I can write her name unconsciously. It seems that she can call me from her paints just as easily. Just as every letter I penned was written in my hand, so, too, is her painting wrought in hers. It lingers as her essence, her watermark in dried paints that even now shimmer as if they are still wet.

She has, perhaps without trying to, painted herself into this portrait. At the outset—and I do not mean any offense to her—she has given me her breasts. Subtle as they may be, the curves and tenderness there do not mesh with the results of hours of my own self-observation and vain indulgences in the mirror. For her, what needed no personalization was my most substantial part, the filler of the frame, my torso. She falls, perhaps, into her default and paints the breast of one of her female models, some other impulse than what I see in the mirror. My legs, shoulders, and hair are also left impersonal, vague, as if she were painting from memory rather than life. She focused instead on two parts: my hand and my face. My hand, so frequently a bond she and I would share in the world outside this encounter, and my face, the source of so much conflict in both. Enlightened by roaring colors, flanked by cheeks and nose nearly red with intoxication, the face erupts from the rest of the portrait. Yet the eyes and the lips, both sealed in blackness, ground all of this fury. They are the only places where the aura of darkness above penetrates.

Surely, I cannot suppose for her some deep-seated anxiety about my gaze, often mistrustful, and my lips, so often the source of empty sweetness as well as honest affections. I can, however, suggest that she has not painted me. She had resolved to paint her idea of me; regardless of whether or not I happened to be physically present, stiff on the bed, her painting would have come into being. The contradictions and inconsistencies now begin to fall into line: my soft breast, not born of a woman but instead a pillow for her head; my shoulders, only vaguely firm, a sign of the timidity she found attractive; my hair less a crown than hers to ruffle. When I see this portrait, I do not see myself. Rather, I see her. I see her hopes, her anxieties, her feeling of capturing me in art and, perhaps, in love. This image is far sweeter than any naked boy could ever be.

But I query this analysis softly as if it were a thought I dare not accidentally accept. For all the presumption and diligence I might commit to this work, I must see that in "seeing" her "seeing" me, I am myself "seeing" an imagined Brittany: one of my own design, one who worries about my gaze and my lips, but wants to project herself onto me as she has with my bosom. For all my presumed authority on what is "me" and what is "her," for all my attempts to break down our encounter and arrange it, piece by piece, those pieces will never add up to a whole. This, I suspect, is because the pieces are infinite and do not fit together as puzzle pieces do. They are ever-changing; even as two pieces fit together, they melt apart, re-form. Inevitably, those notions of "you and I" melt as well. They morph and blend, separate again, rejoin. They flow like waves on a shore or paint on a canvas. Except this paint does not dry—it is ever multiplicitous and often beautiful, even if only for a moment as the perfect color comes and just as quickly goes like a swell stopping for an instant at the height of its surge. Such is the nature of ever trying to know someone, even oneself. I thought I knew myself: the look of my face, the width of my wrist, the slight curve of my hips. But somewhere in the hours of painting, that instantaneous idea of "me" fused and intertwined with the action. Somewhere we became something different from the sum of the parts.

I am sitting in a conference discussing the virtues of a proper history paper. Hanging over the heads of six other writing tutors, a woman I have never seen gazes down at us from the wall. It doesn't feel right to call her a woman; she's not formed of flesh or bone but of paint and time, here reprinted and framed. It doesn't feel right to say she "gazes," either: her eyes are closed, her head nestled in her arm. Sliced from time and superimposed over a conference room wall, it is strange to imagine the woman lying for this work, *Le Repos (The Rest)*, in front of Pablo Picasso. Picasso captured this moment—this woman—decades earlier in a Boisgeloup studio. As I bask in her glowing presence, however, she seems very much present and alive.

Her flesh is a creamy purple, her hair a rich, wheat-yellow, like the high noon sun. Black intrusions hold her together at the edges of her being, but an indigo blue enchants these lines, breaks these corporeal boundaries. It is easy to imagine her dreaming, as if the moment we see now were the very instant she fell asleep. I begin to wonder if she truly was sleeping. I begin to wonder if it matters. That woman is gone; the fascination of this moment, with this painting, remains. Though the subject rests, the strokes are active, the colors vibrant and alive: the stillness nearly breathes. The model is perhaps not the present being I have imagined her to be, but this moment is nonetheless eternal. The frame draws focus to head; she lies on a swath of red, and an eerie green looms to the left. These encroaching colors are aggressive, inching nearly over her own form, just as the black in my own portrait sewed my lips and eyes together. *The Rest* is perhaps the perfect title for this piece: by her stillness, by her dream, the harshness of the red and the souring green are held at bay, held, at least, from her vulnerable eyes. They are closed; they are safe; they are wandering in the unconscious and the surreal, escaping the onslaught of reality. For all she cannot see with eyes softly shut, this dream state has freed her. With vision obscured, this is a moment of clarity. Perhaps we can only hope for an instant of stillness in this tempest of variability. Yet the painting continues.

My eyes flitter back to the conference at hand. I grin at the thought that this print of *The Rest* has indeed been a respite for me, if only for a moment. I take a breath. I look around to the others at the table, gauging whether my distraction has been noticed. Signs point to yes; my grin fades. It seems we live our lives just as a painting does. We are at once present and infinitely progressing, always moving forward from one thing to the next, and yet only ever able to experience the moment. Whether "it" is the moment of the painting or the moment of experiencing the painting, it is undeniably an attempt to recognize the constant flow by holding it constant. *Esse quam videri*. In seizing the moment, the moment is truly something; it does not just seem to be.

The sun is shining down on jagged limestone; I am fastened to a rock that binds the sky above and the waves below. I wear only a bathing suit and a chalk bag; simplicity drives the climb. I am climbing barefoot across Blowing Rocks Preserve, one of the longest stretches of open rock on the Florida shoreline. The waves have mangled and sculpted the alcove I am in now, have made it somehow seem both unreachable and inescapable. In a state almost entirely at sea level, I take my thrills where I can get them. I am cinching meek holes in weathered slabs with hardened fingertips coated in opaque white chalk. My hands appear as ethereal creatures, almost a bridge connecting me to the world of the dead. The rock is made of the ocean's skeletal remains. Its composition is truly a marvel: millions of years of organisms crushed and compacted so that they are no longer disparate parts adrift in the ocean, but a wall, a mausoleum, now facing the thrash of the sea once more. Here, their presence lingers; with my ear close to the wall, I swear I hear a briny coo.

Forcing my feet onto rigid pointe to catch the feint edges afforded me, my calves burn. My toes are wrapped in climbing tape, the skin beneath torn apart. Each step is pain; each grip is gritty. Yet, as conscious as one must be about the fragments of his body—about his limbs, toes, and fingers—in the heat of climbing, my body becomes just like the limestone I crawl across: the disparate parts are unified. Why should I want to do this? I am not entirely sure. It is a curious drive that holds me here. There is no comprehensible reason I should hang here; it is rather something intrinsic that fastens me, something within me that needs an outlet into the world. My first thought was the sport of the climb; then I thought meditation was the motive; then I thought you could use your body to dominate something so much bigger than yourself. Just as soon as I think I have found an answer, the reason changes or falls flat or is complicated by some new facet or shortcoming. If we are always in flux, so too, it seems, are our motivations. But if our reasons are fleeting, they are also permanent. Each vibrates in our grasp, but grows with us, progresses, never truly leaving, only changing. The search is, at once, both an instant realization and the progression of meaning; it is beauty. I plant another foot, twist my knee inward to leverage my hips closer to the wall, and climb on.

Yet nature has no sympathy for such a fluid drive. Even the tide conspires against me. Earlier in January the inward flow consumed this rock face later in the day; later in the month, the swells froth forward earlier and earlier. Even now, I have been here for only an hour and the sea is already catching my feet in its incessant crash. My toes burn as the saltwater seeps through the bandaging and gnaws at the stripped flesh. The adhesive cotton begins to saturate and peel away, and I begin to understand that I am, in a very real way, alone. I thread my left arm through the crescent formed by my right and back up again to grab a solid spire. My left hand envelops it. The dog-toothed edges grip my arm, and, for a moment, my nerves, through their own silent screams, *feel* the rock. The pain fades as I parcel and explain it away: an uncallused palm catching, defying, the momentum that would, unimpeded, cast me to the swell below. For all its discomfort, the caustic motion is deliberate; it is my own, and that is a comforting thought. My fingers field no such complaints; they've long since been petrified in layers of dead skin. They have become like the limestone they hold fast to: organic rocks, compacted by countless crashes, deadened and unified. And yet, just as time and persistence have chipped these monoliths down, I am worn; I am raw; I am falling.

I am underwater. I think I have hit the sand below, but I cannot tell. The churning and swirling would make me sick if my body were not locked at the core, trying to right itself. I open my eyes to the incendiary saline surroundings. There is nothing; there is everything. Dense swathes of sea bend and suck me under. Flecks of sand whip around, muddying the turquoise hue. A bubbling tempest of captured oxygen sprints for the surface. In this moment, I am nothing but the fierce and burning urge to beat back the entire ocean and breathe the sweet air into my lungs; I swear it would taste like honey. The sea takes me, lurches me forward, as if it wanted to spit me out. And so I go where it wills. My right shoulder is first to impact stone. It buckles into my chest as the rest of my body flips over. My left hand blocks the rest of me from slamming into the boulder, but my knees jerk forward into the uneven rock. Something hurts. The tide surges back, satisfied by my beating, as if heeding an unseen master's call. Erupting from the pool, I cough, unsure of where the air has come from. With a final, visceral saltwater-and-phlegm explosion, I suck in the air at last and prop myself up. The current floats gently now, as if I'm not worth the effort. A calm sets in.

The water now at my waist, I stand up. I feel a pulse in my fingertips; I see it pounding in my breast. I am living viciously in my own flesh; I am thinking nothing. I am not a son, a brother, a student, or a climber; I am, for a moment, nothing but this moment. This blissful abyss just is. I just *am*. In this moment of failure, *this* is the reason. It will not be the reason forever, but it is the reason now. It will not be the moment forever, but it is the moment now. Blood begins to drip down my back. I look down: my skin has been ripped off, but I will become a bit more callused for it. I look up: the sun is shining in my eyes, but it can no longer blind me. The moment is gone, yet it remains. I reach for the first ledge. I begin climbing again.

WORKS CITED

Picasso, Pablo. *Le Repos*. 1932. Painting. Richard M. Cohen Collection, Los Angeles. *Christie's*. Web. 7 Mar. 2013.

Measuring by Waves

CLARA KOO

slide, v.
a. To pass from one place or one point to another with a smooth and continuous movement, *esp*. through the air or water, or along a surface.
e. To ride across the face of a wave.
>   —*Oxford English Dictionary Online*

> It is the space of each sentient body's awareness of itself. It is not boundless
> like subjective space: it is always finally bound by the laws of the body, but
> its landmarks, its emphasis, its inner proportions are continually changing.
>   —John Berger, "Rembrandt and the Body" (107)

John Berger tells us that in Rembrandt's *Bathsheba Reading King
David's Letter*, Bathsheba sits, naked, "her nubile stomach and navel" painted
"with love and pity as if they were a face" ("Rembrandt" 108). The stomach,
according to Berger, has become Bathsheba's countenance and thus shows a
kind of emotion, expresses a story—perhaps of love, of tragedy. Her stomach
is full, but sags with a certain disappointment; it imitates her facial expression
as she holds a letter with a sort of silent acquiescence; she submits to the
King's desire for her, her fated pregnancy with the future King Solomon, and
the inevitable death of her husband. Berger explores the notion of a "corporeal space," a physical, bodily place that is often shared and shaped by the people who exist within it. In exploring Rembrandt's depiction of Bathsheba's
stomach, he recognizes this bodily place as "the space of each sentient body's
awareness of itself"; it describes a hyper-awareness of the physical, whether
through pain or pleasure (107). Berger emphasizes that Bathsheba's body
parts live in awareness of each other; her stomach is shaped by the presence
of her face, her lifeless hand, her crossed legs. These "different points of
view," as Berger describes them, "can only exist in a corporeal space which is
incompatible with territorial or architectural space," in that they do not, for
instance, follow the rules of anatomical proportion (109). While grounded in

the physical and the body, this conception of space can also contain an essence of something more. Rembrandt allows viewers to feel as if they can intercept "dialogues between parts gone adrift, and these dialogues are so faithful to a corporeal experience that they speak to something everybody carries within them" (109). For Berger, Rembrandt's awareness of the physical allows us to remember something of our own physical and "inner experience" because of what we see reflected in the painting (109). Yet spectators who manage to share Bathsheba's space possess different experiences that speak individually to their own bodies. Berger reveals that Rembrandt paints not of real space, but of this multifaceted, multi-perspective area that is configured, formed, broken, and reconstructed by the touch of some other essence.

But the space Berger mentions might not only be of essence; it may also partake of time. Virginia Woolf implies that "sliding" helps us live in a present that is forever enriched by the past. That awareness of our bodies that Berger writes about, our physical beings set in an ethereal world, comes from such an act of sliding. Sliding, for Woolf, is a verb, not a noun. In "A Sketch of the Past," she reflects that "[t]he past only comes back when the present runs so smoothly that it is like the sliding surface of a deep river. Then one sees through the surface to the depths. In those moments I find one of my greatest satisfactions, not that I am thinking of the past; but that it is then that I am living most fully in the present" (98). She indicates that a scene must have "the sense of movement and change," to a point that "One must get the feeling of everything approaching and disappearing, getting large, getting small, passing at different rates of speed" (79). In her novel *To the Lighthouse*, Woolf creates the feeling of this motion, as waves crash upon the shore, as the lighthouse beams its light through the windows of the Ramsay house and quietly disappears, as the space between Mr. Ramsay and Mrs. Ramsay pulsates with a certain life that makes intimacy a silent conversation, and as Lily Briscoe moves to capture dead Mrs. Ramsay on canvas. But the word *slide* could possibly be a noun—a shape that forms around each essence, around each piece of work that endeavors to capture it.

In *To the Lighthouse*, Lily Briscoe presents the struggle of an artist—the arduous process of gliding towards another through time and distance, reaching for the subject's core, for intimacy. Lily, in the last section of the novel, continues her portrait of the late Mrs. Ramsay, a woman whom she admired and adored. But on the quiet lawn outside the Ramsay house, where only she and one other houseguest sit, she relives memories and scenes of the past as she paints. Suddenly, we are told, "she lost consciousness of outer things" and "her mind kept throwing up from its depths, scenes, and names, and sayings, and memories and ideas, like a fountain spurting over that glaring, hideously difficult white space" of her canvas (159). This active submission to her "uncompromising" painting, her hand, which quivered with the rhythm of life, and her mind, which pulsated with memories, scenes, and ideas, gives Lily a vision that allows her to start a painting held in mind for ten years (157). Perhaps the interaction between the past and the present, two bodies and essences of Lily and Mrs. Ramsay moving smoothly across each other, makes Mrs. Ramsay more real. As Lily takes green paint onto her brush, she feels something emerging, a kind of clarity in her image of Mrs. Ramsay. At that moment, Mrs. Ramsay's manipulative nature and her flaws, and the beauty that she possessed, that "stilled life—froze it," are all transformed into a visible, corporeal shape (177).

As Mrs. Ramsay seems no longer to be a Greek goddess set in the middle of the dining table, but rather a beautiful woman with a certain shape, like multiple fruits stacked on top of each other, Lily no longer feels her to be unreachable. She is released from Mrs. Ramsay's authority and the beauty that once blinded her; she feels that "now she could stand up to Mrs. Ramsay" (176). The revelation of her flaws makes Mrs. Ramsay an ordinary yet even more extraordinary presence—"to be on a level with ordinary experience, to feel simply that's a chair, that's a table, and yet at the same time, It's a miracle, it's an ecstasy" (202). In fact, by viewing her as a person with imperfections, by warming the beauty that had frozen Mrs. Ramsay, Lily glorifies her even more; she paints Mrs. Ramsay's fleeting essence on a canvas and makes it permanent. Perhaps the key to this unreal yet ordinary experience of Mrs. Ramsay's presence, the key to intimacy itself, is a kind of *distance*. The time that has passed allows Lily to reform and reshape the space between her past and present. Consequently, she is able to see the outline of the relationship she once had with Mrs. Ramsay. In some moments, this increasing time, this swelling space of emptiness, is excruciating, making her long for that space to contract , allowing her to feel close to Mrs. Ramsay again. But this distance also allows her to see an "unornamented beauty," which permits her to envision Mrs. Ramsay as something ephemeral yet permanent. Lily allows time to make the ordinary unreal and the unreal, ordinary (155). Distance, then, permits us to slide. Lily's endeavor to paint Mrs. Ramsay over time allows her to live in multiple places simultaneously; she searches for Mrs. Ramsay in the past, reaches for Mr. Ramsay as he sails off to the lighthouse, and lives within her own corporeal space and shares it, thereby feeling something change within herself and the people who inhabit that space.

Yet what matters to our inquiry, more than capturing an essence, is the act of looking—understanding that searching itself creates intimacy. In "Penelope," John Berger couples Vija Celmins, a Latvian-American artist, with Penelope, the wife of Odysseus, by virtue of their commitment to distance—their patience in depicting something they cannot see, but can only envision from afar. The images that Celmins paints seem hand-made, like Penelope's woven works, which represent images of war and events far off from where she wove her tapestries. Berger imagines Celmins "in her studio shutting her eyes in order to see—because what she wants to see—or has to see—is always far away" (46). But Berger clarifies that Celmins is not looking for a way to replicate reality—she is aware that from such a distance she cannot duplicate a scene; "she transcribes with all the fidelity she knows" what only her mind's eye can see (48). Celmins, like Lily Briscoe, wants to get hold of "that very jar on the nerves, the thing itself before it has been made anything," because a scene, a moment, is most vivid *then* (*Lighthouse* 192-93).

Inevitably, "painting can never get the better of appearances," Berger tells us, implying that a painting will never represent the whole essence of a scene or person, but perhaps will represent only a fragment (47). In our endeavors to capture with fidelity the exact curves of the mountains, the face of a nubile stomach, we tend to create an image that is half essence and half movement; it is always an image "of searching" (47). Berger explains that Celmins wants her fixed image to represent the act of searching, that *To Fix the Image in Memory*—a game in which she takes eleven pebbles, casts them in bronze, and tries to tell them apart—is actually capturing a movement, a gesture that indicates the act of looking, searching for distinct shapes, essences, value. Her ability to recognize a movement towards intimate knowledge allows her to warm "her chilling images of distance" (48). The essence we seek is not in the exact representation, but in something we find before we even reach that representation, the very jar of the nerves Lily mentions—a magnetic field to glide toward and enter, allowing us to distinguish the subject's essence from our own.

There is something in Celmins's attempt to slide across a distance that lets us experience her artwork not only as a representation of an essence or scene, but also as a moment "of searching" (47). Lily turns, at the end of *To the Lighthouse*, to her painting, and looks at it "with all its greens and blues, its lines running up and across, its attempt at something" (208). Both Celmins and Lily, when they look back at their paintings, see them as movements towards that other something, an effort set in motion by a hope of capturing or recapturing an intimacy they have lost. This loss possibly stems from an attempt to represent an ideal image, an impression that seems too perfect, too detailed. In moving across a distance toward someone else, the artist is shaped by what she tries to paint; instead of molding the subject into a fixed ideal, a chilling image of beauty, she attempts a collaboration that will capture the ephemeral and ineffable.

To feel a certain proximity, an artist must move toward the subject to transform it into something that can be touched, made permanent, made more accessible. But the thing an artist wants to capture is not always an essence or intimacy, not always about the past and present; it can also represent a power that can change us in the process of observing, of moving into a relationship. This transformative power is encapsulated in the opening line of Colum McCann's *Let the Great World Spin*: "Those who saw him hushed" (3). Phillipe Petit's high-wire performance between the Twin Towers in 1974 is reminiscent of "sliding"—a word central to McCann's novel and Woolf's vision of the interaction between the present and the past. McCann weaves together the stories of seemingly unrelated New Yorkers and *pulls* them in, as if Petit's walk is a magnet, drawing us from a distance. McCann centers an entire novel on one performance—close to the sky but far from the ground. He tries to transform Petit's walk—by surrounding it with stories that enrich the moment—into something that is not only a performance of sheer beauty, but that also evokes pain, controversy, awe, and love.

Through each character's narrative, we can recapture a dimension that we did not see before—one that allows us to relate, to exist within their world for a moment. At first, the hookers Jazzlyn and Tillie seem to be manipulative, dirty women who suck the life and resources out of those who try to help them. But when Tillie tells her story, she becomes, for us, a wiser character. Her narrative is inundated with the smell of hotels, the fragrance of oily pizza, moments of irony, and self-deprecating regret. As she reflects on Jazzlyn's death, she recalls thinking during her daughter's childhood, "She's never gonna work the stroll. You swear it. Not my baby. She's never gonna be out there. So you work the stroll to keep her off the stroll" (200). But Tillie fails; she cannot get off the stroll; it's an addiction, and she passes it on to Jazzlyn. She lives in penitence and knows she will kill herself soon to escape her pain; but her reflection on her life, in which, as Woolf would describe it, her present flows over her past, is full of humor. Although she knows she is "a fuck-up," Tillie also realizes "how it is in the life. . . . You joke a lot" (210, 201). When we encounter Tillie, we too collide with and accommodate her. Her appearance changes the shape of the novel, the life of other characters within it, and Petit's walk. She changes us. From her narrative, we gain a new feeling of intimacy that results not only from our understanding of Tillie's essence, but also our unconscious movement towards our subject. We, like Celmins and Lily, are molded by another body's essence.

But McCann, through Petit's movement across the wire, shows us that sliding over a distance also separates us from something else—that reaching the sky separates us from the ground. By delving into another's narrative, we are also parting from others, diving into a certain dark emptiness. Claire Soderberg loses her son Joshua, a computer genius, to the Vietnam War; she opens her refrigerator at night, having secret conversations with her dead son through the shivering cold, the humming electricity running through it—"the word was not *snap*, more like *slide*. A word Joshua had liked. I will slide out" (90). But when she *slides* toward Joshua, she loses connection with the outside world, with the ladies she meets every Sunday to reminisce about their sons, with Solomon, her husband, and with herself.

Woolf complicates an analogous problem when Mr. Ramsay and Lily are slowly separating as he sails towards the lighthouse with his two children, James and Cam. But Lily is not disconnected from Mr. Ramsay as he sails from the house, nor does she forget about him as she reaches out for Mrs. Ramsay's presence; she begins to think that "so much depends . . . upon distance: whether people are near us or far from us; for her feeling for Mr. Ramsay changed as he sailed further and further across the bay" (191). Each time Lily drifts toward a past scene with Mrs. Ramsay, she measures the distance Mr. Ramsay has traveled: "'Where are they now?' Lily thought, looking out to sea. Where was he, that very old man who had gone past her silently, holding a brown paper parcel under his arm?" (182). In fact, Mr. Ramsay is crucial to her painting; he is the force that balances Mrs. Ramsay: "she could not achieve that razor edge of balance between two opposite forces; Mr. Ramsay and the picture" (193). As her vision of Mrs. Ramsay morphs when she paints, so does her vision of Mr. Ramsay. The old, widowed tyrant of a man who seemed to demand sympathy, attention, slowly unravels into a softer shape in his beautiful leather boots, a shape that evokes and requires the kind of empathy Rembrandt's Bathsheba elicits.

Along their ride to the Lighthouse, Cam and James feel something of themselves attach to their father; they finally begin to slide over into his presence, to feel and observe the shape of a man they both hate and adore. Throughout the whole scene, Lily, Cam, and James all seem to have silent conversations with him, just as Mrs. Ramsay once had. When Lily finishes her painting, she thinks aloud, "He must have reached it," which makes her feel as if she is stretching her mind and body into his corporeal space (208). All of the characters inhabit that space with him. Unlike McCann, Woolf uses Lily and Mr. Ramsay to remind us that it is possible for someone to move toward something or someone else, without sacrificing themselves entirely; it is possible, too, to balance opposing forces such as Mr. Ramsay and Mrs. Ramsay during such a moment of inhabitation.

"Those who saw him hushed": the silence becomes a corporeal space, a place untouched, yet shared, much like the one Mr. Ramsay, Lily, and Mrs. Ramsay occupy as they have silent conversations with one another. Perhaps, then, it is not that artists are merely attempting to sail through a span of time, of separation, to reveal an essence; they also attempt to put us into a physical place, to stretch us to reach and bend with the characters. When Rembrandt painted those he loved or imagined, "he tried to enter their corporeal space as it existed at that precise moment, he tried to enter their Hôtel-Dieu. And so to find an exit from the darkness" (Berger 111). He looked closely into the darkness, hoping "he might find the presence of a light, damaged and bruised, but a little light all the same" (McCann 20). That darkness is a space that swells with emptiness and loneliness—one we might find impossible to negotiate without the artist's help. Lily is her own kind of Rembrandt, an artist who draws lines and shapes to define spatial relationships among the people she tries to paint. In sharing a space with Mr. Ramsay and Mrs. Ramsay, she begins, finally, to have a dialogue, in which their flaws and beauty are revealed, and she paints a line in the middle of a canvas, establishing a visual symbol of balance and of understanding.

The act of sliding toward intimacy, towards another, is not some linear pathway, that moves us directly from a starting point to a destination; rather, it is a recursive motion, a constant moving about that demands extension. We are trying to expand the body, reach for a light out of our own darkness, extend ourselves to another presence, thereby changing our sense of the world we inhabit.

Bernard, Woolf's writerly presence in *The Waves*, is initially in a self-enclosing bubble, but is constantly touched by others, disturbed by them within his isolation, solitude, darkness; he is in agony in the last section of *The Waves* because he cannot find a way to alleviate the pain of isolation and the constant invasion by other bodies. Although he conjures certain impressions of each of his friends, and seems to take some of their words and make them his own, he begins to think, "Faces recur, faces and faces—they press their beauty to the walls of my bubble—Neville, Susan, Louis, Jinny, Rhoda and a thousand others. How impossible to order them rightly; to detach one separately, or to give the effect of the whole" (256). Woolf chooses Bernard to carry the perspective of all five of his friends near the end of the novel, but he struggles to contain the whole, to capture the entirety of so many selves. Instead, he is constantly trying to enforce "I,I,I" (296). He tries to distinguish himself from the others, to see how *he* perceives things, how he is an utter failure: "I . . . felt my own failure; my desire to be free; to escape; to be bound; to make an end; to continue; to be Louis; to be myself" (257). He desires to make something permanent, something distinctly him—not to be someone who must be triggered by others to create phrases, words that illuminate moments. Bernard longs for solitude, time for himself, but others keep invading his corporeal space—waiters come back and forth, people touch their faces to the walls of his bubble, demanding his attention. But when he begins to feel he is streaming away from Susan, Jinny, Neville, Rhoda, and Louis into his desired isolation, he becomes aware that perhaps "this streaming away...[is] a sort of death? A new assembly of elements? Some hint of what was to come?"—he is not yet sure (279). He realizes finally that the appearance of another, the reaching, the sliding to share a bodily, physical space— "that other clock which marks the approach of a particular person"—is excruciating because appearance inescapably means disappearance (273). As he returns home and stands in the night, he envisions Day as "the eternal renewal, the incessant rise and fall and fall and rise again," and Death as "the enemy" (297). Perhaps Death and darkness, then, disperse forces, essences; they break up the space that all of the characters once shared. And yet Woolf reminds us that "beauty must be broken daily to remain beautiful"; this is perhaps why she depicts the scene of dawn as a sort of rebirth—it is a renewal, a wave breaking into a certain space to create something brilliant again, something different from before . . . and yet a continuance as well (174).

The friction of the canvas and the brush—the gliding between surfaces, essences, is a creation of two worlds merging and giving birth to new forms. The process of creativity, and of creating, requires us to exchange and expand, to constantly break the space we inhabit, to create distance, and to close in on it again. This creative activity is a process of transformation. As Woolf might suggest, sliding is both a verb and a noun—it creates a shape that captures an act of intimacy and convergence. It is both a life-preserving and life-giving act.

WORKS CITED

Berger, John. *The Shape of a Pocket*. New York: Vintage, 2001. Print.
  "Penelope." 45-48.
  "Rembrandt and the Body." 105-11.
McCann, Colum. *Let the Great World Spin*. New York: Random, 2009. Print.
Woolf, Virginia. "A Sketch of the Past." *Moments of Being*. Orlando:
  Harcourt, 1985. 61-160. Print.
—. *To the Lighthouse*. Orlando: Harcourt, 1981. Print.
—. *The Waves*. Orlando: Harcourt, 1959. Print.

Ode to a Witch

HANNA NOVAK

I.

the spirit of re-creation which masters this earthly form
loves most the pivoting point where you are no longer yourself.

—Rainer Maria Rilke, "Sonnet XII" (157)

These three lines surely spoke to Mrs. Ramsay, even though she never picked up Rilke's *The Sonnets to Orpheus*. Or, if she had, she might have skipped past the section while "zigzagging this way and that" through poetry, as she is so prone to doing in *To the Lighthouse* (119). During her nightly fireside reading rituals with her husband, she flips pages at random, slipping in and out of different texts and worlds: nineteenth-century poet Charles Elton's "Luriana, Lurilee" is followed by a one-line interlude from Browne, and then pieces of Shakespeare's "Sonnet 98." Here, the concern is not to move chronologically, abiding by rules of literal understanding; rather, Mrs. Ramsay seeks the "essence" of the texts, letting their spirits ordain meaning (121).

Words and images, here, seem to have a kind of autonomous power, one independent of the reader. They need no interpreting; rather, they are imbued with a force of their own. This spirit of the text moves Mrs. Ramsay "backwards" and "upwards," and "under," pulling at the different parts of her mind, stretching her in many directions (119, 121). George Steiner would say she is reading "*as if,*" letting the meaning of the text—a meaning separate from that which we, the reader, might presume—take us over, allowing it to color and inform our "remembrance and [our] sense of the future," pulling us both back and forth through time (34, 35). The text should incarnate some "*presence of significant being*" in us; we should allow it to inhabit us, to create *in* us (35).

Steiner suggests that we be a subordinate to the text's own power, but also a kind of participant in the nature of its workings; we should be made "responsible" and "answerable" to the text's calls, "as a host is to a guest" (35). Mrs. Ramsay is, indeed, subordinate to her texts, though Steiner does not suggest that such a process is devoid of pleasure. Rather, this covenant between "guest" and "host" raises the reader up in a climactic ascent. Mrs. Ramsay is pushed "on to the top" of a "summit" (121). And, though a plaything for the forces that unfold in her reading, she seems also to participate in their making. Out of this climax comes something "suddenly entire . . . beautiful and reasonable, clear and complete"; she holds the product of the encounter in her hand, victorious (121). She and some force have been able to "celebrate [their] nuptials," by the fireside, "in darkness," or, as Virginia Woolf would say, having "*incarnate[d]*" a "*presence of significant being*" out of a cross-pollination of sensations (*Room* 103; Steiner 35).

Mr. Ramsay, sitting across from his wife, does not recognize her transcendent encounter with words, images, and this *thing* one might call *the force*. He does not register her making. Rather, he attributes Mrs. Ramsay's ecstatic and sleepy stupor to "ignorance" and "simplicity"; he doubts if she even understands what she is reading (121). Little does he know that this moment is one of the many "pivoting points"—of conjuring and of creation—at which his wife has arrived that day and, I surmise, every day of her life. In this moment, as Rilke would say, Mrs. Ramsay is no longer herself.

The creative path seems, for Mrs. Ramsay, to be imbued with a sense of dark magic, both on the part of the force at hand and the mind that it plays with. All parts of her making—both process and product—go unseen, are unrecognizable to their human witness, Mr. Ramsay. And while the outcome of Mrs. Ramsay's experience is, to her, tangible and definite—she "held it in her hands" and it was "complete"—the thing itself is inaccessible to the mind across from her, a mind like nearly all of our minds, which can capture the literal far better than the "essence" (121). The mind which does not read "*as if*."

Such "essences" are at the crux of Virginia Woolf's novel, an ever-complicating nexus of fleeting, generative images and the minds that try to make sense of them. At the novel's core is a witch of sorts, a mother of countless children, male and female, mortal and omnipresent. Above all seeming contradictions, she is a human host of *the force* that others cannot see or touch. This is the simultaneously all-powerful and destructible Mrs. Ramsay. Not unlike the narrators of Woolf's other novels, she is attuned to seemingly invisible, intangible powers. And yet, she is embodied. In Mrs. Ramsay, both the supernatural and corporeal are presented to us at once. And that should give us hope.

II.

In spite of all the farmer's work and worry,
He can't reach down to where the seed is slowly
Transmuted into summer. The earth bestows.

—Rainer Maria Rilke, "Sonnet XII" (105)

"That sounds like a personal problem," my writing teacher says. He is responding to a remark I have made in class about E. M Foster's *A Passage to India*, in which *the force* is ever-present but, in the absence of a character like Mrs. Ramsay, can never be called on, grasped, and made generative by the individual. The novel is bereft of *witch*. Instead, set against the backdrop of the British Raj, English and Indians alike fumble in each other's midst, not understanding, losing control. Mistakes are always being made; clumsiness and error reign; West and East slide past one another and refuse to be made sense of. The novel's plot hinges on a false accusation made by a young British woman, Miss Adela Quested, implicating an Indian doctor, Aziz, in sexual assault. Such grave errors as these, which tear personal relationships asunder, are made all the darker against the landscape of India, which Forster seems to admire more than he does any human, always turning us back to the earth.

A Passage to India opens and closes with Nature. In the first chapter, it is magisterial, imbued with divine power. Forster writes:

> [W]hen the sky chooses, glory can rain into the Chandrapore bazaars or a benediction pass from horizon to horizon. The sky can do this because it is so strong and so enormous. Strength comes from the sun, infused in it daily; size from the prostrate earth. . . . League after league the earth lies flat, heaves a little, is flat again. Only in the south, where a group of fists and fingers are thrust up through the soil, is the endless expanse interrupted. These fists and fingers are the Marabar Hills, containing the extraordinary caves. (5-6)

Here, as much as the words on the pages that Mrs. Ramsay reads, elements of the earth seem to have an autonomous power, a force of their own. The sky alone chooses when to rain glory upon the bazaars; its relationships to the man-made are not influenced by human power, but rather by the sun and the "prostrate earth." In the novel's opening section, Forster seems to be asking us never to forget the power of nature, its unique ability to turn the earthly divine. And yet, as all-powerful as these natural elements seem, they are also personified, brought down to a human scale: the earth "heaves" while mountains are "group[s] of fists and fingers." The corporeal is interlocked with divine power, and yet no human can intervene. The Earth "bestows," but, Forster seems to be saying, no individual can take what it gives and make something whole of it. The Earth's charges are human, animal and inanimate already. There is no need to interpret them, to find their human "host." There is no Mrs. Ramsay in India, nor, perhaps, is there a need for one.

The novel's last words belong to the sky. In the closing scene of the book, recently united long-lost friends, one British and the other Indian, reluctantly say goodbye to one another as they ride on horseback through India. They are nameless in the scene, their individuality taken away to invoke a broader meaning: "Why can't we be friends now?" one of them says. "It's what I want. It's what you want" (362).

Nature stops them. This all-seeing narrating voice, dictating to us from some higher realm, tells readers that the non-human forces at work—"the temples, the tank, the jail, the palace, the birds, the carrion, the Guest House"—do not want them to be together (362). Just as the sky and the Marabar caves, in the novel's first chapter, are personified, so, too, are the inanimate and animal, here, made human. They, "in their hundred voices," answer the man's question: "No, not yet" (362). This is a tentative conclusion that leaves the much larger question of "when" outside the frame of Forster's work. The narrator leaves his readers behind—joining "the temples, the tank, the jail, the palace, the birds, the carrion, the Guest House" in shared understanding, deriding us with his godly knowledge, his "religious truth[s]" (307).

But how insulting! Animals and buildings can dictate fate, can know more than I do, be actors and confronters of *the force*, more than I can! This is a personal problem indeed, one that Forster seems to know his Western reader will butt up against and resist, just as the human characters in his book do. Failure and undersatnding seem tangled in resistance.

Though images and impressions of the godly are always close by, hovering above the action of the novel, dictating the fate of its human players, they stand apart, stay separate. While a little repose may come in a scene near the end of the novel, when the Indian Professor Godbole seemingly "transcends human processes," and "stands in the presence of God," we are quickly made aware that the distance between human and divine—within the "host" of the individual—is once again vast (317). Godbole and God (note the names) stand "at opposite ends of the same strip of carpet"; while the *individual human* and the *divine* inhabit the same space, a physical closeness is denied them (317). Sensual knowledge, the erotic pursuit of the ephemeral and divine, is unattainable.

III.

Plump apple, smooth banana, melon, peach
gooseberry . . . How all this affluence
speaks death and life into the mouth . . . I sense . . .

What miracle is happening in your mouth?

—Rainer Maria Rilke, "Sonnet XIII" (107)

In only one scene of *To the Lighthouse* are we given access to Mrs. Ramsay's mind as she sits alone: a Mrs. Ramsay without form, without a role—no easy frame to contain her. As a mother of eight children and the backbone for a needy husband, Mrs. Ramsey perpetually needs to care for others and is usually given to us in the midst of action, caught in the "being and the doing" of maternal and domestic duties, even if her mind travels beyond these simultaneously self-assigned and socially ordained roles (62). She is always in the process of interacting with others: reading a story to her son, hosting a dinner party or taking a walk with her houseguest, Charles Tansley. Even while conjuring *the force* by the fireside that evening, she'll be interrupted by her own insuppressible need to mother: the sound of Mr. Ramsay "slapping his thighs," and his reason for doing so, will preoccupy her before she allows herself to delight in the makings of her own individual mind (119). But, in this central scene, this one-time occurrence, she sits "by herself, with herself," ready for the "strangest adventures" (62).

Indeed, such adventures do confound our expectations. I seek Mrs. Ramsay freed from the social roles that I'd like to think oppress her; I want her gleefully unhinged from husband and child. In a wash of her "personal problems," of presumptions—a resistance to something more complex—I seek access to the mind of a witch—a dark and fertile magician. And she does not disappoint.

Mrs. Ramsay not only has a summoning power, she is also imbued with a *transformative* power. She "sit[s] and look[s], sit[s] and look[s], with her work in her hands until she bec[omes] the thing she look[s] at—that light, for example" (63). She is pushed towards a limitless, invisible, ego-less self, capable of merging with the inanimate. Personality dissolves when she is alone, without her inherent need to care. She becomes an abstraction, self-consciously identifying as "a wedge-shaped core of darkness" (62).

Our previous access to Mrs. Ramsay's mind as she sits and reads shows us that the loss of the tangible and visible self, this unification with the inanimate—the "text" or the "light"—is indeed generative. It is a process by which the "fret[s]" and "hurr[ies]" of everyday life are shattered and can give way to ecstasies, to "irrational tenderness" towards the inanimate (63). However, though a generative process, it is also overwhelming and destructive and unchallengeable. Mrs. Ramsay's encounter with texts erupted into ecstatic ascendance, but here, the moment climaxes in death. Her mind recites in hypnotic incantations, "It will end, it will end. . . . It will come, it will come. . . . We are in the hands of the Lord" (63). Though the transcendence of selfhood—the bindings of many selves—rises in triumph and exultation, it finishes with a moment of horror.

Here, Mrs. Ramsay's abilities to *summon* and to *transform* are complicated by her limited powers of control. Though she is capable of both perceiving and being open to the forces—inanimate and earthly—to which no others, in the novel's world, have access, they still overtake and overwhelm her. In effect, they push her under, perhaps into a kind of momentary Hades. She is reminded of her inevitable mortality: she will die. This particular process, one of control and divine knowledge dissolving into fear and limitation—suggests that Mrs. Ramsay is imbued with a double-consciousness: one open to both the forces of the living and the dead. One part of her reigns over the powers of the earth and calls upon them; the other is open to a force of the underworld. Death and abundance lock their hands inside her body, a body of many bodies: such is her "miracle." She stands a little closer to God on the same carpet. Perhaps this should suggest that she is our Orpheus incarnate, a mortal granted godly powers—rising as a divine maker, lowering as a commoner among the dead.

IV.

In this immeasurable darkness, be the power
that rounds your senses in their magic ring,
the sense of their mysterious encounter.

—Rainer Maria Rilke, "Sonnet XXIX" (191)

Bernard, one of the seven narrators of *The Waves*, necessarily complicates notions of *the force* present in *A Passage to India* and *To the Lighthouse* by establishing the power of *the collective*. If Mrs. Ramsay has two consciences, perhaps Bernard has eight, fusing in the novel's final pages all the presences that have spun the whole: six friends, a fallen hero, and Time. At the beginning of the novel, these forces are seemingly separate; the novel's form designates them as distinctive entities. We are presented with the sun's movement in italicized prose, followed then by separated, pseudo-interior monologues of six friends: such monologues are the workings of each mind, but always claimed by Woolf to be spoken aloud, a transmogrification of genres, of prose and plays and poetry.

Following the death of their collectively loved and carnally yearned-for friend, Percival, we start to lose sense of individual identities. By the last section of the novel, Bernard remains as a seemingly singular voice. But he, not unlike Mrs. Ramsay, has been experiencing, evaluating the "text" of the human psyche, reading it "*as if.*" His five friends, Percival, and Time have *created* in him an eight-bound self that causes him to give up his own ego, to house and adopt an *other*. A hallmark of his individuality, his penchant for "phrases," is surrendered: "I have done with phrases. How much better is silence" (295). There is, now, "a gradual coming together, running into one, acceleration and unification"; Bernard adopts the encountering charges of the inanimate and the human around him—of a clock ticking, a woman sneezing, the creak of a door (294). He adopts the voice of Time, appropriating the tone of the omnipresent narrator who gives us accounts of the sun's movement through a day in nine sections of the novel. In an exhaustive whirlwind of this renewal of the limitless self—made up of infinite, collective energies, a "magic ring" of forces (Rilke 191)—Bernard does not shy away from, but flings himself towards "Death" (*Waves* 297).

This flinging oneself towards what we might call *the force*, which I have evoked through Mrs. Ramsay, is both destructive and creative, rooted equally in the fleeting nature of the corporeal and the sense of "forever" in the sacramental. Bernard has indeed collapsed gender and genre, becoming one with fellow humans and objects—even the ephemeral patterns of time and space; he has let forces *create* within him, but in doing so, he loses his mortal self. He joins the ranks of the heroes, of myth, likening himself to Percival. He "ride[s] with [his] spear couched and [his] hair flying back like a young man's, like Percival's, when he galloped in India," boldly riding like a warrior in the face of "Death" (297). For among the aggregate of forces, Bernard, too, encounters death, as Mrs. Ramsay does while she sits alone and "be[comes] the thing[s] she look[s]," unhinged from her limitless self as she awakens to her own mortality (63). But, unlike Mrs. Ramsay, Bernard faces Death head on, and addresses him directly: "O Death!" he cries valiantly. He "fling[s] [him]self, unvanquished and unyielding" in the face of it (297). Here, he is without mortal limitation, stripped of the human fear of death, his own servitude and helplessness in the face of it dissolved. He joins the ranks of heroes, leaving the corporeal behind. Bernard is no Orpheus. He does not rise and fall, slipping in and out of divine power and mortal status. Having surrendered his eight-fold consciousness in pursuit of mythic ventures, of immortality, he has perhaps ascended among the gods. And while climactic and perhaps even sensational, his ascension can perhaps teach us less about being immortal, about employing dark magic, than can the character of Mrs. Ramsay.

V.

Does it really exist, Time, the Destroyer?
When will it crush the fortress on the peaceful height?
This heart, which belongs to the infinite gods forever,
When will the Demiurge violate it?

—Rainer Maria Rilke, "Sonnet XXVII" (187)

Mrs. Ramsay is reported dead to us amidst the force of Time. Woolf states it in a single sentence, in parentheses. Death may be something greater, then: something that has not yet been quite achieved, and is not necessarily finite. At least not for Mrs. Ramsay, who continues to inhabit the forces infused in time's passing, and to cradle the human characters that remain past her death. In the second section of the novel, mothering and birth proliferate. In the wake of Mrs. Ramsay's death, human agency is restored to the earth, but not with the same dominance and divine power that Forster gives it. Rather, the earth here is fertile, teeming with life: the "poppy seed itself and the carnation mate with the cabbage," "the thistle thrust[s] itself between the tiles," and "the broken glass and the china lie out on the lawn and be[come] tangled over with grass and wild berries" (138). All is chaos: strange species of plants are born, while the inanimate and the living intertwine. And yet such chaos, such loss of order, breeds new life and a mothering spirit. The restoration of the house, after all the time has passed, is compared now to a "laborious birth" (139). Woolf's nature is lustful, erotic, and fertile, while

Forster's is simplistic in its autonomy and power. Though perhaps personified, it does not pursue the corporeal. Forster's earth does not generate; it dictates.

Mrs. Ramsay is infused in the rest of the novel, not just in nature but also in collective memory. Other characters are in constant pursuit of their lost mother, trying to conjure her. But they are more consumed with the material world—with production—than with witchcraft; they know not of Mrs. Ramsay's entanglement with the earth's spirit. Her spirit does not suffice for them; a vision must occur. Lily Briscoe, perhaps the novel's Demiurge, belongs to the material world—to an ultimate goal of production. She is trying to reconstruct something whole out of a fragmented present, born out of a seed from the past. She seeks to complete a painting she started a decade earlier, at the start of the novel.

To help her with her painting, Lily conjures the image of Mrs. Ramsay so that she is beside her, seeming to sit with Lily on the beach. And though Lily has "her vision" and creates something representative of her experience, she is not capable of transforming—of hosting—the spirit she has summoned. Perhaps the spirit of Mrs. Ramsay cannot be captured or appropriated by another. Perhaps, indeed, Lily is no Bernard. Rather, Mrs. Ramsay stays whole, sitting beside Lily—a mere witness, and not a participant, to her presence—on the beach "making of the moment something permanent" (172). Mrs. Ramsay is still a maker: a motherly, erotic, and singular presence, even after death.

Standing in a wash of personal problems, I try to make whole a force that cannot be reduced into one shape. Mrs. Ramsay is human, though equally belonging to nature's life force and divine power, unlike the separated friends in *A Passage to India*. She is a host of the collective, yet, unlike Bernard of *The Waves*, always autonomous and singular—a presence discernibly human—a fertile mother—even after her death. She is at once limited and limitless; afraid of mortality, though she herself is immortal. The synergy between that thing we might call *the force* and the human is harbored in Mrs. Ramsay's ever-abundant womb of creation, of magic both erotic and dark.

"Oh, Mrs. Ramsay! . . . Mrs. Ramsay!" (*Lighthouse* 41).

you, strength and purpose of how many worlds!
—Rainer Maria Rilke, "Sonnet V" (143)

WORKS CITED

Forster, E. M. *A Passage To India*. New York: Harcourt, 1965. Print.

Rilke, Rainer Maria. *Duino Elegies and Sonnets to Orpheus*. Trans. Stephen Mitchell. New York: Vintage, 2009. Print.

Steiner, George. "Real Presences." *No Passion Spent: Essays 1978-1995*. New Haven: Yale UP, 1998. 20-39. Print.

Woolf, Virginia. *To The Lighthouse*. New York: Harcourt, 1989. Print.

—. *A Room of One's Own*. Boston: Mariner, 2005. Print.

—. *The Waves*. New York: Harcourt, 1950. Print.

MERCER
street

NOTABLE ESSAYS OF 2013 - 2014